Cross-Functional Teams

Cross-Functional Teams

Working with Allies, Enemies, and Other Strangers

Completely Revised and Updated

Glenn M. Parker

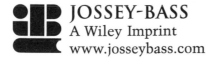

JOSSEY-BASS
A Wiley Imprint
www.josseybass.com

Published by Jossey-Bass
A Wiley Imprint
989 Market Street, San Francisco, CA 94103-1741   www.josseybass.com

Survey of Cross-Functional Teamwork © 1992 by Glenn M. Parker.

Jossey-Bass books and products are available through most bookstores. To contact Jossey-Bass directly call our Customer Care Department within the U.S. at 800-956-7739 or outside the U.S. at 317-572-3986, or fax 317-572-4002.

Jossey-Bass also publishes its books in a variety of electronic formats. Some content that appears in print may not be available in electronic books.

Library of Congress Cataloging-in-Publication Data

Parker, Glenn M., (date)
  Cross-functional teams : working with allies, enemies, and other strangers / by Glenn M. Parker.—2nd Ed.
    p. cm. — (The Jossey-Bass business & management series)
  Includes bibliographical references and index.
  ISBN 0-7879-6085-3 (alk. paper)
  1. Cross-functional teams. 2. Intergroup relations. 3. Interorganizational relations.
4. Complex organizations. I. Title. II. Series.
  HD66 .P345 2003
  658.4'02—dc21   2002011849

Printed in the United States of America
SECOND EDITION
HB Printing   10 9 8 7 6 5 4 3 2 1

The Jossey-Bass
Business & Management Series

Contents

For Jake, Max, and Emily

Preface

When I wrote *Cross-Functional Teams* ten years ago, cross-functional teams were found to a considerable extent in health care, specifically, in hospitals and pharmaceutical companies and to a lesser degree in telecommunications and computer technology. Stories were beginning to be told and research was starting to take place in other venues such as engineering, consumer products, automobiles, and insurance. Organizations were just getting the idea that cross-functional teams made sense for speeding up the product development process, providing comprehensive customer service, recommending process improvements, and managing major sales accounts.

In many of America's most successful and competitive organizations, cross-functional teams were making for some strange bedfellows.

Research scientists were meeting with marketing professionals; design engineers were working with suppliers; cost accountants were teaming up with operations managers; and software developers and business managers were serving together on systems development teams. In many organizations, eight or more disciplines were working together on cross-functional teams to bring a new product to the marketplace, develop a next-generation computer system, design a new layout for a factory floor, produce an important new drug, engineer a complex telecommunications network, prepare a long-term corporate strategy, or implement a procedure to upgrade service quality in a government agency.

As more and more organizations began to use cross-functional teams during the last decade, the need for clear, specific advice and tangible examples became apparent. And while there have been more articles on the subject, there is still no other book that brings together best practices and provides a cookbook for managers, team leaders, consultants, and coaches. I said at the time that cross-functional teams are the most difficult form of teamwork to pull off. In many ways, it has become more difficult, with the recent explosion of geographically dispersed teams, global teams, and virtual teams. It is now evident that cross-functional teams are different from traditional functional teams and require different approaches. Although many standard team-building practices are applicable to cross-functional teams, the keys to success lie in the extent to which the organizational environment provides the requisite supports for teamwork. We now know that the real barriers to success come not from the team itself but from organizational factors such as strategy, structure, systems, and culture.

As cross-functional teams have increased in number in the past ten years, we still need to know how to make them successful. During this time, I have added to my knowledge of the success factors, only to conclude that we were on the right track in 1994 but some of the ideas needed to be better developed with more specific examples. In addition, cross-functional teams are now operating in a world characterized by organizations that are mostly technology-based, often global, usually multicultural, universally leaner and flatter, more highly competitive, and almost always cost-conscious.

Background and Purpose of the Book

Cross-Functional Teams provides specific advice and practical help for people in organizations who have decided that cross-functional teams are going to be an important factor in their business strategy. I hope the book will also convince others of the value of such teams and will give them the courage to begin the process of incorporating these teams into their day-to-day business operations.

The book had its genesis in questions posed by clients, workshop participants, and audience members at conference presentations. The questions reflected the frustration of people who believed in the concept of cross-functional teams but were missing the answers to some key questions:

What role should senior management play?
How do we select an effective team leader?

What type of person makes the best team member?

What is the optimal size of a team?

What type of training should teams receive?

When and how should a team be empowered to take action?

How do you account for the contributions of team members in the performance management system?

How does the organization acknowledge team and individual successes with team rewards and recognition?

How does a team manage their relationships with key stakeholders?

How do global teams manage cross-cultural relationships among team members?

How do virtual teams make the best use of communications technology?

The data that form the basis of this book come from a number of sources. For the first edition of the book, I conducted a survey of public and private organizations. Before conducting the survey, I searched the literature and my networks to find organizations that seemed to be in the forefront of cross-functional teamwork. I then mailed the survey to the organizations I had targeted and to the top one hundred companies on the 1992 *Fortune* list of America's most admired corporations.

I also conducted telephone and face-to-face interviews with people who had worked with cross-functional teams. The purpose of the survey was to find answers to the questions listed earlier and perhaps to others I had not yet thought of. In the end, I was looking for a catalogue of "best principles" that would inspire and help others who are struggling with the potential of cross-functional teams.

For the revision of the book, I conducted both telephone and on-site interviews with managers, team leaders, and team members in a number of other organizations. These organizations were selected because they included examples of successful cross-functional teams. I was looking for "lessons learned" that will help other organizations deal with the same issues. In all of these interviews, I worked from a structured interview guide that included fifteen open-ended questions.

In four interviews, I decided that the situations provided such important learnings that they should be expanded into a case study. In each situation, the organization agreed to work with me to create a case study that provides the foundation for a high-level learning experience for the reader. The four cases are found in the Resources section of the book.

In addition, I reviewed the literature again to locate both examples and research findings that tell us more about what seems to help teams succeed and what factors derail them.

Audience for the Book

Cross-Functional Teams is written with practitioners in mind: executives and high-level managers who are trying to create the right vision and cultural supports, team leaders who are struggling with the twin goals of getting a job done and keeping a diverse group of people moving toward that end, managers who are wondering how to handle all these people in their organization who are constantly running off to team meetings, and human resource professionals who are being asked to provide training and coaching for leaders and members of cross-functional teams.

The most consistent comment I received about the first edition of the book was that it was both practical and readable. This is, once again, one of my key goals because I know that practitioners want strategies they can realistically apply to their work environment. This book will answer questions and provide strategies for a varied audience.

Executives and high-level managers in the private and public sectors are looking for ways to create an organization that encourages and supports cross-functional teamwork. They want to know what type of message they should send, what type of direction they should provide, and in what ways they should change their organization to fit this new direction. *Cross-Functional Teams* offers recommendations drawn from the lessons of other successful organizations. Senior managers will be especially interested in the chapters on the challenges faced by cross-functional teams on team empowerment and, of course, on management's role in building a team-based organization.

Leaders of cross-functional teams will find that many of the issues they are dealing with are not dissimilar to those that leaders face in other organizations. This book will describe approaches that have worked and should be tried and those that are sure to fail. Team leaders will want to pay special attention to the chapters on team leadership, team empowerment, team goals, and team size, and on the team working together.

Mid-level managers and supervisors who are trying to figure out how to manage people in a team-based organization will find answers here. With many of their people spending an increasing amount of time on teams directed by others, the challenge is how to manage the work, time, and performance of their subordinates while getting their own work done. *Cross-Functional Teams* discusses procedures that seem to be working. Particularly relevant will be the chapters on performance appraisal, bridge building, and the role of management.

Human resource professionals will find much of value here. They will be able to use the Survey of Cross-Functional Teamwork at the end of the book to understand teams in their own organizations. They will also be able to apply ideas from the chapter on team learning to training people for cross-functional teams. In addition, they will learn about organizational interventions that other professionals have used to facilitate successful teamwork. The chapters on rewarding teamwork and on team learning will be of special interest.

Students of organizational behavior and human resource development will find the book a valuable resource for course curricula and research. As cross-functional teamwork becomes a widespread corporate strategy, the academic community will look to this book for answers from the business world. Students will find Chapters One, Two, and Three especially useful. Chapter One provides an overview of the team landscape, Chapter Two outlines the competitive advantages of cross-functional teams, and Chapter Three outlines the obstacles faced by cross-functional teams. In addition, the four case studies and the accompanying discussion guides are intended to augment the concepts in the book.

Overview of the Contents

Cross-Functional Teams begins with a scan of the team landscape, with the goal of placing cross-functional teams in the lexicon of work teams in organizations. I look at the benefits of functional teams, self-directed teams, and cross-functional teams and note where each type seems to work best. I also describe the composition of a cross-functional team from the perspective of strangers, colleagues, friends, and enemies.

Chapter Two begins with a discussion of the six competitive advantages that cross-functional teams provide for an organization. With examples from more than twenty organizations, I show how cross-functional teams are helping to speed up the product development process, improve customer focus, increase the creative capacity of the organization, provide a forum for organizational learning, and serve as a single point of contact for customers, suppliers, and other key stakeholders.

In Chapter Three, I discuss the challenges of cross-functional teamwork. Specifically, I outline the obstacles to success. I explain the various factors that can derail a team, such as ineffective leadership, unclear authority, ambiguous goals, poor boundary management, performance appraisal that overlooks teamwork, lack of rewards and recognition, interpersonal problems, too many people on a team, and lack of management support.

In Chapter Four, I tackle the key role of team leadership. I show how the leadership requirements of a cross-functional team are different from and more difficult to meet than those of a functional team. I outline the unique characteristics of a successful cross-functional team leader.

Chapter Five describes the issue of team empowerment. Using business examples, I show how empowered cross-functional teams get things done faster, build ownership, encourage creativity, demonstrate respect, and motivate team members. Then I discuss how empowered teams get empowered, including what the team can do and what top management can do to encourage empowerment. Finally, I look at the importance of member empowerment.

Chapter Six focuses on team goals. Although goal setting is critical to all teams, it is especially important for cross-functional teams. In this chapter, I make the point that clear goals reduce conflicts, build partnerships, provide an incentive, and establish a scoreboard. I also describe a process for setting goals in a team environment.

In Chapter Seven, I focus on the need for cross-functional teams to build bridges to key stakeholders inside and sometimes outside the organization. I describe the key stakeholders, the inherent barriers to relationships with them, and strategies for building effective interorganizational relationships.

Chapter Eight addresses the sticky issue of performance appraisal. I look at the need to incorporate performance on cross-functional teams into the organization's appraisal process, and I discuss how some companies are currently doing this. I also describe the concept of peer appraisals where other members of their team evaluate members of a cross-functional team.

In Chapter Nine, I try to boil down some of the best ideas on how to reward cross-functional teamwork. I review the three main types of plans: team recognition, project team rewards, and group incentives. In each case, I provide one detailed case study along with other, related examples. The chapter concludes with recommendations for designing a team rewards program for cross-functional teams.

Cross-functional team learning is highlighted in Chapter Ten. Here I discuss the cross-functional team as a learning community, team training in interpersonal skills, cross-cultural learning, leader development, team building, and technical training. I introduce and provide examples of blended learning solutions.

In Chapter Eleven, I discuss team size and make the point that smaller is better. I examine the tendency for cross-functional teams to be larger than is necessary and the negative impact of oversized teams on team productivity and on the involvement, participation, and trust of team members. I discuss optimal team size and what to do if your team is just too large.

Chapter Twelve focuses on the internal dynamics of a cross-functional team. Here I describe both barriers and methods of addressing issues such as conflicts among team members, lack of trust and openness, meeting management, getting the right mix of people, involvement of suppliers and customers, and virtual teamwork, including the effective use of communications technology.

In Chapter Thirteen, I focus on management's role in building an organization that is aligned with and supports cross-functional teamwork. Here I provide a specific prescription for leaders of organizations who want to know what they can do to make teamwork thrive in their organizations.

Finally, in Chapter Fourteen, I outline what to do after you read this book and are ready to initiate a change. But first I discuss when to use and when to avoid the use of cross-functional teams. I provide specific advice for senior managers, team leaders, functional managers, team members, and human resource professionals.

The book ends with Resources for Cross-Functional Teams, consisting of several supplements to the ideas presented here. First, I provide team leaders with a list of ten things that will keep them up at night along with a prescription for getting a good night's sleep. Then follows a series of four case studies: (1) the creation of a climate for cross-functional collaboration at Parke-Davis (2) a virtual cross-functional team at IBM, (3) a network of cross-functional teams at IBM that responded to the September 11, 2001, terrorists' attacks on the World Trade Center, and (4) a permanent cross-functional team in the public sector. Each case includes a list of discussion questions that help you understand the issues and apply the lessons to your organization. Finally, you can use the Survey of Cross-Functional Teamwork to assess the strengths and weaknesses of your team and begin to build an action plan for improvement.

Acknowledgments

I begin by acknowledging the person who encouraged and supported me throughout the writing of this book and just about everything of value in my life: my wife, Judy Parker.

Several people were especially helpful in locating case examples and setting up interviews for me. In that regard, I would like to thank Larry Raymond, Marsha Frady, and Mal Conway of IBM, Donna Lipari and Don West of Xerox, Deborah Harrington-Mackin of New Directions Consulting, and Debra Gmerek of Parke-Davis.

I also want to acknowledge the research assistance of Christine Rosena and Shirley Casiano, who helped with the literature search.

Julianna Gustafson of Jossey-Bass, my initial editor on the project, helped me frame out the structure for the revision of the book. Later, Susan Williams picked up the editorial ball and saw the project through with me to completion. Cedric Crocker, a great editor and a great guy, was my editor on the original book. Cedric also provided some solid advice on how to approach this revision.

Finally, I especially want to thank all of the people who gave freely of their time and ideas during the course of the many interviews that give this book its unique flavor. You will see their names associated with the many quotes that are sprinkled throughout this book.

Skillman, New Jersey   GLENN M. PARKER
November 2002

The Author

Glenn M. Parker, author and consultant, works with organizations to create and sustain high-performing teams, effective team players, and team-based systems. His best-selling book, *Team Players and Teamwork* (Jossey-Bass, 1990), was selected as one of the ten best business books of 1990. Now in a paperback edition, *Team Players and Teamwork* (1996) has been published in several languages and has been brought to the screen in the best-selling video, *Team Building: What Makes a Good Team Player?* (CRM Learning, 1995). His training and team-building instrument, the Parker Team Player Survey, has become a standard in the field.

Parker has created an innovative Web-based course titled "Being a Team Player" for distribution by Interactive Training, Inc. He also teaches a course titled "Team Management" at Rider University, where he is an adjunct faculty member. He is one of only seventy-five management experts recognized in *The Guru Guide* (Wiley, 1998).

Parker is coauthor of *50 Activities For Team Building,* volume 1 (HRD Press, 1991), which was selected by *Human Resource Executive* as one of 1992's Top Ten Training Tools. He is the author of two resources for cross-functional teams: the book, *Cross-Functional Teams: Working With Allies, Enemies, and Other Strangers* (Jossey-Bass, 1994), and a facilitator's manual, *Cross-Functional Teams Toolkit* (Pfeiffer, 1997). Parker is coauthor of *50 Activities for Self-Directed Teams* (HRD Press, 1994) and author of a collection of training resources and job aids: *The Team Kit* (HRD Press, 1995). He is also editor of the HRD Press's *Best Practices for Teams,* volume 1 (1996) and volume 2 (1998).

Parker's latest publications are *25 Instruments for Team Building* (HRD Press, 1998), *Teamwork: 20 Steps for Building Powerful Teams*

(Successories, 1998), *Teamwork and Teamplay: Games and Activities for Training and Building Teams* (Pfeiffer, 1999), *Rewarding Teams: Lessons from the Trenches* (Jossey-Bass, 2000), *Team Workout* (HRD Press, 2000), and *Team Depot: A Warehouse of 585 Tools to Reassess, Rejuvenate, and Rehabilitate Your Team* (Jossey-Bass/Pfeiffer, 2002).

In addition to writing about teamwork, Parker is a hands-on consultant and trainer who works with start-up and ongoing teams of all types in a variety of industries. He facilitates team building, conducts training workshops, consults with management, and gives presentations for organizations across a wide variety of industries. His clients have included pharmaceutical companies such as Merck, Johnson & Johnson, Bristol-Myers Squibb, Pfizer, Rhône-Poulenc Rorer, Novo Nordisk, Aventis, and Abbott Laboratories; a variety of industrial organizations such as 3M, Kimberly-Clark, The Budd Company, Penntech Papers, Allied Signal, Pratt & Whitney, LEGO, BOC Gases, and Sun MicroSystems; companies in telecommunications, including AT&T, Pacific Bell, NYNEX, Lucent/Bell Labs, Telcordia Technologies (Bellcore), and Siemens/ROLM Communications; service businesses such as Commerce Clearing House's Legal Information Service, Asea Brown Boveri (ABB) Environmental Services, American Express, Promus Hotels (Embassy Suites, Hampton Inns), CDI Corp., and the *New England Journal of Medicine;* the sales and marketing organizations of Roche Laboratories and the Pontiac Division of General Motors; health care providers such as Pocono Medical Center, Palomar-Pomerado Health System, St. Rita's Medical Center, Monmouth Medical Center, and Riverside Health Care Center; retailers such as Ann Taylor and Phillips Van Heusen, and several government agencies: U.S. Department of the Navy, the Environmental Protection Agency, the U.S. Coast Guard, and the National Institutes of Health.

Parker holds a bachelor's degree from City College of New York and a master's degree from the University of Illinois; he studied for the doctorate at Cornell University. He is much in demand as a speaker at corporate meetings and at national conferences sponsored by the American Society for Training and Development (ASTD), Lakewood Conferences, and Center for the Study of Work Teams. He keynoted a recent "Best of Teams" conference sponsored by Linkage and corporate meetings sponsored by Pfizer and

Blue Cross and Blue Shield of America. He is past president of the ASTD Mid-New Jersey chapter and chairperson of the ASTD publishing review committee.

Parker is the father of three grown children and currently lives in central New Jersey with his wife, Judy. In his spare time, he plays with his grandchildren, rides his bike, volunteers with the American Cancer Society, roots for the Philadelphia 76ers, and plans his next vacation. For more information, go to *www.glennparker.com*.

Cross-Functional Teams

Chapter One

The World of Cross-Functional Teams

Cross-functional teams are at the heart of every motorcycle produced at Harley-Davidson Motor Company.
LEROY ZIMDARS, DIRECTOR, SUPPLY CHAIN MANAGEMENT,
HARLEY DAVIDSON, INC.[1]

The world and the world of business are changing. Individualism is out; teamwork is in. Specialization is out; a new-style generalism is in. Rigid organizational lines are out; fluid collaboration is in. Power is out; empowerment is in. Hierarchical organizations are out, replaced by network organizations, adaptive organizations, informational organizations, and horizontal organizations. Right smack in the middle of all this sit cross-functional teams, composed of experts ready to move quickly and flexibly to adapt to changing business needs.

Types of Teams

Despite what we call them, not all "teams" are teams. Some so-called teams are simply groups masquerading as teams, because in today's world it's important to be on something called a team. Keep in mind that there is nothing wrong with being a part of an effective group. For example, nine group leaders report to a division head.

---

[1]Brunelli, 1999, p. 148.

Each group leader has a set of objectives for which he or she is accountable. However, there is no overarching goal for which all nine are mutually accountable; interdependence only exists among several subsets of the group leaders. There is no joint product or service for which the whole group is responsible. Therefore, this is a group, not a team. Nevertheless, this can be a very effective structure.

A team is a group of people with a high degree of interdependence, geared toward the achievement of a goal or the completion of a task. In other words, team members agree on a goal and agree that the only way to achieve the goal is to work together. Many groups with common goals are not teams. The key is the requirement for interdependence. The three best-known types of teams today are functional teams, self-directed teams, and cross-functional teams.

The Functional Team

The classic functional team is made up of a boss and his or her direct reports. This so-called military model has been the staple of modern business. Despite all the talk about change, most organization charts still look like a pyramid. It may be a flatter pyramid but it is a pyramid nevertheless. There is comfort in having all the design engineers report to the same manager. Engineers like hanging out with other engineers, and other people like knowing where they can easily find an engineer. Issues such as authority, relationships, decision making, leadership, and boundary management are simple and clear.

The Self-Directed Team

There are as many ways of describing a self-directed team as there are consulting firms specializing in the process. For example, Development Dimensions International says that "a self directed team is an intact group of employees who are responsible for a 'whole' work process or segment that delivers a product or service to an internal or external customer. To varying degrees, team members work together to improve their operations, handle day-to-day problems, and plan and control their work. In other words, they are responsible not only for getting their work done but also for managing themselves" (Wellins, Byham, and Wilson, 1991, p. 3).

Zenger-Miller emphasizes team size, cross-training, and individual team member responsibility when it defines a self-directed team as

> a highly trained group of employees, from 6 to 18, on average, fully responsible for turning out a well-defined segment of finished work. The segment could be a final product, like a refrigerator or ball bearing; or a service like a fully processed insurance claim. It could also be a complete but intermediate product or service, like a finished refrigerator motor, an aircraft fuselage, or the circuit plans for a television set. Because every member of the team shares equal responsibility for this finished segment of work, self-directed teams represent the conceptual opposite of the assembly line, where each worker assumes responsibility for a narrow technical function [Orsburn, Moran, Musselwhite, and Zenger, 1990, p. 8].

From Pfeiffer and Company, we get a narrower conception of a self-directed team. Consultants Torres and Spiegel seem to limit self-directed teams to a functional area in the production side of organizations. In their view, "A self-directed team is a functional group of employees (usually between eight and fifteen members) who share responsibility for a particular unit of production. The work team consists of trained individuals who possess the technical skills and abilities necessary to complete all assigned tasks. Management has delegated to the self-directed work team the authority to plan, implement, control, and improve all work processes" (Torres and Spiegel, 1990, p. 3). Although it is true that self-directed teams are more prevalent in production operations, especially in manufacturing, they also operate in the service side of a business. For example, many insurance companies have established self-directed teams in policyholder services.

Self-directed teams have been particularly successful in start-up sites. In these locations, there is no history or culture to change, there are no supervisors to retrain, and no power shift needs to be negotiated. But in spite of many advantages to self-directed teams, there are tremendous obstacles to successful implementation, especially in hierarchical organizations that have

no tradition of participative management or employee involvement. Many organizations are experimenting with self-directed
teams for the wrong reasons—the most attractive reason being
that it looks like an easy way to reduce the middle-management
and supervisory ranks. However, a small number of quality companies are sincerely dedicated to successful self-management, and
they are making it work.

The Cross-Functional Team

Sometimes called multidisciplinary teams (in educational settings,
interdisciplinary teams), cross-functional teams are part of the
quiet revolution that is sweeping across organizations today. There
seems to be no limit to the possibilities for cross-functional teams.
I have found them in a wide variety of industries doing an equally
wide spectrum of business functions that were once done in isolation. To begin, it is important to understand that "a standard cross-
functional team is composed of those individuals from
departments within the firm whose competencies are essential in
achieving an optimal evaluation. Successful teams combine skill-
sets which no single individual possesses" (Doyle, 1991, p. 20). In
addition, "an increasing number of firms are entrusting the product development task to teams composed of individuals from a variety of functional areas such as marketing, research and
development, manufacturing, and purchasing" (Sethi, 2000, p. 2).
It is important to note that the role of the cross-functional team in
using the expertise of many different people is coupled with the
task of *enlisting support* for the work of the team. This is critical for
successful cross-functional teamwork (I will discuss this further in
Chapter Seven).

Team Composition

Although some people question the viability of mixing people
from different levels on the same team, at Motorola's assembly
plant in Austin, Texas, this is not seen as a problem but as an
advantage. People at Motorola believe that "members of a true
cross-functional team should consist of all levels of management,
operators, and technicians, and members from different organizations, including vendors and customers" (Kumar and Gupta,

1991, p. 32). In addition to including all levels, at some organizations, "leading customers, technology suppliers, and other contributors . . . are defined as insiders, interdependent with the organization and capable of being trusted and engaged in the new product development process" (Jassawalla and Sashittal, 1999, p. 58). Chapter Seven discusses the value of involving suppliers and customers.

At 3M's Industrial Specialties Division, cross-functional teams literally manage the whole business. Each product family (for example, adhesives, fasteners, urethane films) is managed by a cross-functional team that includes people from the laboratory, manufacturing, and sales who are responsible for the daily operation of the business, as well as new-product development (McKeown, 1990). Other companies, such as Pratt & Whitney and Hoffman La Roche, have reorganized parts of their businesses into product centers or specific lines of business with cross-functional teams driving the process. In some parts of the electronics industry, product development teams are called core teams, which are composed of eight to ten people from different functions involved in the day-to-day development of new products. They are "the single point of contact for all corporate functions involved in a development project, both for those involved in day-to-day development work and for managers within each function" (Whiting, 1991, p. 50).

Many consulting firms have reorganized their staffs into permanent multidisciplinary teams aligned with specific customers or market segments. For example, one of our clients, an environmental consulting organization, eliminated all its functional departments in favor of ongoing customer-focused teams composed of geologists, hydrogeologists, environmental engineers, chemists, and other specialists. What's new about this approach is that the teams are part of the permanent structure of the organization.

Talk of permanent team structures causes some cynics to suggest that cross-functional teams are simply a warmed-over version of the matrix organization popular in the 1960s (Davis and Lawrence, 1977). Although some of the issues (such as the sharing of resources) are similar, no cross-functional team leaders I know or have studied see themselves as the typical two-boss manager found in matrix structures. Cross-functional teams are more akin to project organizations that must integrate various resource groups to achieve an agreed-upon product.

For the purposes of this book, I define a cross-functional team as *a group of people with a clear purpose representing a variety of functions or disciplines in the organization whose combined efforts are necessary for achieving the team's purpose.* The team may be permanent or ad hoc and may include vendors and customers as appropriate.

Which Team? When and Where?

Each type of team has its advantages and works best in a particular organizational setting.

- *Functional teams* work well in traditional hierarchical organizations in stable, slow-growth industries with predictable markets.
- *Self-directed teams* can be used in some of the same industries as functional teams and in many others as well, particularly in start-up sites or in organizations with an embedded base of participative management and a history of employee involvement.
- *Cross-functional teams* seem to be most effective in companies with fast-changing markets, such as the computer, telecommunications, pharmaceuticals, and similar industries that value adaptability, speed, and an intense focus on responding to customer needs.

So far, all of this looks pretty rosy. Just put together a group of people from different parts of the organization and let them go. Not so. Unspoken in all this discussion are the potential differences among the team players who come from different functions, different levels, and from outside the formal organization. Some players may be friendly colleagues with positive team experiences; some may be antagonists with memories of past wars; still others may simply have never met. It is extremely important for everyone involved to see the team as more than a joining of functions; they must also see it as a blend of real people with different histories, team-player styles, and priorities.

Working with Diverse Team Members

Recent survey results, the large number of books (see the References section) and conferences, and plain old-fashioned observation tell us that teams have become an important business strategy in today's competitive environment. Central to this shift are a series of unusual collaborative efforts. These new-styled teams are composed of people from a variety of functions who may know and like each other, or who may be enemies, or who may simply be strangers.

Some Are Strangers

Sometimes team members have never met before the first team meeting. An automobile design engineer from Detroit may never have talked with a Ford dealer from Langhorne, Pennsylvania. The reason may not be simple geographical separation, however; a marketing professional may never have run into the government affairs attorney, even though they work in the same building for the same company. One key dynamic of a cross-functional team is that many team members do not know each other. Sit in on the first meeting of a new cross-functional team and you will probably see (or hear) member introductions as one of the first activities.

Some Are Colleagues

Sometimes team members may have worked together on past project teams or were colleagues in the same department. For example, if the research scientist and the manufacturing manager have a common understanding of customer needs, their past association can help jump-start the team. However, if they are old turf-war enemies, the team will begin with a conflict to resolve.

Some Are Friends

Sometimes team members know each other but have never worked together. For instance, the social studies teacher and the English teacher have shared lunch together for years in the faculty room.

Now, however, they are part of the seventh-grade team, which must develop a coordinated curriculum. The computer programmer and the accountant have carpooled together, but now they must team up to develop a new tracking system. Sometimes informal associations play out well in more serious cross-functional team environments, but not always.

Some Are Enemies

Some team members have worked together in the past, and it has not worked out well. They did not get along. They fought over the issues. However, although some interpersonal conflict does lead to people becoming enemies, more often team members come to the team from "warring" departments. They may not know each other, but they make certain assumptions about the other person that are based on the function he or she represents. They may have had bad experiences with people from that area in the past, and they assume they will encounter similar problems with this person. For example, "as an engineer I know that the people in marketing always give us a hard time." Similarly, "the lawyers in the legal department usually begin by telling us why we can't do something rather than figure out a way to get it done." As a recent study in technological organizations points out, there is a long-standing rivalry between engineers and marketing people "because engineers accustomed to having a lot of clout fear sharing power with marketers and often mistrust the quality of marketing information they receive" (Yu, 2001, p. 1). Stereotypes abound and lead to endemic obstacles that must be overcome.

Dimensions of Cross-Functional Teams

There are many ways to categorize cross-functional teams. One way is to look at them in terms of three dimensions: (1) purpose, (2) duration, and (3) membership.

Purpose

Teams vary in their purpose or goal; for example, they may be devoted to product development, systems development, quality improvement, problem solving, or reengineering. The mission of the IBM PDxT Team was to deliver a course for managers of remote employees, the University of Alabama's Distance Education Task Force was charged with improving the quality of distance education, and the Project Team in Boeing's Aerospace Division was responsible for developing new products and improving existing products. There is almost no end to the possible purposes for which organizations create cross-functional teams.

Duration

Teams tend to be either permanent or temporary (sometimes referred to as ad hoc). Permanent teams include the functional department teams and others that are built into the ongoing organizational structure. In other words, you can find them on the company's organization chart. The Clark County (Nevada) Major Projects Review Team is a permanent team in the county government organization responsible for review and action on applications for land use development. Temporary teams include task forces, problem-solving teams, project teams, and a variety of short-term teams set up to develop, analyze, or study a business issue. The COMET team at BOC Gases was an ad hoc team charged with developing a new incentive plan.

Membership

The membership of a cross-functional team can be as varied as the organization itself. The team is almost always composed of people from various functional departments but may also include vendors, suppliers, consultants, and customers. For example, the IBM PDxT Team included a customer project manager as a full-time team member whose presence was considered a real benefit because it speeded up the overall process. In global teams, membership may be cross-cultural, which adds a more diverse point of view to the team's deliberations. Some global teams may also be so-called virtual teams because members complete their task using electronic means of communication without the benefit of in-person meetings. You can find more on cross-cultural and virtual teams in Chapter Twelve.

The Culture of Cross-Functional Teams

The diversity of cross-functional team players creates a new culture. Therefore, it is important to understand that in creating a cross-functional team, you are fashioning a potentially powerful organizational vehicle. Although it lacks the simplicity of a functional team composed of, for example, six engineers all reporting to the engineering manager, a cross-functional team has a greater chance of realizing the potential synergy of that old axiom: *the whole is greater than the sum of its parts.* This group of allies, enemies, and strangers can weave together a cross-functional design that is an amalgam of many cultures.

Team sponsors and team players must understand that the beauty of the idea of putting together a diverse group of people to launch a product, develop a new system, or solve a business problem is not enough. A good concept is not enough. Diversity is not enough. Sethi's study of new product teams found that "merely having a functionally diverse team is not sufficient for the emergence of quality. Instead, product quality seems to depend on how effectively members from different functional areas integrate information and perspectives" (Sethi, 2000, p. 11). In practice, it requires the migration from a parochial view of the world—my function, my values, and my goals are paramount—to a broader view that "we're all in this together." We need to understand, appreciate, and utilize the data and opinions that each person brings to the team. Success is team success; rewards are team rewards. And if the team fails, the members share the blame.

Implications

For a manager responsible for team development or a leader of a cross-functional team, the implications are clear:

- Insist on having a clear team goal and a plan to achieve it.
- Work hard to gain the commitment of team members and other stakeholders to the team's goal.
- Emphasize collaborative efforts and team rewards.
- Provide training on how to work with a diverse group of people.
- Create a set of policies and procedures that support a team-based environment.

Looking Back: Some Issues to Consider

1. What do you think of Motorola's practice of including people from different levels on cross-functional teams? How would that work in your organization?

2. Who are the "warring departments" in your organization? What is their impact on cross-functional teams?

3. Review the list of where each type of team (functional, self-directed, cross-functional) seems to work best? Do you agree? Are there other settings in which each type can be used?

4. Look around at the team landscape in your organization. Where can you see a greater use of cross-functional teams?

5. Think about the culture of your organization. To what extent is it supportive of the practice of creating a team composed of people from different parts of the organization?

Chapter Two

The Competitive Advantages of Cross-Functional Teams

The change in speed was extraordinary.
DEBRA GMEREK, DIRECTOR, TEAM LEADERS, PARKE-DAVIS[1]

Effective cross-functional teams have many advantages. Although some of the pluses apply to other types of teams, too, these advantages have a unique flavor when played out in the context of a cross-functional team. I have found that cross-functional teams bring six important competitive advantages to organizations that successfully implement and manage them:

1. *Speed.* Cross-functional teams reduce the time it takes to get things done, especially in the product development process.
2. *Complexity.* Cross-functional teams improve an organization's ability to solve complex problems.
3. *Customer focus.* Cross-functional teams focus the organization's resources on satisfying the customer's needs.
4. *Creativity.* By bringing together people with a variety of experiences and backgrounds, cross-functional teams increase the creative capacity of an organization.
5. *Organizational learning.* Members of cross-functional teams are more easily able to develop new technical and professional skills, learn more about other disciplines, and learn how to

---

[1]Interview with the author, October 2001.

work with people who have different team-player styles and cultural backgrounds than those who do not participate in cross-functional teams.

6. *Single point of contact.* The cross-functional team promotes a more effective cross-team effort by identifying one place to go for information and for decisions about a project or customer.

Importance of Speed

Speed—the ability to get things done faster—is now so important for business success that time-based management is a topic of critical importance to businesses in competitive markets. Speed is a critical differentiating factor in product and systems development and in customer service.

In product development, cross-functional teams are central to reducing the time spent in the development cycle or what is now called *time to market* or *time to value.* According to a McKinsey and Company study, the cost of arriving late to market by five months reduces gross profits by 25 percent (Wallace and Halverson, 1992). Cross-functional teams replace serial development with parallel development. In the past, the process was like a relay race, with completed work serving as the baton. When the people in a function completed their work (conducting basic research, prototyping, testing, engineering, carrying out operations, marketing), they handed it off to the next group of people, who did their work and passed it on to strangers or colleagues in the next group, who did their work and passed it on to the next group.

Cross-functional teams allow many pieces of the development process to be done at the same time. The team approach also eliminates many of the features of the serial process that added time and costs to the final product. Operating in isolation, a department might add features that would seem valuable to them but not to others, including the customer. For example, engineers might give a product features that would make it difficult to manufacture or sell. Or salespeople might like to see features that make the product easier to sell but would add excessive production costs. All this isolated development activity can slow down the time to market because it leads to errors and other factors that require time-consuming changes down the line. Cross-functional teams discover these problems at the front end or simply catch them before they occur.

Honeywell's Building Controls Division uses cross-functional teams to cut product development time by at least 50 percent through minimizing changes in specifications and therefore in the subsequent rework. As the following description of Honeywell's process also makes clear, these same capabilities are critical for a successful total quality effort.

> The reduction in changes and rework is achieved in part through an emphasis on the front end of the product development process. Through disciplined planning, team members produce a "frozen spec" that, once agreed to by the team, can only be changed by a "no-go" decision based on a major shift in the market's requirements. The team itself enforces the discipline necessary to defer small design changes to the second issue of the product under development. In addition to shortening the product development cycle, the process of arriving at a stable product design also benefits product manufacturability, cost, and quality. Getting production involved in the product development process from the start focuses the development team on designs that are compatible with existing manufacturing processes. It also enables the team to identify any hurdles in the early stages that will affect product cost, performance, or delivery [Larson, 1988, p. 23].

In all, the cross-functional teams at Honeywell's Building Controls Division are credited with

- Cutting product development time by at least 50 percent
- Reducing product costs by 5 to 10 percent
- Producing products that are 97.6 percent defect-free
- Enhancing the performance of new products in the market
- Delivering products that meet customer requirements

Systems developers are finding that cross-organizational teams that bring users together with information systems professionals cut time and cost from the development of new systems. Team techniques such as IBM's Joint Application Design (JAD), WISE Integrated Systems Development Method (WISDM) from the Western Institute of Systems Engineering, and the method developed by Performance Resources are group design methodologies that facilitate user-developer team dynamics. Cigna Insurance in Philadelphia, CNA Insurance in Chicago, Chase Manhattan Bank, and Ford Motor Company in Dearborn, Michigan, are all committed to team techniques in systems design. Studies indicate that the development cycle can be cut in half with effective teamwork, resulting in an overall return on investment of 10 to 15 percent (Leavitt, 1987). In a study of thirty-six computer companies, Eisenhardt and Tabrizi (1995) found that the use of cross-functional teams was positively linked to rapid development time.

One of the most dramatic stories concerns Cincinnati Milacron, an old-line machinery manufacturer. The company used a new cross-functional team process to develop a plastic injection-molding machine in record time, at reduced cost, and with increased functionality (Nulty, 1990). Instead of the engineering department designing a machine in their cubbyhole and then tossing it over the wall to manufacturing, purchasing, marketing, and others, a team composed of people from all the relevant departments was formed. They began with clear goals: to make the machine competitive with foreign imports by reducing costs by 40 percent, to increase functionality, and to cut the usual development cycle from two years to one. In the end, they cut the cycle time to 270 days (the project became known as the P-270) and met other cost and quality goals. And more important, the new machine is selling. In the first full year of production, the company has sold two and one-half times as many of the new machines as it had in the best year of the earlier model.

A famous and often-cited example of the success of cross-functional teamwork is AT&T's development of the 4200 cordless telephone (Dumaine, 1989). The vice president of product development, John Hanley, decided that the old development process, which took two years, was just not acceptable. Getting to the market faster was simply good business because the company could charge a premium while everyone else played catch-up. Hanley replaced the traditional hand-off approach with small teams of engineers, manufacturers, and marketers who had the authority to make decisions on functionality, cost, production, and appearance. The teams set strict deadlines for freezing all design specs and held to them. As a result, they cut the development time from two years to twelve months while improving quality and, of course, lowering costs. Thus there may be no need to form a new team, obtain other resources, or renegotiate the timeline for providing the product or service to the customer. All customer needs can be met by the cross-functional team.

More recently, PrestigeSoft, a developer of low-cost consumer software, used cross-functional, global development teams to reduce time to market significantly (Carmel, 1999). Most projects take about six months, but a recent screen-saver package took only three months from concept to release. In the same vein, Parke-Davis's submissions team was able to reduce the time from the last patient visit to the final NDA (new drug application) from the usual nine to twelve months to twelve weeks, according to team leader Mary Sylvain (interview with the author, October 2002). In another interview, Debra Gmerek, director of team leaders at Parke-Davis (October, 2001), said, "The change in speed was extraordinary. The average time to create a database went from nine months to three weeks." In another study, Brown and Eisenhardt (1995) found that cross-functional teams shorten the time from concept to commercialization if project tasks are conducted simultaneously.

Guidelines for Speeding Up the Process

The examples just discussed provide some clues as to how cross-functional teams speed up the development process. Successful teams

- Have a clear goal
- Include all the relevant functions
- Conduct many tasks currently
- Empower the team to act without checking every decision
- Involve all the key players from the very beginning of the process
- Enforce the discipline necessary to keep to a schedule

Although teams are a key to improving an organization's time to market, it should be understood that other things must be in place if an organization is to effectively implement the concept of speed. Other factors include simplifying the approval process and the other red tape that slows down development, using electronic communication tools, using the latest software tools to support development, and—here's a big one—top-management support for the team's goal.

The Issue of Complexity

Cross-functional teams are in a better position than a series of functional teams to solve complex business problems, because most of these problems transcend disciplines or functions. The old view that you can put a genius alone in a laboratory or in front of a computer terminal, water and feed him or her periodically, and then wait for a solution to emerge is losing ground. As a manager in a telecommunications research and development company told me, "Network architecture planning is so broad a field that no one person can do it alone." The cross-functional team provides the framework for putting together scientists and engineers with a variety of backgrounds and diverse training to solve a complex business problem, design a new system, develop a new product, or reorganize the company. As the authors of a highly regarded study of new-product teams said, "As products become more complex, it is no longer possible for a single engineer or scientist to complete a project alone" (Ancona and Caldwell, 1990b, p. 25). And as Bill Baker, leader of the OM Team at BOC Gases pointed out, "The nature and complexity of the team problem was the main reason for having a cross-functional team. One function could not accomplish this task" (interview with the author, December 2001).

In our survey of cross-functional teamwork, the ability to deal with complex issues came up often as an outcome of cross-functional product development teams. Bringing people together from different parts of the company with different skill sets, a wide variety of orientations, and training in diverse disciplines means that the product outcomes will be more creative. It is not just reduced cycle time but, as Barbara Bennett, vice president of The Stanley Works, put it in responding to my survey: "More innovative products result from cross-functional product development teams." More specifically, Debra Gmerek of Parke-Davis reported that "the problem of how to get treatment codes into the database was extremely complicated, but we sat down with team members, and we were able to get it in twenty-four hours instead of two weeks" (interview with the author, October 2001).

In a functional organization, many groups might be given the same problem to solve and then go off and work at it in isolation from each other. When the various solutions and recommendations come back, one person or a task force will sift through them and try to come up with a synthesis or simply pick one of the ideas. In this model, it is assumed that each group has enough information and background to look at the whole problem. This model offers no possibility of group interaction, cross-learning, or synergy.

Under the old system at Ford Motor Company, there was no collaboration between people who designed the exterior of the car and those who designed the interior. However, Mimi Vandermolen, an executive with Ford, saw the need for looking at the total design of the Probe as the problem to be solved. The problem was how to design an automobile that had appeal for both young men and young women. As a result, she created an overall design team that began with a common vision of the target market for the car. Together this cross-functional team of people who design the hood, fenders, and doors worked together with those who design the seats, steering wheel, and rearview mirror. Vandermolen reported that a cross-functional team of interior and exterior car designers "would allow us to avoid making mistakes in exterior design that would ultimately cause problems in interior design. For example, if the shape of the roof is already set in stone when you get ready to do the interior, you may have to sacrifice passenger space. But if you plan the interior and exterior together, you can create harmony between the two" ("Shifting the Corporate Culture," 1992, pp. 25, 28). In the end, this new team approach would save the company 20 percent on the cost of the design *and* produce a better vehicle. Similarly, Helena Gordon of Penn National Insurance reported that "we got to a workable solution to some complex problems because business analysts saw how it worked on the job, and the technical people brought what was technically possible" (interview with the author, October 2001).

In some cases, cross-functional teams in manufacturing are responsible for end-to-end product development. For example, at TRW in Cleveland, Ohio, Ian Ziskin, director of leadership and organizational effectiveness, reported that a transportation electronics team included people from engineering, manufacturing, quality, operations, finance, marketing, and even suppliers such as Sony. The team was charged with the development of a remote, keyless entry for the automobile industry. They took responsibility for the product's design and manufacturing and, ultimately, taking it to market (interview with the author, January 1993).

Guidelines for Addressing Complex Issues

Keys to using cross-functional teams to solve complex business problems include having

- A leader with a creative vision
- Freedom from unnecessary restrictions, including the freedom to fail
- A wide range of diverse opinion
- An openness on the part of team members to new ideas

Need for Customer Focus

Every type of team—product development, systems development, sales, quality, or any other cross-functional team—has a customer; often these customers are internal to the organization. Therefore, by definition, all teams should have a customer focus.

As organizations around the world jump on the quality bandwagon, we are seeing a resurgence of teamwork as a serious business strategy. Every serious quality effort is a team-based effort. Every winner of the Malcolm Baldrige National Quality Award has made teams an integral part of the quality process. In fact, effective teamwork is one of the Baldrige criteria. And in quality improvement, cross-functional teams are seen as an important tool, especially when the product or service spans several functions. In two studies (Kessler and Chakrabarti, 1996, and Patti, Gilbert, and Hartman, 1997), cross-functional new-product teams produced higher-quality products.

As the work process becomes more complex and as quality is defined as "satisfying the customer," cross-functional teams become a necessity for achieving quality improvements. For many products and services, one person or one department simply cannot know enough to understand the total process, identify the breakdown points, and suggest ways to reduce errors, waste, or other drains on quality. For example, the beginning of most quality improvement efforts is the creation of a process flowchart. In working this process with one of my clients, it became clear that producing the flowchart required the combined input of at least six people, each with a unique view of the work process. In another case, we found that the production of a customer invoice involved several functions within a department, as well as two other groups in other departments.

There are many examples of small and large companies, government agencies, and school systems using cross-functional teams to improve the quality of their products and services. Teams are part of corporatewide quality programs in major corporations, as well as in small, homegrown quality improvement efforts, school reform projects, and government agencies seeking ways to better serve their clients. Because we know how Motorola, Xerox, IBM, Federal Express, and other high-profile companies are using teams to drive their successful quality efforts, let's look at some not-so-famous but effective organizations.

Storage Technology Corporation, a worldwide producer of storage and retrieval systems for the computer industry headquartered in Louisville, Colorado, used a team-based quality process that helped achieve an impressive business comeback (Stratton, 1991). The company went from the depths of Chapter 11 in 1984 to revenues in excess of $1 billion in 1991, buttressed by significant increases in customer satisfaction ratings and revenue per employee.

Donald Stratton, StorageTek's vice president of corporate quality and education, reported that cross-functional teams, supported by an extensive training program, have been critical to quality improvements and the company's turnaround (interview with the author, January 1993). For example, a cross-functional metrology team, winner of the 1992 Chairman's Quality Award, made recommendations that led to a reduced inventory of test sets (from 350 to 50) and decreased interval of testing (twenty-eight days to three days). This saved StorageTek $500,000.

Some people may think that the stodgy bureaucracy of a government agency would not be amenable to the team-based quality process, much less the idea of people working with others outside their immediate work area. These cynics only see resistance to change in government agencies, compounded by a view that says, "What's the point of process improvements? If we show we can do more with less, they'll just cut our budget next year." But the cynics would be wrong. I see many government agencies at all levels using cross-functional teamwork to improve services to the public.

Although many people would not point to the U.S. Department of Veterans Affairs as a paragon of innovation and change, they would miss an important example of successful teamwork. At the Philadelphia Regional Office and Insurance Center (ROIC), more than forty cross-functional quality teams were formed. The initial results of some of the teams were impressive.

> One of the first teams tackled problems within the Veterans Insurance Phone Service, where each day telephone operators handle between 2,600 and 3,000 calls from veterans and their beneficiaries. In the 21 months that the eight-person team met, it reduced the percentage of multiple calls reps receive (when a customer calls more than once to get the same information) from a high of 12.9 percent in January 1990 to a low of 3.3 percent the following August. . . . Another team saved the department an estimated $168,000 by simplifying the office's loan-default processes (veterans can borrow mortgage funds from the ROIC) [Penzer, 1991, p. 36].

The interesting aspect of this team-based quality program is that whereas cost savings are a natural outcome of teamwork, other factors may prove more important in the long term. Less tangible but potentially more powerful is the learning that comes from understanding the total work process, including all the tasks and how they fit together. Serving on a cross-functional team has helped employees understand how a screw-up in their area affects work in other areas. In addition, individual employees get a sense of ownership and empowerment from participating on a team that generates ideas that eventually see the light of day.

One radical innovation using cross-functional teams took place in the Kentucky school system. The power to make key decisions about textbooks, courses, and teacher selection was taken from local school boards and handed over to school-based councils made up of the principal, three teachers, and two parents. In this case, the customers are parents and students. Although each of

Kentucky's 1,366 schools has considerable control over the education of their children, they are also accountable for results. Each school is also rewarded if test scores, attendance records, graduation rates, and other standards increase significantly. The rewards involve monetary payments, which can be used to supplement teachers' salaries or make school improvements. The reward system is also designed to encourage teamwork in the school among teachers and other professionals because the awards are given to the schools rather than to individuals. In other words, if the school does well, the staff does well. Therefore, they are more likely to share ideas and resources with their colleagues. However, schools that do poorly will be declared "in crisis," which will trigger the dispatching of a team of experts to devise a rescue plan.

Here in one place we find some important factors for achieving success in cross-functional teamwork. The factors are (1) a small group of key players who are given sufficient authority to make important decisions, (2) measures of success provided in advance, and (3) rewards for success given to the entire team (Henkoff, 1991b; Dowler, 1991).

In a local school district in New Jersey, junior high school teachers in a variety of disciplines teamed up to provide quality education. For example, an eighth-grade-level team includes five teachers—English, social studies, math, science, and foreign language—and specialists in areas such as physical education, industrial arts, the library, art, and music. The team met regularly to correlate the learning between subjects.

- When the English class is reading a novel set during the American Revolution, the social studies teacher devotes several lessons to the historical background.
- The art teacher presents a unit on lettering at the same time the English teacher leads a unit titled "Designs in Art and Poetry."
- When the math teacher is teaching a unit on probability and statistics, the science teacher has a lesson on analyzing data.

The team coordinates field trips and midterm examinations. When one teacher takes the class to a museum, the other teachers do lessons related to the museum topic. The team can also schedule tests so they do not all fall on the same day. In addition, teachers can discuss and develop a coordinated game plan for students with behavior problems. Thus far, teachers in the program report that students are more motivated and there are fewer discipline problems. The students realize they are part of a team and seem to enjoy the competitive spirit that is associated with the team concept. In the future, the cross-functional team concept in a school should result in some positive shifts in the total organization. For example, assistant principals would be able to spend more time on real administrative and planning work and less on discipline. Perhaps there would be fewer curriculum coordinators and department heads or their role would change to focus more on strategic planning, coaching, and staff development.

In many ways, the advent of teamwork in the sales area amounts to the most radical application of the cross-functional team model. Think about it. The sales area is considered the last bastion of rugged individualism and entrepreneurship in most organizations. And yet, even here—especially here—organizations are finding a real payoff from cross-functional teamwork.

One reason cross-functional selling teams are emerging is that customers are demanding them. People in client companies are saying, "We're tired of dealing with a cadre of salespeople from your company. Most of your people do not even know each other, and as a result there is no coordination among the product lines." In an often-repeated story, two sales representatives from the same company meet each other at the elevator in a client's office and begin trading stories about the client. At that moment, the client comes by and proceeds to introduce them to each other. Only then do they realize that they work for the same company. Aside from the embarrassment, this is just plain bad business practice. It is quite possible that the two organizations and probably others could have a cross-functional account team that provides the customer with better service and ultimately yields increased sales and revenue from the company.

One of the innovators in this area was Procter & Gamble, which years ago acted to reduce the number of salespeople calling on retailers (Sellers, 1992). In addition, people from marketing, finance, distribution, and operations work with sales to coordinate efforts with large customers. These sales teams help big accounts such as Eckerd Drugs and Kroger solve practical business problems, which ultimately helps these large retailers sell more Procter & Gamble products.

Another large company using a team approach to oversee sales to large accounts is Black and Decker. One successful strategy they used was this:

> [The company] set up Wal-Mart and Home Depot divisions to cater specifically to those fast-growing accounts. In each, a vice president oversees a group composed of salespeople, marketer, an information systems expert, a sales forecaster, and a financial analyst. The team can be rallied to create a promotion, such as a specially designed package containing a drill and drill bits for the retailer. The result: Black and Decker sales to Wal-Mart were up over 10 percent last year, and those to Home Depot climbed almost 40 percent [Sellers, 1992, p. 102].

Cross-functional team selling does not work just for major corporations. Small businesses can bring together all the key players to increase sales and customer service. The mortgage banking industry is one such example. The number of mortgage bankers has increased dramatically, as a number of independent mortgage companies have sprung up. These companies aggressively sell mortgages to the home buyers and owners who are refinancing and then resell the "paper" to major lending institutions. As a refinancing customer of a local mortgage company, I can attest to the cross-functional teamwork required to close a deal. The team I dealt with included the sales representative, loan processor, underwriter, file clerk, receptionist, and other back-office people I never actually saw; most customers do not. Ancillary, but no less important, team members included the mortgage insurer, an appraiser, and an attorney. In the case of a home purchase, the realtor is also a key member of the sales team.

In a totally different market, BSD, a software inventory control company, uses cross-functional teams that are responsible for selling, designing, installing, and servicing specific customers in a particular area (Belasco, 1991). BSD is the most profitable business of its kind, with sales in excess of $500 million, built on the strength of seven hundred people organized into sixty-two teams around the world, according to James Belasco, a San Diego–based consultant to the company (interview with the author, January 1993).

Each team is responsible for hiring, training, and maintaining sales and service to customers in their area. Their success is built on the cross-training of all team members and a reward system tied to team success.

Cross-functional team selling lends itself to high-tech industries where product sales and after-sales support require a high level of technical expertise. The computer industry is a good example because selling computers requires working with the buyer to get the right mix of hardware, software, and support. Cathy Hyatt Hills, a sales-training consultant from Novato, California, says that sales teams include sales representatives, engineers, programmers, and, perhaps, lawyers, accountants, financing experts, and others (interview with the author, January 1993).

According to Hills, Pacific Bell is one company that has encouraged vendors to not only use cross-functional sales teams but to integrate them into their internal project teams. This cross-functional and cross-organizational team approach has "prevented costly mistakes . . . and improved the company's bottom line by getting new technology up and running more quickly than otherwise would have been possible" (Hills, 1992, p. 56).

The point is that many cross-functional teams arise because of demands from customers for a more coordinated, efficient, and cost-effective team approach to doing business with them. In an unrelated field, public service customers who also happen to be voters and taxpayers are demanding better cross-functional teaming. For example, the Major Projects Review Team in Clark County, Nevada, came into being as a result of demands from developers for better service. As team leader Marta Brown said, "The team was created based on demands from developers for a more efficient, customized approach to review of projects" (interview with the author, October 2001).

Guidelines for Maintaining Customer Focus

Using cross-functional teams to put the customer first requires

- A clear understanding of who the team's customer is
- Involving the customer closely, either directly as a team member or indirectly with consistent communication

- Training for team members in process-improvement techniques and team dynamics
- Empowerment of the team to make decisions that satisfy customer needs
- Rewards that support and encourage collaboration

The Fostering of Creativity

Cross-functional teams provide the basis for a creative mix of people with different backgrounds, orientations, cultural values, and styles. Although this diversity can be difficult to manage, the possibilities for bright new ideas and innovations to bubble up are great. In some organizations, these teams spring up like wildflowers; people with an idea or a problem simply call other people and say, "Let's get together and talk about making this part withstand heat better," or "How about a brainstorming session on making it easier for the customer to get this service on the weekend?" Some organizations foster this type of ad hoc collaboration by providing such simple things as flip charts or white boards in offices and hallways, as well as more substantive support, such as time and budget, to pursue an idea.

In every organization, an informal organization exists side-by-side with the formal bureaucracy. Sometimes called the emergent organization or adaptive organization, it is the latter-day version of what, more than thirty years ago, Warren Bennis labeled "the temporary society" (Bennis and Slater, 1968). Cross-functional teams embody the positive features of the informal organization because they provide the opportunity for creative expression usually reserved for small entrepreneurial companies. The team achieves this by being a venue for aligning what the organization seeks—innovation—with what excites creative people—an opportunity to use their heads and learn from each other (Dumaine, 1991).

Companies in computers, telecommunications, pharmaceuticals, and automobiles are especially supportive of cross-functional teams because of those industries' rapidly changing markets and the need for constant innovation. Other companies that bet their future on product innovations use cross-functional teams to drive the process. Some highly innovative companies have a goal that says 30 percent of their sales will come from products introduced in the last five years. Effective cross-functional teams foster creativity among their members. As Jassawalla and Sashittal (1999) found in their study of cross-functional teams in high-technology companies, the most collaborative teams "infused high levels of creativity in new product development processes, and better harnessed the energies, talents and creative potential of their cross-functionally trained members" (p. 4).

As Motorola has shown, cross-functional teams at all levels in the organization have been a vehicle for creative problem solving. "The Ronamakers [are] a group of workers around the world who manage inventory for Motorola's automotive and industrial group, which stocks things such as microprocessors and transistors. These employees, mostly high school graduates, started using basic industrial engineering techniques to analyze inventory and ultimately reduce average levels of supply to four weeks from nearly seven, saving $2.4 million a year" (Hill and Yamada, 1992, p. A18).

Creativity can be found in all parts of the organization when teams of colleagues and strangers from different parts of the company come together with the freedom to look at new ways of doing business. The structure, as well as the management style of the organization, can hamper freedom. As Paul Hartley, director, corporate strategy for Xerox, points out, "Prior to our use of cross-functional teams, we had stifled creativity because we were too cumbersome, too compartmentalized" (interview with the author, December 2001). At Southwest Industries, a high-technology aerospace engineering company, cross-functional shift teams have produced some dramatic breakthroughs in quality improvement. Composed of machine operators, electricians, maintenance mechanics, and tool and dye makers, the teams were given responsibilities for quality previously handled by quality control inspectors.

> Under the previous system, by the time quality control inspectors found a problem, 25 to 30 more airplane frames had been run before the operation could be closed down and the cause found and corrected. Now the team members usually find the problem early on and correct it. Work in progress inventory is down, output per shift is up, and the two inspectors are no longer needed [Robinson, Oswald, Swinehart, and Thomas, 1991, p. 14].

Guidelines for Fostering Creativity

Cross-functional teams can be a vehicle for fostering creativity if

- The culture supports informal problem solving.
- Communication among team members is open and candid.
- The structure is fluid and open across organizational lines.
- Risk taking is encouraged and rewarded.
- Product and service innovations are seen as critical to the organization's future.

Value of Organizational Learning

The value of the cross-functional team as a "learning community" is rarely proposed. Because the emphasis is on the ever-present bottom line, "soft" benefits such as education and training are not given sufficient emphasis. However, it is all those things "above the line" that make for a profitable bottom line. Knowledge management is being seen more and more as an important management strategy.

In many cases, employee learning in cross-functional teams is informal; it happens as a natural result of opportunities to interact with colleagues and strangers who have knowledge and skills to share. At team meetings, presentations of proposals and status reports on topics related to the team's goals are a source of development. In addition, opportunities to ask questions and participate in discussions take place throughout the life of the team. Teams often use ad hoc subgroups, which offer another way to learn from colleagues. The great thing about the informal learning that is taking place all the time on cross-functional teams is that, as Pat Pendell, vice president–chief engineer in Xerox's document systems and solutions group, notes, "people begin to learn from outside of their discipline" (interview with the author, December 2001).

Even less formal is the networking that is part of the team process. People tell me that the cross-functional team is a place to learn from colleagues and strangers during those periods prior to meetings, during breaks, after the meetings, or over lunch. These contacts become resources for development in other settings and on other topics. An engineer at a telecommunications company told me she learned more about the business through interactions with associates at project team meetings than from any other source. Some of the learning may have a direct impact on the success of the project. As Dr. Katherine Erlick of Boeing pointed out, "The cause of our success was that technical writers who prepare the manuals learn from hearing the engineers and are better able to write documents, and engineers understand what the writers require" (interview with the author, October 2001). Similarly, Debra Gmerek of Parke-Davis said that "getting people involved with folks in other areas helped them understand how their work impacted other areas" (interview with the author, October 2001).

Formal training is, of course, a major benefit of cross-functional teams. For teams that are part of the quality improvement process, the members usually receive training in a variety of problem-solving techniques. Although the training is the usual fare, it pops up in some unusual places. For example, the Philadelphia office of the Department of Veterans Affairs (referred to earlier in this chapter) set up some forty cross-functional quality teams to improve the focus on the customer. The training included "learning about the customer-centered culture, statistical process control, group dynamics and error prevention" (Penzer, 1991, p. 34). Although the advantages to the organization on one level were apparent—costs were reduced; customers were satisfied—on another level they created a multiskilled workforce. A knowledge of group dynamics and problem-solving tools will be helpful to the company in the future when employees team up with people from other functions. In contrast to ten years ago, organizations are now providing specific training in team effectiveness, conflict resolution, meeting management, and team leadership skills for cross-functional teams. These organizations have come to realize the importance of cross-functional teams and, therefore, the importance of providing training to support these teams.

I recall one of my clients saying that although he valued the teamwork skills that his people were acquiring as they dealt with solving the current business problem, he was really interested in building a team-based culture over the long term. Over time, his organization did just that: it had a recognition program; the visible support of the managers; inclusion of team behaviors in performance appraisal; and a management team that served as a model of teamwork. In subsequent chapters, I discuss each of these areas and provide examples of organization supports for cross-functional teams.

Cross-functional teams are often involved in what I call formal technical training. There are two types of technical training: (1) the entire team learns the tools and techniques necessary for completing the work of the team, and (2) individual team members acquire the skills and knowledge of other jobs on the team. An offshoot of individual training is cross-training, in which individual team members train each other in their specific skills and job knowledge.

Team Learning

The work of many teams requires the use of tools and technology. For example, many engineering project teams, using a concept called concurrent engineering, need to learn how to use new hardware and software tools to support the design and development process. Litton Guidance and Control Systems in Woodland Hills, California, purchased Valid Logic Systems software and Sun Microsystems workstations. The company then provided classroom training on how to use the new tools, and an applications person from Valid came on-site every two weeks to answer questions. After some field experience, the classroom sessions were repeated in order to give the engineers an opportunity to ask questions and reinforce the learning based on actual use of the system (Beckert, 1991).

Team learning may also involve sessions conducted at team meetings covering basic information about the technical aspects of the team's project. Members of the team with the expertise conduct subject-matter training and orientation classes for other team members.

Individual Learning

In many cross-functional teams in manufacturing, cross-training is the key to a successful team. In this model, each team member acquires the skills of other team members' jobs and is therefore able to back up team members, detect errors in work, and participate more effectively in problem solving on intricate technical issues. Sometimes this training is done by other team members; other times it is conducted by supervisors and plant trainers. Companies such as Johnson and Johnson and Motorola have knowledge-based (also called skill-based) pay systems that provide pay increments for team members who successfully complete training programs and can demonstrate the new skill or knowledge.

Many organizations offer workshops in team communications that focus on learning to understand, appreciate, and communicate with a variety of team members with a variety of team-player styles. It is also important to include knowledge of different cultures and what people from these cultures bring to the team. Teams that are both cross-functional and cross-cultural provide rich opportunities to learn how to work with a diverse group of people (Halverson, 1992). In Chapter Ten, I outline a variety of training and development activities for cross-functional teams.

Guidelines for Organizational Learning

To take advantage of the learning opportunities provided by cross-functional teams, it helps to

- Provide training that breaks down the barriers between strangers.
- Conduct technical training that demystifies the work of the various functions on the team.
- Create an open environment, which allows informal learning to flourish.
- Provide team training in group dynamics, being a team player, conflict resolution, and meeting management.
- Reward team members who share information and expertise and team members who are active learners.

Need for a Single Point of Contact

In the functional team structure, it is often difficult to figure out where to go for information when working on a complex, long-term project. Because development in this structure is done serially, it is often hard to get an accurate and complete overview of the status, resources, and impact of the project. A major drawback of this approach is the lack of a shared vision. Functional team participants are usually more concerned about getting their piece of the puzzle complete than they are about seeing that the total project gets done. When a conflict arises between the project and their own department, you can be sure who wins.

In addition to the lack of a shared vision and commitment to the project, there is no good mechanism to coordinate the varied efforts. Some years ago, organizations using a matrix management structure resorted to the creation of "integrators" whose job it was to facilitate the coordination of the various allies, enemies, and strangers assigned to a project. The cross-functional team structure and process plays this role now.

> [A cross-functional] team becomes the single point of contact for all corporate functions involved in day-to-day development work and for managers within each function. The manufacturing team member, for example, serves as the core team's liaison with the manufacturing vice president and the manufacturing engineers assigned to the project. . . . The team system shifts employee focus away from specific divisions, departments, or other functional groups to the project itself, as the team members become accountable for achieving the project's goals [Whiting, 1991, p. 50].

External customers also like the idea of the team as the single point of contact. In Clark County, Nevada, for example, the Major Projects Review Team is "the one place to go for information about projects. A developer no longer has to go to three different departments for the status of their project" (Marta Brown, interview with the author, October 2001). Dr. Katherine Erlick reported that the cross-functional teams in Boeing's engineering organization found that "the customer really benefited because she or he could find out what was going on at any phase within a project via a single source, the project manager, who represented the team" (interview with the author, October 2001).

The automobile industry uses the cross-functional team as the single point of contact for the complex job of bringing a vehicle to market. In the past, the design process at Chrysler "was organized around a very traditional, sequential, component-based process characterized by vertically oriented functions or 'chimneys.' Most departments were in separate buildings, literally insulated by brick and mortar. . . . Designers worked . . . in a vacuum, creating a product and 'throwing it over the wall' to engineering in the next building, which would do the same to procurement and supply, down the line" (Lockwood, 2001, p. 5).

The company replaced this process with completely horizontal, cross-functional "platform teams." Chrysler coined the term *platform teams* to describe cross-functional groups charged with "bringing a vehicle to market—on time, within budget, and with world class quality characteristics" (Vasilash, 1992, p. 59). Platform teams include engineers, manufacturing experts, marketing professionals, and suppliers, among others. And the teams are effective. They have reduced time to market by twelve months and improved quality. One way they did this was to run pilot production vehicles earlier in the cycle. In the early 1990s, a team developed the LH midsize sedans (Chrysler Concorde, Dodge Intrepid, Eagle Vision) as a platform, discovering 93 percent of all problems by week thirty-five and resolving 55 percent of all problems by then as well.

Does this new use of cross-functional teams make a difference? Industry watchers seem to think so. In its year-end roundup of 1992's new-product innovations, *Fortune* (December 28) highlighted the Chrysler LH Series for its "groundbreaking design" and surprisingly moderate price. Platform teams are given credit for the success of the LH series, which was named Car of the Year for 1992 by *Automobile Magazine.*

Amoco Production Company provides us with another unusual example of cross-functional teamwork (Henkoff, 1991a). Several years ago, in an era of higher production costs and cheaper oil, the company decided that it needed to lower overhead and improve its operating effectiveness. A cornerstone of the strategy was the creation of cross-functional teams invested with authority to make decisions and charged with being the focal point for coordinating the various change efforts.

In one example, the Offshore Business Unit in New Orleans formed a cross-functional team made up of geologists, geophysicists, engineers, and computer scientists. The team was responsible for obtaining more oil from fields in the Gulf of Mexico. Using powerful new workstations and no longer reliant on the company's mainframe computer, the team worked together to find more oil in an area that had already been explored. In the old functional organization, each of these specialists would have been off in his or her own little world, linked to a vertical chain of command. Now, with the authority to act, the necessary technological support, and effective teamwork, this team continues to show results. For example,

"Last year (1990) the offshore unit replaced more than 100 percent of its depleted reserves, an exceptionally good record in a mature province" (Henkoff, 1991a, p. 84).

In the sales arena, account teams (discussed earlier) serve as the single point of contact for all communication with the key company players and the client. In fact, it's inaccurate to call these major account teams "sales teams" because they include many other functions besides sales.

One of my clients uses cross-functional teams to do a wide variety of things, from developing a new system to creating a vision for the future of the organization to planning the annual division conference. Anyone in the organization who has an idea, comment, or criticism knows where to go and can be sure it will get consideration. Team members also serve as a communication link with their groups, keeping them informed about the progress of the team's work and soliciting their ideas on the team's project.

Some years ago, the U.S. Environmental Protection Agency (EPA) began a fascinating experiment in cross-functional teamwork aimed at, among other things, creating one clear agency voice to speak to its "customers" (industry and environmental groups). These EPA "cluster teams" brought together people from many different offices to create a total approach to specific environmental issues (Cleland-Hamnett and Retzer, 1993). It was projected that the regulated community (EPA's customers) would benefit from this collaborative effort because it would eliminate duplication of efforts by various agency offices, reduce compliance costs and hassles, send a consistent EPA message to the community, and result in more innovative alternatives to environmental problems. Although the cultural and structural barriers in the agency were significant, the EPA moved forward with more than a dozen cluster teams because they saw some tangible benefits from a single point of contact. For example, the Pulp and Paper Industry Cluster decided to develop two key air and water regulations together, which will result in "an optimal combination of technologies to meet air and water requirements, avoid unnecessary cross-media pollution transfers . . . minimize releases to air and water . . . and reduce compliance costs to the industry" (Cleland-Hamnett and Retzer, 1993, pp. 19–20). I had had a chance to work with the EPA cluster program, and I see it as a model for cross-functional teamwork throughout government and other complex bureaucracies. For example, as John Dew, director of continuous quality improvement at the University of Alabama, pointed out, "Universities are very complex organizations, so it's hard to get clear information about a project issue. The team is a partial solution to this barrier" (interview with the author, September 2001).

Guidelines for Teams as the Single Point of Contact

To take full advantage of the cross-functional team as the single point of contact,

- Clearly communicate to the stakeholders that the team or the team leader is the point of contact for information about the project or team-related issues. As Sue Whitt, vice president of Parke-Davis, said, "We made it clear to everyone, 'If you want to know where your data base is, ask the team leader. If you want to know where your statistical analysis is, ask the team leader'" (interview with the author, October 2001).
- Tighten up internal team communication so that the leader has all the relevant information so that he or she can carry out the contact role effectively.
- Provide regular communication from the team to the key stakeholders about team progress and related issues.

Much can be learned from the experiences of organizations that have experimented with cross-functional teams. From these reports of successful teams, the keys to successful cross-functional teamwork appear to be as follows:

- Management support in the form of tangible resources, encouragement of risk taking, and empowerment is critical.
- A clear, overarching goal that transcends individual functional priorities and commands the commitment of team members is essential.
- The team should identify their customer or key customers and maintain focus on satisfying their customer.
- Team rewards must correspond to and support collaborative efforts.

- The organization should provide training to help colleagues, enemies, and strangers work together effectively with the goal of encouraging an open learning environment.
- The team should include the right mix of players, including a leader able to pull together a diverse group of people in support of the team's goals.
- The team should be empowered to act in a way that's consistent with its responsibilities.
- The organization should encourage and support the effort to establish the team as the single point of contact for information about a project.

Looking Back: Some Issues to Consider

1. Speed is one important reason for using cross-functional teams. What are short- and long-term advantages and disadvantages of the current obsession with speed in organizations? How important is speed in your organization?

2. Some people feel that working as a team rather than producing more creative outcomes actually results in watered-down compromises and bland solutions. What do you think? What is the situation in your organization?

3. Other people believe that the way to get breakthroughs in new products or services is to send an expert off by him- or herself to work on the problem. They see teamwork as a series of exercises in "sharing ignorance." What do you think?

4. Why should we care about the cross-functional team as a "learning community?"

5. Among all the competitive advantages of cross-functional teams, which one is the most important? How has your organization benefited from cross-functional teams? Are there benefits that have yet not been realized?

Chapter Three

Overcoming Barriers and Obstacles to Teamwork

Merely having a functionally diverse team is not sufficient for the emergence of quality.
RAJESH SETHI, ASSISTANT PROFESSOR OF MARKETING, SCHOOL OF BUSINESS, CLARKSON UNIVERSITY.[1]

Despite the obvious advantages of cross-functional teamwork, it is not as easy as it looks. There are many obstacles. Each obstacle is significant, can limit the effectiveness of cross-functional collaboration, and can even bring down a team. That's the bad news. The good news is that we know how to deal with each of these barriers. The remainder of this book is devoted to a detailed exploration of each of these issues and to a series of recommendations for overcoming the barriers. However, before we look at the barriers, let's look at the natural history of a cross-functional team (Parker, McAdams, and Zeilinski, 2000) and the potential barriers at each stage.

The Natural History of a Cross-Functional Team

Although it is risky to generalize about "all teams" because the details vary significantly from team to team, most cross-functional teams follow a pattern in their development. This pattern provides

---

[1]Sethi, 2000, p. 11.

a helpful framework for looking at potential barriers that can pop up during the journey.

Creation

Most cross-functional teams begin in the mind of a person, usually an executive or senior manager, who sees a problem or an opportunity for the organization and envisions a collaborative approach to addressing the issue. He or she has a vision of a better way—a new product, better customer service, a new system—and believes that a functionally diverse team is the way to get there. Usually, the vision is translated into an overarching goal ("to improve turn-around time on customer requests") or a new way to do business. At this point, the person, often referred to as the sponsor or champion, should hand the problem or opportunity off to the team leader for further development. However, that is not the way it always happens, and we encounter our first obstacles.

Potential problems at this stage include the following:

- The sponsor provides too much direction to the team by either making the goal too specific or telling the team how the problem should be solved, or both.
- The team's flexibility and freedom to use its expertise is limited because the leader has created restrictive boundaries.
- The team sees its goal as simply trying to satisfy the sponsor.
- The team lacks accountability and, therefore, commitment to the goal because "it's the sponsor's goal."

Formation

The sponsor, with the overarching goal in hand, begins the team-forming process with the selection of the leader. The leader of the team should be a person with both a working knowledge of the technical issues and the interpersonal skills to lead a diverse group of people. The leader has to know enough about the subject to understand the issues and follow the discussions but need not necessarily be the most knowledgeable in the field. However, he or she must have the expertise and skills in team process issues such as conflict resolution, consensus building, and meeting management (see Chapter Four for much more background of leadership requirements).

In conjunction with the team leader, the sponsor selects team members from the various functional areas necessary to address the team goal. In some cases, the manager of the functional department is asked to provide a person for the team. In the best of all possible worlds, the leader or the sponsor will meet with the department manager to explain the role of the team and the type of person the team needs.

The formation stage can produce some significant obstacles that often remain for the life of the team. Barriers created at this stage include the following:

- The leader is a technical guru but lacks the team leadership style and interpersonal skills to manage a cross-functional team.
- Team members are selected for the wrong reasons, such as (1) they are the only people with time available, (2) they are new to the organization and need development opportunities, (3) they are not on any other teams, and (4) the best people are busy working on department projects.
- The team is too large, because either too many departments are involved or each department is sending several members.

Launch

A team kick-off meeting is a critical milestone. A launch meeting should be designed to present the management's expectations for the team, the overarching goal, and any restrictions or limitations on the work of the team. The meeting should be attended by the sponsor, the leader, and of course the members. Some teams also invite functional managers and other key stakeholders to the meeting. At the meeting, team members should have an opportunity to ask questions and present concerns about the team and their role on the team. This is also an opportunity for the sponsor to both address the concerns and questions and hear the issues that could derail the team in the future.

After the kick-off meeting, the team should translate the overarching goal and management's expectations into specific performance objectives, milestones, and a project plan or what some organizations call a Statement of Work. The sponsor then reviews the Statement of Work. Once the sponsor and the team agree on the objectives and the plan, the team should be empowered to do whatever it takes to achieve the objectives in the context of the plan. A well-thought-out launch is very important because, as I often say to team leaders, "The way you start out is a good predictor of how you will finish."

Barriers encountered here get embedded in the foundation of the team and include the following:

• Member concerns and questions that are not addressed emerge later in the life of the team and are more difficult to handle.
• Lack of clear objectives, specific milestones, and a well-developed plan make it difficult to establish team accountability, develop member commitment, and track team progress.
• Lack of empowerment or confusion about empowerment slows progress and dampens morale.

Development

Following launch, most organizations provide some form of team building or team training. Training may involve classes and coaching for the leader, workshops for members, and briefings for senior management. Team building may involve work directly, with the full team designed to put in place norms for communicating, making decisions, solving problems, resolving conflicts, and managing meetings, as well as other areas of internal and external dynamics (for more on types of team learning, see Chapter Ten). Development provides the team with the skills and knowledge needed to work together to accomplish the objectives and carry out the plan. Obstacles at this stage are important but not critical to success. Often these obstacles can be overcome during later stages.

Barriers encountered during this stage include the following:

• The team is launched without any training or team building.
• The training or team building is inadequate or ineffective.
• The training or team building comes too late; it comes after the team has already experienced problems.

Initial Success

When the creation, formation, launch, and development goes well, the team hits the ground running. Members are energized and, as a result, usually score some early successes. In fact, team coaches and trainers often encourage the team to get some quick wins as a way of establishing a positive team climate early in the life of the team. Often there is so-called low-hanging fruit in the form of new processes, policy changes, or the updating of outmoded procedures that can be quickly and easily addressed and successfully completed. In other cases, there is "fat" in the system, time requirements that are unrealistic, or silly rules that are amenable to a quick fix. Even though all this early success is positive, it can create internal barriers that can create problems in the future.

Barriers that can develop here include

- An overemphasis on short-term tasks at the expense of long-term goals and outcomes
- An obsession with quick fixes to the exclusion of an examination of fundamental change
- An obscuring of the need to address team process issues critical to moving to the next stage

Cynicism

The low-hanging fruit dries up or disappears; the easy wins are nowhere to be found; the honeymoon is over. Cynicism sets in, or what Tuckman (1965) called *storming* takes over. Except in corporate cultures that allow it, overt conflict characterized by loud disagreements and nasty e-mails is rare. Rather, team members express their disagreement with passive-aggressive behaviors such as showing up late for meetings, not completing assignments, or failing to participate. You can also observe cynicism in nonverbal messages such as smirks, rolled eyes, and bored expressions. Quite often, I find these reactions expressed outside of meetings in hallway conversations and over lunch in the cafeteria where small groups of team members congregate. At this point, team members are frustrated by the failure to make progress, a perceived lack of management support, and a belief that their teammates lack commitment.

This is a dangerous stage because it is here that teams derail and have great difficulty getting back on track. Even though the team may have established norms during the forming stage, they are not sufficiently embedded to act as a self-correcting force. Team members are still not sufficiently comfortable with each other to engage in a candid diagnosis of the problem and the development of an improvement plan.

Barriers associated with this stage include the following:

- Lack of embedded norms to serve as a self-correcting mechanism
- Quickly declining morale among team members
- Members retreating to focus on work in their functional area
- Few leaders with the process skills to address these issues
- Loss of faith in the team concept, especially in the cross-functional team approach

The Zone

Athletes and sports commentators often refer to someone who is playing very well as "being in a zone." The zone is not a place but a feeling that you can do no wrong; it is a time when everything is working in a perfect harmony or a feeling that you will succeed no matter what the obstacle. Your jump shot never misses; your tee shot is long and straight every time; every swing of the bat produces a solid connection with the ball. Artists and musicians experience a similar situation when the creative juices flow in a new and unique way and they are able to translate them into creative outcomes that chart a new course.

Teams also experience a kind of zone where it all comes together for them. After they have worked through the hard times of the cynical period, the full force of the team process is unleashed. There is a recommitment to the goals, member accountability for task completion soars, people are "living" the norms, milestones are hit, management interest and support is re-ignited, members are having fun again, and, most important, there is meaningful progress toward the goals. But just as success seems so close at hand, obstacles, subtle at first, begin to emerge.

During this stage, some significant barriers interrupt the sweet smell of success:

- Members wake up to the realization that the predominant management style is still command-and-control.
- Despite the talk that teamwork is important, the performance management system still favors technical experts who care little for collaboration with colleagues.
- Although the team has forged effective cross-functional collaboration in its little world, the organization is still dominated by rigid functional silos.
- Although the team has received some informal forms of recognition, the corporate rewards program is still competitive ("employee of the month"), focused on individuals rather than teams, and does not encourage or acknowledge collaborative behavior by teams.

In order to take cross-functional team success to the next level—to a place where they are not solely dependent on the team being in a zone—the organization must create an environment that incorporates factors that facilitate team success rather than block it. In this world,

- There is a cadre of team leaders capable of leading a diverse group of members and working with a diverse group of stakeholders.
- Teams are empowered to act, based on a set of objectives and a plan that is developed jointly by management and the team.
- Management holds functional department heads and other stakeholders accountable for their efforts to support the work of cross-functional teams.
- There is systemic support for cross-functional teams in the areas of performance management, rewards, and recognition, as well as organizational development and training.

In the next section, we look at the specific obstacles and issues that need to be addressed by the team and the organization.

Obstacles to Success

On the face of it, cross-functional teamwork looks like a great idea and an easy one to implement. Simply get together a group of people from different parts of the organization who have something to contribute about a subject, and good things will happen. There is something very logical about identifying a problem and then asking eight or ten people with a variety of backgrounds, experiences, and opinions to share their ideas and develop a plan of action. But like many good theories about group behavior, when it gets tested in the field, barriers to its success emerge. As Hutt, Walker, and Frankwick (1995), in their study of new-product teams point out, "Each department has common judgments and procedures that produce a qualitatively different understanding of product innovation. For example, marketing personnel are interested in products that will be successful in the near term while R&D personnel are interested in more radical breakthrough projects" (p. 23).

In the following sections, I describe the key barriers and then refer to the subsequent chapters that provide advice on how to overcome them.

Limitations of Team Leadership

Although the leader plays an important role on any team, leadership of a cross-functional team is both more important and more difficult. By definition, the team is dealing with a complex subject and a diverse group of team members. The team leader has to have the technical background to understand both the subject and the contributions made by people from a wide variety of backgrounds. The team leader must also have the "people management" skills to facilitate the interactions of a group of people who either have had little experience working together or have had some negative experiences in working together. Few people combine high-level technical expertise with exceptional team process skills. As Debra Gmerek of Parke-Davis pointed out, "It's not easy to find good team leaders because leader skills are not naturally developed in other roles. Leaders need more influence, project management, motivation and empowerment skills" (interview with the author, October 2001). In my experience, organizations tend to select the most logical person from a technical point of view, ignoring expertise in team dynamics. As a result, our surveys of cross-functional teams show that the major complaints about team leaders include their inability to run good meetings, involve everyone in discussions, resolve conflicts, and effectively use all of the team's human resources.

Think about the leadership of your cross-functional team; does the leader have

- The breadth of technical know-how to understand the big picture and the contributions of the broad range of team members?
- Sufficient process skills to manage the participation and involvement of team members who have a variety of past team experiences and a mixture of team player styles?

If you have some concerns about cross-functional team leaders in your organization, take a look at the suggestions in Chapter Four.

Confusion About the Team's Authority

One of the most persistent problems for cross-functional teams is their lack of empowerment. To be effective, they must have the authority to make decisions and implement them. A related obstacle is the lack of clarity about just how empowered the team really is. This confusion leads to a lack of consistency. "We didn't realize what the authority of the team was and, as a result, we were always going back to the coach (supervisor) for advice" (Dave Prochaska, training and development coach, Delta Faucet, October, 2001). Some teams, however—usually on the strength of the leader's skills—simply assume they have the requisite authority and therefore act in an empowered fashion. These cross-functional teams operate on the old axiom, "It's easier to get forgiveness than permission." Cross-functional teams with a more conservative leadership feel the need to seek approval for every key decision and in some cases actually send up trial balloons before making recommendations, much less taking action. In other situations, it is a matter of trial and error. For example, Marta Brown of the Clark County (Nevada) Major Projects Review Team noted, "We're still feeling out what things we need to go to the functional departments for and what things we can decide for ourselves. There have been times when the team had a problem because a department manager felt she should have been involved" (interview with the author, October 2001).

Is your cross-functional team

- Clear about the team's authority to make and implement key decisions?
- Clear about what decisions they want to be empowered to make?
- Empowered to act to the extent necessary to effectively carry out its responsibilities?

For help on addressing team empowerment issues, turn to Chapter Five.

Goal Ambiguity

Much of my work with cross-functional teams indicates a lack of a clear vision of where they want to be or what they want to accomplish. Many teams have action items, due dates, PERT charts, and other short-term planning tools, but they often have no long-term sense of the future. Often, members of a team are clear about what pieces they themselves have to deliver but little sense of where their pieces fit into the whole. As a result, team members are committed only to making sure their deliverables are accomplished. They care little for the work of the total project or for the need to pitch in to make it work. When the customer criticizes the team's performance, individual team members often respond with, "Well, I got my work in on time." Goal clarity is essential for team success because, as Frank Brinkman of IBM Software Group Data Management pointed out, "A team will disintegrate with goal ambiguity" (interview with the author, January 2002).

Assess your cross-functional team by asking these questions:

- Does the team have clear goals that are understood and accepted by everyone? (A quick test: Ask everyone to write down the team's goals, then collect and analyze the statements for both consistency and accuracy.)

- To what extent were team members involved in setting team goals?
- How often does the team review the goals to assess both progress and continued relevance?
- Have the goals been translated into specific performance objectives, milestones, and a plan?

If you feel this particular barrier is impeding your team, Chapter Six can help.

Stakeholder Relations

A team leader reported to me his disappointment that senior management had stepped in and, in a seemingly arbitrary fashion, terminated the work of his project team. When we sat down and analyzed the functioning of the team, he reluctantly admitted they had done a poor job of communicating with senior management about the team's work. In fact, team members were just arrogant enough to feel that their individual expertise was so great that the product produced by the team would be recognized for its brilliance. The team felt that management would not fully appreciate the team's work (translation: management is not smart enough), and the team did not need any management involvement (translation: management always screws things up). In the end, it was this attitude that led to the downfall of the project because the team did a poor job of interfacing with senior management to gain its support. In some organizations, this type of attitude is not acceptable. For example, at Parke-Davis, senior management said to team leaders, "It's *not* OK for you to have ineffective relationships with stakeholders" (interview with Mary Sylvain, team leader, October 2001). Cross-functional team stakeholders include senior management but also functional department managers, customers, support groups, and major vendors. The IBM PDxT Team included a customer as a member of the team to ensure that the customers' perspective was included in the final products. Participation of the customer came to be seen as the most natural thing. As one member of the team said, "After a while, team members viewed the customer as just another teammate rather than as the customer."

Has your team taken the time to

• Identify the key stakeholders outside the team?
• Develop a plan for building positive relationships with these stakeholders?
• Assign responsibility to team members for facilitating the interfaces?
• Identify opportunities for specific stakeholders to actively participate as either a core team member or an adjunct member.

Teams lacking good stakeholder relationships will find help in Chapter Seven.

Performance Appraisal

A nagging issue, and one that is likely to increase in intensity, is that of giving team members "credit" for their performance on cross-functional teams. Many cross-functional teams take people out of their departments, but their department managers must still assess their performance; team members often complain that their work on teams does not get seriously evaluated during performance reviews.

As more and more people spend more and more time serving on cross-functional teams, this will become a significant problem for organizations. I worked with a group of technical experts whose sole responsibility was to participate on different cross-functional teams. I use the word *group* to describe them because they rarely worked together as a department team. Because their department manager rarely saw them perform—because they usually worked on teams outside the department—she could not judge them by the quality of their written work. The only way for her to get a complete view of their performance was to obtain input from the cross-functional team leaders. Still, the process for incorporating team member performance into the corporate performance appraisal system is, more often than not, informal and ad hoc. As Pat Pendell of Xerox reported, "Participation on cross-functional teams is considered in the goal-setting and performance management process (PMP). I encourage team members to include team goals in their personal goals. I also tell them I will give input to their manager for their PMP" (interview with the author, December 2001).

In your organization, does the performance appraisal process

- Include cross-functional team participation as a factor in an employee's appraisal?
- Require or even encourage department managers to use feedback from leaders of cross-functional teams?

See Chapter Eight for ideas about what other companies have done to overcome this barrier.

Rewards and Recognition

As more work is done with teams, organizations will have to shift the emphasis of their rewards programs from individual to team awards. At the present time, one important barrier to the success of cross-functional teams is that the focus of many awards programs is still on individual performance. Although there will always be a need to recognize the individual who goes above and beyond, a good awards program must reward the collaborative efforts of teams as well. We must get away from the "star system" that rewards individuals who stand out from the crowd and begin to reward people who "help the crowd perform better." In other words, even our individual awards must acknowledge people who are effective team players—people who freely share their expertise, people who pitch in and help out when necessary, people who can effectively facilitate a meeting, and people who challenge the team to do better. Perhaps even more important, we have to take the risk of using project team incentives that reward team members based on a pre-announced formula when the team meets or exceeds its goals (Parker, McAdams, and Zeilinski, 2000). In the absence of such rewards, we run the even greater risk of decreased motivation on the part of team members because they do not believe the organization really values their efforts. For example, at Parke-Davis, "team members, at times, felt unappreciated for what they saw as significant progress" (interview with Mary Sylvain, team leader, October 2001).

Take a look at your current rewards program and ask these questions:

- Does it reward individuals who are effective team players?
- Does it provide awards to teams that accomplish their goals?

If you need ideas on team awards and recognition, you can find them in Chapter Nine.

Interpersonal Dynamics

Another persistent barrier to effective cross-functional teamwork is the failure of people to work well together in groups. Despite the increased number of people participating in recreational team sports, most people come to the workplace poorly prepared to function as a team player. Few people take courses in group dynamics, and even fewer develop group process skills naturally. In comparison with functional teams, cross-functional teams are more susceptible to poor interpersonal relationships, conflicts among team members, and a lack of trust and candor. Members bring to the team their ingrained work styles, developed as a result of their associations with people in their functional area. Members also bring differing priorities, past turf battles, negative attitudes about other functional disciplines, cultural biases, and other baggage—all of which sets up interpersonal barriers.

In your cross-functional team, do you see

- Serious interpersonal conflicts among team members?
- A willingness to openly discuss professional, personal, and cultural differences?
- Team members with the necessary interpersonal skills to facilitate good communication, effective conflict resolution, and member participation in decision making?
- Opportunities for team members to participate in team training programs?

If these are issues for your team, Chapter Ten contains ideas on training to overcome these barriers; Chapter Twelve describes interpersonal dynamics and how to improve them.

Team Size

Many teams violate one of the fundamental principles of effective teams: smaller is better. Just about everyone knows intuitively what researchers have proven over and over again about the size of a team: about four to six members, but certainly no more than ten members, works best. Yet cross-functional teams continue to try to operate with teams of twenty-five, thirty-five, and even fifty members. In fact, cross-functional teams seem especially willing to increase their membership rosters to a number that ultimately makes them unwieldy and ineffective. There seems to be a drive to involve as many people as possible as if, in some peculiar way, large membership is an indicator of successful teamwork. Paradoxically, a large membership is likely to be an impediment. As Paul Hartley of Xerox noted, large teams "had stifled creativity" (interview with the author, December 2001). In some organizations, many unnecessary people are invited to join the team because it is assumed that they would be offended if they were overlooked. Quite the contrary. They would probably be delighted to have one less meeting to attend and one less responsibility to worry about.

Take a hard look at the membership of your team and ask these questions:

- Are there simply too many people on the team? Could you do just as well or better with fewer members?
- If the membership is large, do you use a core team to make key decisions?
- If the membership is large, do you break down into small task groups to accomplish most of the real work?

If your team is too large, go to Chapter Eleven for ideas on how to deal with size.

Lack of Management Support

There is very little a team can accomplish without the support of management, both senior management and functional department management. This is often the "killer" barrier. The team can overcome many of the other barriers by team actions such as training, good leadership, planning, and communication, but if key management stakeholders either do not cooperate or, worse, sabotage the team, there is little the team can do about it. Sometimes senior management "talks the talk" but does not "walk the talk" in providing the tangible supports such as budget, people, time, and interest. That team will fail. In addition, functional department managers "can feel a loss of power and control over . . . projects" (Sethi, 2000, p. 13), which makes it difficult for the team to make effective use of department resources. Effective boundary management can only go so far.

In your organization,

- Does senior management have a clear goal of supporting and encouraging cross-functional teamwork?
- Does senior management act in a way that demonstrates tangible support for cross-functional teamwork?
- Do functional department managers understand the priorities of cross-functional teams in relation to the managers' own departments?
- Do department managers support the work of cross-functional teams that require use of department resources?

Senior managers can refer to Chapter Thirteen for advice on how to build a team-based environment in the organization.

In this chapter, we have looked at team and organizational barriers to successful cross-functional teamwork. In the chapters that follow, we look at each of these barriers and suggest specific methods for overcoming them.

Looking Back: Some Issues to Consider

1. How would you rank order the barriers? Start with "1" as the most difficult barrier to overcome for a cross-functional team.

2. New research reports that team size has little impact on team success. What does your experience tell you about the impact of size on team success?

3. If management does not provide sufficient support for the work of a cross-functional team, is there anything the team can do about it?

4. If your team has an ineffective team leader who has been appointed by senior management, what can the team do to overcome this barrier?

5. In your experience, what are some of the other obstacles that cross-functional teams face?

Chapter Four

Leading Cross-Functional Teams
It's a Tough Job!

*I don't have all the answers. My role is to facilitate
making it happen.*
MICHAEL HEIL, TEAM LEADER, BOC GASES[1]

Over the years, leadership has been a subject of great discussion
and much debate. Various people have emphasized visionary leadership, shared leadership, empowered leadership, values-based
leadership, charismatic leadership, and even tough-minded leadership. Leaders of cross-functional teams must possess all of these
characteristics and more. This is a tough job!

Leaders of cross-functional teams must manage a diverse group
of people, often with a wide variety of backgrounds, cultural values, languages, team-player styles, training, and interests. In addition to the people-management skills required, a team leader must
also follow the often highly technical and scientific nature of the
team's work. Frequently, all of this must be accomplished without
the authority that is usually associated with a team leadership position in a functional organization.

---

[1]Interview with the author, November 2001.

In today's world, an added leadership challenge is the cross-functional team that operates in a virtual world where members communicate electronically and may never experience a face-to-face meeting. In some cases, team members are dispersed around the world, making even a teleconference meeting of the full team difficult because of time zone differences. It's a tough job!

Would you apply for or accept this position? Your job, as leader of a cross-functional team, would be something like this: you'll be managing a group of people from different departments, functions, countries, and cultures who have little or no experience in working together (given the choice, those people would probably choose *not* to work with these strangers). You will be given little or no authority over their performance; however, you will be held accountable for the success of the team. You must have sufficient knowledge of the team's task to follow the discussions and reports. And you should have the group process skills to facilitate the participation of team members, resolve conflicts, and gain a consensus on key issues. By the way, much of this facilitation will take place electronically, using various technology-based tools that you will need to master.

Given this job description, few people would apply for the position, and even fewer would be able to meet these standards. As Xerox Vice President Pat Pendell said, "It's a difficult assignment. Sometimes we try to grow people too fast because we just don't have enough people to go around. In those cases, their direct manager has to provide support" (interview with the author, December 2001). As I said, it's a tough job! Yet it must be done.

Needed: A New Breed of Leader

Most organizations select the cross-functional team leader based on his or her knowledge of the technical, scientific, or business issues. In some other cases, especially where the ranks have been thinned by downsizing, the selection is based on availability. However, the most logical person from a task or subject-matter perspective may not be the best person to lead a cross-functional team.

Many technically trained professionals lack the experience of working effectively in groups. In fact, they often chose their profession because it involves working independently, with minimal supervision and interpersonal contact. The doctor, the engineer, the computer scientist, and many other professionals who may prefer to work alone and with limited outside interference must now lead teams that include people from strange places such as marketing, sales, and human resources. As leaders, they must also communicate with senior executives and department managers, as well as external stakeholders such as regulatory agencies, vendors, and even customers. Functional heads and other stakeholders want and need this ongoing communication. As Barbara Gledill, manager of a key functional area at Parke-Davis, pointed out, "The effective team leader is available to the functional heads. In addition to the informal communication, they schedule regular one-on-ones with us" (interview with the author, October 2001).

Simply appointing the smartest physician or electrical engineer to head a project team does not ensure success. The key to the success of these teams is the ability to meld the talents of this diverse group. Our data show that the people typically selected to lead these teams tend to be task-oriented team players I call Contributors (Parker, 1996). Contributors tend to be excellent at getting the team to focus on the immediate task in an organized and efficient manner (see Chapter Twelve for more discussion of these styles). They emphasize short-term, specific outcomes, with a great concern for the quality of the product. The strengths of the Contributor are sometimes offset by a failure to have a vision and to set long-term goals. And Contributors usually do not see the value of positive group process—a concern for good interpersonal relationships, effective involvement by team members, open communication, conflict resolution, and consensus decision making. Some companies are beginning to recognize the importance of good process skills to the success of cross-functional teams. In one situation, a drug development team in a pharmaceutical company was falling behind schedule to bring an important new compound to the market. The company replaced the team leader—a highly trained physician—with a scientist who had the interpersonal skills to pull the group together and meet the original milestones for submitting an NDA.

What is becoming more evident is that leading a key cross-functional team is a high-visibility opportunity for a high-potential person in the organization. Unfortunately, the skills that help identify a person as "high potential" are often not the same skills required to be a successful cross-functional team leader. In a study of the leadership practices of one highly regarded multinational company, reported by Morgan McCall (1998) in his wonderful book *High Flyers,* "the culture strongly emphasized and subsequently assessed and rewarded *individual* achievement, when at the higher levels, many of the skills needed for success shifted toward teamwork, coordination and cooperation with others and working through others to achieve synergy" (p. 57).

Leaders with Technical, Scientific, and Business Knowledge

I am a very good facilitator, but I could not lead most cross-functional teams. I lack sufficient knowledge of the subject matter to be able to follow the discussion and understand the implications of key decisions. A leader requires what I call a working knowledge of the subject or functional area. What this *doesn't* mean is that you have to know more than everyone else on the team. But it does mean you have to know enough to ask the right questions, to understand the answers, and to know if something doesn't feel right or smell right. As Paul Hartley, a Xerox senior executive put it, "You have to be more than a facilitator because pure facilitators don't have the knowledge base to make the tough call" (interview with the author, December 2001).

Although technical knowledge is not sufficient, it is necessary. It is necessary to establish the credibility and respect of the leader at the forming stage of the team when team members are looking to the leader for direction. As a leader, you must be able to present the overarching goal, the expectations of senior management, and the potential obstacles in a way that provides team members with the confidence that you have a grasp of the issues. In much the same way, you must project that same sort of technical leadership to senior management sponsors who may be investing a great deal in the work of the team. Mark Waxenberg, a vice president and general manager in Xerox's Production Systems Group, said in no uncertain terms: "You have to be respected by both management and the team" (interview with the author, December 2001).

However, it should be clear that you gain respect by "being authentic about what you know and what you don't know" (interview with Mary Sylvain, team leader, Parke-Davis, October 2001). Once again, other team members are there to provide their expertise; therefore, you do not need to know everything about every area. But you have to, as Ms. Sylvain said, "have a good b.s. detector!" In other words, you have to have enough technical training and experience to know when a team member is not being completely honest and forthright. It is helpful to know how long a test should take, whether a proposed approach is necessary, or if a suggested solution will work in the real world. You do not have to know how to do any of these things but know enough to tell, as one team leader said, "if someone is 'jiving.' me." Dr. Katherine Erlick, a project manager with Boeing, put it quite succinctly: "You have to be technically competent and be able to handle people" (interview with the author, October 2001). It is the "handling people" area that seems to be the differentiating factor for cross-functional team leaders.

Leaders with Group Process Skills

The successful leader of a cross-functional team must have the necessary technical expertise to understand the issues and keep the team focused on the goal. Many team leaders are able to meet this requirement. However, although an understanding of the technical issues is necessary, it is not sufficient to ensure the success of the team. The successful leader is also able to understand and facilitate the human dynamics of the team—what I call providing "positive process leadership." Process leadership involves bringing together the strangers who do not know each other, colleagues who have worked together on other tasks, and, perhaps, enemies who have participated in some past organizational battles.

Some of these positive process skills include the following:

- *Asking questions that bring out ideas and stimulate discussion.* As Marta Brown, team leader of the Clark County (Nevada) Major Projects Review Team, said, "You have to be very good at helping the team get to the heart of the matter" (interview with the author, October 2001).
- *Using paraphrasing and other listening skills to ensure effective communication.* Many people in our study reported that a willingness to listen and having the skills to do it well were critical to a successful leader of a cross-functional team.

- *Managing group discussions to encourage quiet members to partici-pate and talkative members to adhere to limits.* Because many teams are too large, the ability to facilitate group interaction is tough but essential.
- *Establishing an informal, relaxed climate where members feel free to candidly express their point of view.* It is important for a leader to present him- or herself as open to new ideas, reasonable risks, and out-of-the-box thinking.
- *Using the consensus method to reach decisions on key team issues.* Although sometimes the leader has to be willing to, as Pat Pendell of Xerox said, "make a decision, take action and move on," *key* decisions are best made with the active involve-ment and commitment of the team.
- *Involving members in the setting of team goals, objectives, and plan.* Overall goals (for example, to deliver the macro soft-ware by December 31) are handed to the team by the senior manager sponsor; the team leader then works with team mem-bers to develop the specific plan by which the team will accom-plish the overall goal.
- *Implementing good team meeting guidelines, including agenda plan-ning and time management.* Because the team meeting is the most visible team activity, it is essential that your team meeting be well planned and well run. Nothing turns off team mem-bers faster than a boring, unproductive meeting.
- *Insisting that team members respect each other and that each person's contribution is valued.* Because team members come from dif-ferent parts of the organization, it is important that everyone realize that all functions have a different but essential role to play in the success of the team.
- *Facilitating interaction among members.* Effective team leaders "encourage team members to express whatever differences they have in task-productive ways . . . [and] leaders can give constructive feedback regarding team members' work, thus setting an expectation that some disagreement is nor-mal and expected" (Lovelace, Shapiro, and Weingart, 2001, p. 784).
- *Identifying and dealing with dysfunctional team member behaviors.* In leadership training sessions, we help team leaders develop coping strategies for dealing with members who dominate

discussions, come late or leave early, or engage in side conversations and similar antigroup behaviors.

- *Celebrating the achievement of milestones and other team accomplishments.* Great team leaders encourage team members to plan celebrations to acknowledge the attainment of team successes. For ideas on celebrations, see Parker (2002).
- *Using recognition methods, task assignments, and other techniques to motivate team members.* "Great project managers share the credit and take the blame" (Melymuka, 2000, p. 64).

Leaders Who Are Empowered

Another key requirement is the ability to work in an environment where you are expected to have a great deal of responsibility but little, or at best murky, authority. The challenge for the team leader is to either clarify the team's authority or act as if empowered. In fact, for project teams composed mostly of technical or scientific professionals, it is probably true that empowerment "is only important to the project leader whose name may be prominently associated with the project's success or failure" (Cohen and Bailey, 1997, p. 20). Many team leaders have become frustrated with their inability to control the resources on the team. The point is that you cannot control or manage the people on the team; rather, you have to *lead* them. Sheila Mello, vice president of BBN Communications in Cambridge, Massachusetts, and a team leader herself, put it this way: "Team members have their own functional managers, so I cannot tell them what to do" (Whiting, 1991, p. 54; see Chapter Five for more discussion of empowerment).

Leaders Who Can Set Goals

Effective leadership also involves setting a direction for the team. Setting goals is, of course, important to the success of any team. However, it appears to be especially critical to the success of cross-functional teams. My colleague Ira Asherman, a New York–based consultant to the pharmaceutical industry, points out that the failure to set goals is one of the most persistent criticisms of leaders of project teams who are responsible for bringing new drugs to the market. In addition to the typical reasons for having team goals, leaders of cross-functional teams are able to use the goals to resolve conflicts among members and obtain needed resources from important stakeholders. For example, Pearson points out that the inevitable conflicts that emerge among professionals on interdisciplinary child assessment teams can be resolved more easily if the team has "agreed on common goals" (Pearson, 1983, p. 395; see Chapter Six for a discussion of team goals).

Leaders Who Are Flexible

Flexibility is another key characteristic of the effective leader of a cross-functional team. A rigid, highly structured person who likes lots of clear rules and regulations will have great difficulty in this environment. Cross-functional teams operate in a fluid, changing arena. As hard as we try to clarify authority, establish policies, and publish manuals, the day-to-day functioning of the team will be changeable. As team leader, you must be prepared to react and adapt with ease. As Mike Waters, vice president, human resources and quality of Xerox's Office Systems Group, points out, "A team leader must have an ability to deal with ambiguity because you will never have complete information. You have to accept that and move forward (interview with the author, December 2001).

Leaders Who Can Resolve Conflicts

One of the most important process skills is the ability to resolve conflict. We assume there will be some conflict on a cross-functional team. In fact, it is a given; it is even encouraged. The diversity of ideas, expertise, and styles is the very strength of a cross-functional team.

However, a strength can turn into a weakness if it is not handled with skill. First, the effective leader needs to understand that conflict is not bad and that disagreements on the team are to be expected. Viewed from a different perspective, if there is total agreement throughout the life of the team, something is wrong. Either we don't have a diverse membership or the diversity exists but is being suppressed or smoothed over. The effective leader encourages the expression of opinion, helps the team look at both sides of issues, forms subgroups to study problems, keeps the team goals and the customer in view, and uses the consensus method to make key team decisions. However, beyond the internal dynamics issues such as goal setting, conflict resolution, and empowerment, the effective leader must also address a series of external factors, which are discussed in the next sections.

Leaders Who Can Maintain Good Stakeholder Relationships

It is virtually impossible for a cross-functional team to be exclusively focused on the internal operation of the team. Even with the best technical work and group process, the team will fail if members are unable to work effectively with other key stakeholders outside the team. Stakeholders may run the gamut from the directors of functional departments represented on the team, to upper management who funds and supports the work, to government agencies who influence or approve the work, to community groups who care about the team's work, to other departments in the company who will make, sell, or service the team's product. The team leader is often the key facilitator of the interactions with the team's stakeholders. This function requires good communications skills such as listening, negotiating, and resolving conflict. (See Chapter Seven for ideas on how to build effective stakeholder relationships.)

Leaders Who Can Obtain Resources

Jane Perlmutter, a former manager with Bell Communications Research (now Telcordia Technologies, Inc.), suggested that the effective leader of a cross-functional team in telecommunications is able to "simply get team members what they need, when they need it" (interview with the author, January 1993). The needs of team members vary widely from laboratory time, computer support, and the development of prototypes to less tangible items such as fast turnarounds on approvals, freeing up of team members' time to allow them to work on team projects, and recognition for team member accomplishments. In some cases, extra help may mean additional human resources in the form of experts that the team needs to understand an issue or solve a knotty problem. Effective team leaders have "to be tenacious and want to make things happen . . . and they must be willing to make noise at the top and ask embarrassing questions when obstacles arise," according to Theresa Pratt, a team leader at Codex Corporation, an electronics company in Mansfield, Massachusetts (Whiting, 1991, p. 54). The effective leader knows how to work the system to get the team what is needed to get the job done.

Leaders Who Can Orchestrate Communications

Sometimes what the teams need is simply to be left alone. They do not want outsiders, including (and especially) top management, poking around them. They need time to work on the problem or do some development work, unencumbered with the need to make progress reports, answer questions, or deliver presentations. The effective team leader runs "interference" for the team by providing upper management and other stakeholders with enough information to satisfy their curiosity and keep the team insulated. In a study of project team leaders in a high-tech firm, Hansen (1995) found that team leaders consistently orchestrated their communication to management "to keep them at bay." In other situations, the liaison role of the team leader involves, as Geri Weber of Bell Communications Research (now Telcordia Technologies, Inc.) noted, "obtaining systematic feedback from management" (interview with the author, January 1993).

Cross-functional team members need to know that management supports the project; therefore, they want to get regular feedback from the management sponsors of the team. Because it is often difficult to get top managers to come to team meetings, the team leader has to communicate with these managers about the team's work, get their reactions, and report back to the team. In the electronics industry, which makes heavy use of cross-functional teams, "the team leader is a communicator, serving as the project's main point of contact between the company's executive ranks and the [team]" (Whiting, 1991, p. 54; boundary management is discussed in Chapter Seven).

Leadership Alternatives

As organizations understand the difficulty of identifying effective leaders for their cross-functional teams, they are looking for alternative solutions. There are a number of possibilities.

Coleadership

Coleadership is an approach being tried in a number of organizations. When there is a natural division of responsibility, this approach makes sense. One division of leadership roles that seems to work is the splitting of technical and process leadership functions. In this model, the expert-leader (for example, an engineer or physician) focuses on the task while the facilitator-leader, with group dynamics and team management experience, addresses the team meeting and other process issues.

Facilitation Support

Some organizations provide the team leader with a trained facilitator to help run the team. In this model, there is one team leader, usually a technical expert, backed up by a human resources staff person or other professional with good group process skills. The facilitator helps the team leader prepare for the meeting, offers advice and coaching on process issues, intervenes as necessary during team meetings, and works with individual team members outside the meetings.

Project Manager as Team Leader

Some organizations opt for a professional project manager to serve as team leader. These organizations believe that the technical and scientific input will be provided by the members of the team. This approach simply bypasses the technical leader in favor of a trained project manager. Certified project managers typically possess the tools and techniques to help the team

- Define a project
- Generate required tasks
- Determine responsibilities
- Define task sequence and critical path
- Develop a project schedule
- Analyze resource availability and scheduling
- Develop a project budget
- Track and manage a project
- Conduct project reviews
- Manage project relationships

Rotation of Team Leaders

This model applies to long-term projects that have a series of key phases. The leader changes as the project moves into a new phase, with the leader coming from the function that is carrying the ball during the particular phase. As a result, the leader is the person most knowledgeable about the current work of the team. It also means that the leadership burden is shared; it often means that the various phase leaders tend to support each other.

Leadership Training

This approach simply says that every cross-functional team leader needs solid leadership training. The training tends to be focused on the group process aspects of the position because these skills are usually the most poorly developed. (See Chapter Ten for ideas about team leader training.)

Leadership Requirements for Cross-Functional Teams

Effective leadership is effective leadership. Some universal truths cut across types of teams. There are some common characteristics of effective team leaders that apply to self-directed work teams, top management planning teams, temporary task forces, quality action teams, committees, and plain old-fashioned business teams. Effective leaders have a clear vision and are able to communicate that vision to the members of the team. They develop a sense of urgency about the team's work, involve team members in goal setting and decision making, and foster a climate of openness and honesty. People want to work for them; they have, dare we say it, charisma! Beyond these common characteristics, however, leaders of cross-functional teams need something more. The unique features of a cross-functional team call for some special characteristics—or a different spin on some familiar qualities.

Leaders of cross-functional teams have a difficult job because it requires pulling together a group of people who may be close friends, archenemies, or just strangers. It requires dealing with upper management, functional department heads, support groups, and other stakeholders who may or may not support the team's goal. The keys to success are to (1) select the right person, based on the criteria suggested in this chapter, and (2) provide training and support on an ongoing basis. See Figure 4.1 for a list of qualities a leader needs.

In the next chapter, one of the most difficult issues for team leaders is discussed: empowerment. For the leader, it often comes down to this: How do you get things done when you are not in charge?

Figure 4.1. Dimensions of Successful Cross-Functional Team Leadership.

- *Know Your Cookies.* Demonstrate a working knowledge of the technical, scientific, and business issues.
- *Work and Play Well with Others.* Have the skills or the potential to develop the skills to facilitate the group process issues of a diverse team of people and make it fun.
- *Initiate, Interact, Influence.* Be able to work with little, no, or at best unclear authority.
- *Stoke (and Stroke) the Stakeholders.* Practice effective relationship management up, down, and across the organization.
- *Set and Stay the Course.* Facilitate the establishment of team goals and an implementation plan and then keep focused on their targets.
- *Get the Goods.* Be assertive about obtaining the resources necessary for the team to be successful.
- *Bar the Door.* Protect the team from undue and unproductive outside interference.
- *Show Persistence, Perseverance, and Passion.* Demonstrate a commitment to and belief in the value of the work and a willingness to work through obstacles.
- *Bend Without Breaking.* Be open to change and help the team adjust to changing conditions and priorities.
- *Be Comfortable with Lack of Clarity.* Be able to deal with ambiguity and act without complete information.
- *Keep It Real.* Be authentic; make honest commitments, tell the truth, and act with integrity.

Looking Back: Some Issues to Consider

1. Think about a team leader of a cross-functional team that you find to be effective. What are the person's strengths? What does he or she do well?

2. How do you react to the conclusion of this chapter that group process skills are the critical differentiating characteristic of effective team leaders? To what extent is it consistent with your experience?

3. In the list of group process skills for a team leader (pp. 57–60), which is the most important for leaders in your organization?

4. How would you feel about selecting a leader for a project team that was developing a new engineering product who was weak technically but very strong in group process skills? Would such a person be selected in your organization? If you did select such a person, what would you do to ensure that the leader and the team would be successful?

5. How do you react to the notion that the *team leader* and not the team should be empowered? What are the advantages and disadvantages of such an approach? How does it work in your organization? Is the team or the team leader empowered?

Chapter Five

Empowering Teams to Do the Job

A team really gets empowered after they have made a decision, and you support it.
PAUL HARTLEY, DIRECTOR, XEROX[1]

In the last ten years, empowerment has come out of the closet. When I wrote the first edition of this book, empowerment was primarily something that management experts and team advocates proposed and debated. It was seen as more important for plant-based teams that were moving toward self-direction (Wellins, Byham, and Wilson, 1991). All that has changed dramatically. Now, as I predicted in 1994, empowerment is seen as an essential ingredient of a successful cross-functional team. And its importance has extended to just about every type and manner of cross-functional team, including those composed of scientists, technical personnel, service staff, administrative people, and even managers. In addition, as *cross-functional* comes to mean *cross-cultural,* empowerment is critical because "all the research on numerous global teams indicates that decentralization of authority is a key to improving decision-making processes" (O'Hara-Devereaux and Johansen, 1994, p. 154).

---

[1]Interview with the author, December 2001.

Empowerment Is . . .

An empowered team is one that has both the responsibility and the authority to carry out its mission and exercises ownership and control over its task and process. What does that mean? It is not carte blanche. It's all about boundaries. According to Pat Pendell of Xerox, it means "there is a defined set of boundaries within which the team can operate without outside influence in terms of key areas such as performance and budget" (interview with the author, December 2001). In a practical sense, it means a group of people who make decisions about certain defined aspects of their work without checking with anyone. As Vogt and Murrell (1990) put it, "In simple definitional terms, the verb to empower means to enable, to allow or to permit and can be conceived as both self-initiated and initiated by others" (p. 8). In other words, a cross-functional team can be empowered by management or can empower themselves by taking action in the absence of any prescription from management. I often advise teams to "go for it" as long as their actions or decisions are legal and ethical and not contrary to any company policy. This is called taking initiative.

For cross-functional new-product development teams,

> empowerment is defined as the range of decisions the team is authorized to make in order to get its job done. A team makes decisions in certain areas during new product development: setting technical and business specifications; determining product and process design content; scheduling and budgeting; obtaining resources (people, tools and facilities); coordinating with vendors, customers and other teams; and monitoring progress and evaluating performance. The team's empowerment increases as it obtains the right to make more decisions in these areas [Gerwin, July 1999, p. 12].

It is important to understand that empowerment is a moving target. A team's authority can expand and contract during the life of a project, sometimes in unplanned ways. Reasons for a change in team empowerment include

- *New information.* During the life of a team, new information about the task may come to light that makes it reasonable for the team to take on added responsibilities, along with the authority to make the key decisions in these areas.

- *Success.* When a team demonstrates the ability to make important decisions in a responsible manner, management is willing to shift more decision making to the team.
- *Failure.* When a team makes decisions that lead to a loss of confidence on the part of management, this can lead to a reduction in team empowerment.
- *Leadership change.* When a new manager arrives on the scene who does not support significant delegation of power to the team, he or she may pull back and reserve more decisions for him- or herself. In other cases, a change in team leadership may cause management to be less comfortable empowering the team if they do not have faith in the new leader.
- *Business pressure.* Stress caused by issues such as demands to bring a new product to the market faster or a rash of customer complaints can lead to a lack of patience with the team process and a reduction in the range of decisions under their control.
- *Lack of or unclear communication.* In some situations, the team is operating under one set of understandings and management is under another in regard to the degree of empowerment. When this conflict comes to light, the reaction is usually something like, "That's not what I meant." The net result is a change in the team's decision-making discretion.

Empowerment Is Not . . .

Some managers think that to empower a team means to adopt a completely hands-off posture. However, empowerment does not translate to abdication. It does *not* mean, "You're empowered; call me if you need anything." This is *abandonment.* Part of the problem, as I have observed it, is that some managers just don't know what to do.

In a team-based organization where cross-functional teams are the norm, managers are available to

- *Coach not control.* Managers help the team, often through coaching the team leader, to see the big picture, look at opportunities, be aware of obstacles, and anticipate problems down the road. They do not solve the problems or make the decisions but rather provide guidance that helps the team make the decisions. In one organization, the senior vice president pointed out a potential problem in a proposal that the team was considering, but he did not suggest what the outcome should be and did not even recommend a process; he allowed the team to work out the solution.

- *Champion not command.* The team should not look to the manager to make decisions for them but to be a cheerleader for their efforts. Some cross-functional team members are fearful of failure and, therefore, want management to tell them what to do and when to do it. They don't want to be empowered because they don't want to be held accountable. So they try to "socialize" a proposed decision in a draft form to find out how the manager feels about it. Management should resist all such efforts.

- *Advocate not abdicate.* When asked, the manager should support the work of the team with senior management, key stakeholders, support groups, customers, vendors, and others who can help the team or who are providing obstacles. The operative phrase is "when asked." Manager advocates work both on behalf of and at the behest of their teams.

- *Teach not preach.* A manager in a team-based organization began or ended many meetings with cross-functional teams in his organization with the phrase, "The way we used to do it in the Big Rock plant was . . . " and then proceeded to lecture them on how things should be done. The effective manager, by contrast, provides the team with the skills and knowledge to create their own road to success.

- *Facilitate rather than obfuscate.* Your job as an empowering manager is make it easier for the team to be successful by providing an inspiring vision, clear expectations, and support, along with the education and training that creates the conditions and the environment for the team to be successful. Sometimes this can mean direct involvement, as in the case of floundering cross-functional new-product teams at Microsoft. Breakthroughs "came only after senior management began to facilitate team meetings and teach fundamental principles of communication and team effectiveness" (Smart and Barnum, 2000, p. 21).

Four Levels of Empowerment

In an effort to help both coaches (managers) and teams clarify and get comfortable with the transfer of authority, the Delta Faucet plant in Tennessee developed four levels of empowerment:[2]

Level 1: Coach Decides[3]

Level 2: Team Has Increasing Input, Coach Decides

Level 3: Team Recommmends, with Considerable Input, Coach Decides

Level 4: Team Decides and Informs the Coach, Prior to Taking Action

Level 5: Team Decides, Implements Decision, Informs Coach

Level 6: Team Decides, No Further Action Required

A similar formulation was developed by Rees (1997), using four questions for management to ponder before they empower a team:

1. What decisions will be the *sole responsibility* of the team?
2. What decisions will be made *collaboratively* by the team and management?
3. What decisions will be *reserved for management* but *with* team input?
4. What decisions will be *reserved for management* but *without* team input?

Empowerment: So What?

What's all the fuss about? How does being empowered help a cross-functional team succeed, and what are the implications of little or no empowerment?

Let's begin with the negative end of the continuum. Lack of empowerment or confusion about the team's authority causes problems and limits success. Turf battles among team members can stymie a team's progress. Consider this scenario:

---

[2]Dave Prochaska, manager of training and development, Delta Faucet; interview with the author, October 2001.

[3]At Delta Faucet, the coach is typically a supervisor.

In 1990, Becton Dickinson developed a new instrument called the Bactec 860, designed to process blood samples. A team leader was assigned and immediately put together a project team of engineers, marketers, manufacturers, and suppliers. While the group eventually launched the Bactec 860 some 25 percent faster than its previous best efforts, (CEO Raymond) Gilmartin wasn't satisfied. There was still too much time-wasting debate between marketing and engineering over product specifications. Marketing argued that Bactec needed more features to please the customer, while engineering countered that the features would take too long to design and be too costly. Further inquiry led management to the nub of the problem: *because the team leader reported to the head of engineering, he didn't have sufficient clout to resolve the conflict between the two sides.* Today the company makes sure all its team leaders have access to a division head, which gives them the authority to settle disputes between different functions [Dumaine, 1991, p. 42, emphasis added].

In response to its large and growing number of managed health care customers, a major pharmaceutical company established a market planning team composed of top-level marketers from its key product lines. The managed care customers were demanding a coordinated corporate offering and a single point of contact for dealing with the company. Although the marketing representatives on the team recognized the necessity of cross-functional teamwork to respond to the needs of these customers, their bosses did not buy into the concept. As a result, after investing considerable effort in developing business plans for each major account, the team died. Cause? Good idea, customer focus, technical support, but no authority to act.

When cross-functional teams are empowered to act, however, great things can happen. In some organizations, empowerment means the freedom to act with minimal reporting and accounting restrictions and the flexibility to work around the system. In organizations where rapid response time is valued and in fact produces value, eliminating excessive approvals is equated with empowerment. And it works. At Calgon Corporation, Frank Daniher, director of water management research and development, reported that a cross-functional team with the freedom and flexibility to respond quickly to customer demands was able to cut the time it takes to commercialize a new polymer from twelve to four months (Wolff, 1988).

Finn Knudsen, director of research and development for the Adolph Coors Company, said that a team composed of people from research, marketing, sales, production scheduling, production, quality control and assurance, and packaging was able to cut by 50 percent the time it usually takes to launch a new product. The new product, Winterfest, a seasonal beer, was driven by a cross-functional team that was empowered by top management to do whatever it took to get the product to the market in time for the Christmas holiday season (Wolff, 1988).

The well-known story of AT&T's development of the cordless phone known as the 4200 also demonstrates the success of a cross-functional team empowered to act. John Hanley, vice president of product development,

> formed teams of six to 12, including engineers, manufacturers, and marketers, with *authority to make every decision on how the product would work, look, be made, and cost. The key was to set rigid speed requirements—six weeks, say, for freezing all design specs. Because the team didn't need to send each decision up the line for approval, it could meet these strict deadlines.* With this new approach, AT&T cut development time for the 4200 phone from two years to just a year while lowering costs and increasing quality [Dumaine, 1989, p. 57 emphasis added].

The Technical Services Division of Parke-Davis Pharmaceutical Company was in trouble prior to their transition to cross-functional teams in 1996. The company needed to improve the turnaround time on its ability to deliver data management, statistics, and research reports to the clinical development arm of the drug development process. Empowering the new cross-functional teams in conjunction with other changes in management and technology led to significant decreases in time for deliverables, in some cases up to 75 percent. For more on this story, see the first case, "Creating the Climate for Cross-Functional Teams," in the Resources section of this book.

One client organization—the Common Language Products Business Unit of Telcordia Technologies, Inc.—established a cross-functional team called Common Link. The team's goals for the year 2001 were, among other things, to improve intergroup communication, propose solutions to employee morale issues, serve as a communication link between the management team and employees, and plan and implement the monthly business unit meetings. Since cost-containment was an important company priority during this period, the boundary of the team's empowerment was defined in dollar terms. Although the team was empowered to implement any project that furthered its mission, any idea that required a "significant" financial expenditure required approval of the management team. This limitation on the team's level of empowerment proved to have an unintended salutary effect. It required team members to learn and effectively employ the discipline of preparing a business case that analyzed the problem, looked at alternatives, presented the recommendation, outlined the costs, and described the intended benefits. It also challenged the team to look for low-cost but effective solutions.

At another client organization—the Izod Retail Division of Phillips Van Heusen—cross-functional teams were established to develop recommendations to improve the quality of working life in five different but related areas. These teams, composed of a mix of people from all areas of the business, were empowered to "do whatever it takes" to study the issues and prepare a proposal that described their recommendations. Each team had a senior management sponsor who was available to advise and support the team. The team's boundary was clear: they could propose, but all recommendations had to be approved by the senior management team. In the end, proposals from all five teams were approved and ultimately implemented. The results were significant. Between 1999 and 2000, overall employee satisfaction rose in all five areas measured, and the division experienced significant sales growth. More than thirty new stores were opened, and many new product lines were introduced.

At BSD—a software inventory control firm—empowered multidisciplinary teams are the key to the company's success (Belasco, 1991). The teams are organized around a specific customer or a set of customers. Each team includes all the necessary sales, service, and technical experts to support a given customer. These teams are responsible for making all decisions on how to best serve their customer, including their own training and development.

James Belasco, a consultant to the company, reports that empowerment is working to make BSD "one of the most profitable businesses of its kind" (interview with the author, January 1993).

Empowered teams are also having a positive impact on buyer-seller relationships when cross-functional teams integrate cross-technological components. "For example, a new automobile brake, which combines traditional metallurgical and mechanical engineering with advanced electronics and microcomputer technologies, requires the integration of departments and personnel that have never worked together before" (Lyons, Krachenberg, and Henke, 1990, p. 30). These cross-functional teams make all the decisions about the product involved, including the selection of vendors. A core team from six different departments joined with purchasing to manage the total process. Other functional specialties, including, at times, supplier representatives, augment the team.

The Downside of Empowerment

Is there a downside to team empowerment? Perry, Pearce, and Sims (2000) point out three areas of concern:

- *Overzealousness.* A team may overreach its boundary in an earnest effort to be successful and thus cause unintended problems in other parts of the business. For example, in an effort to please the customer and close the deal, a sales team may make promises that result in additional work or difficult changes for other departments.
- *Perceived loss of status for middle managers.* Managers may perceive the transfer of authority to the team as a diminution of their authority and importance in the organization. These same managers may engage in various forms of resistance, including failing to provide coaching or help in overcoming barriers and obtaining resources. The organization needs to provide education and training to help them perform their new roles.
- *The empowered team as counterculture.* If hierarchy, top-down management, importance of silos, and no history of cross-organizational collaboration characterize the organization's primary culture, a cross-functional empowered team may be a disruptive force.

Empowerment: How to Get It and How to Give It

There are two important empowerment issues for a cross-functional team: the degree of clarity and the degree of authority the team may exercise.

Degree of Clarity About Authority

Many cross-functional teams are set up without any thought given to the degree of team empowerment. In other cases, authority is given to the team but the team simply does not use it. They either don't believe they have authority or they simply feel more comfortable checking their decisions with management. However, many cross-functional teams were never intended to be empowered teams; yet because the authority of the team was never clarified, the team wanders around frustrated by what they perceive as their ineffectiveness.

Degree of Authority

The first thing to understand is that team empowerment is not a gift. A team cannot be given real, operating authority as a present from senior management. Real empowerment, just like motivation, comes from within the team. Members act as if they are empowered. Bill Hines, an executive director with Bellcore (now Telcordia Technologies) in New Jersey, spent almost a year working on a policy statement empowering project managers (and their cross-functional teams) to make key decisions about project costs, deliverables, and resource allocation based on customer needs. Although all the right words were down on paper and the policy statement had been approved by top management, as Hines put it, "Now the trick [was] to get someone to stick their toe in the water and make a decision which benefits the customer" (interview with the author, January 1993).

This is not to denigrate the importance of a clear policy statement on empowerment. Such a written document is an important first step in the process. However, it cannot stand alone. Statements and actions by senior management must buttress the policy. Cross-functional teams must continually hear the message that they are empowered to act as long as their actions are in the best interests of the organization and "are not outside the boundary within which the team can make a decision without checking with a higher authority" (Paul Hartley, Xerox, interview with the author, December 2001).

Teams must also see actions that reinforce the written policy and verbal remarks. They must see senior management keeping a hands-off position in regard to cross-functional teams. For example, one of the fastest ways to "unempower" a team is to second-guess or, worse, change a decision made by the team because a senior manager got nervous or a functional department manager complained. As a director with a *Fortune* 100 company told me, "Around here, the authority of our project teams is, at best, ambiguous. We are told 'you can make decisions.' But, in reality, if they (senior management) don't like it, it won't fly."

Team Road Map to Empowerment

Here's how empowered teams get to be that way.

Empowered Teams Act Empowered

These teams take responsibility and assume they have the authority to act. They do not wait for top management's approval. Jim Kochanski, former director of human resources for Northern Telecom in Research Triangle Park, North Carolina, said that the question he hears often from leaders of cross-functional teams is, "How do I get the right kind of commitment, behavior, and decisions out of them if I don't have straight-line authority over them?" What they probably mean is, "If I don't have the authority to fire them" (interview with the author, January 1993). Kochanski used that statement to facilitate a discussion of what the team can do instead to become empowered or to act empowered to get done what needs to get done. The focus has to be on taking action rather than waiting for someone else to make it happen for you. Sometimes you just have to assume you are empowered. As Frank Brinkman, coleader of the IBM Post 9/11 Team said, "We just assumed our role was to get the customer up and running again and we should do whatever it takes to make that happen" (interview with the author, January 2002).

Empowered Teams Have a Clear Focus and a Plan

You can't ask for empowerment unless you can answer the questions, "For what?" or "To do what?" No one is going to give you carte blanche empowerment like an open line of credit. You need to be clear what you want to do, how you plan to get there, what the benefits will be, and what it will cost. IBM uses a formal process built around a Statement of Work (SOW) that outlines goals, activities, deliverables, and a timeline. As members of the Professional Development and Training Team told me in a group interview (December 2001), "Because the SOW is signed off on by all parties, including the management sponsor, we don't have to go back to management for approvals." In other organizations that lack a formal process, an inspiring goal can motivate a team to move forward as if they are empowered. An engaging vision or a challenging goal will move team members to positive action. It will create its own empowerment. (Chapter Six discusses the importance of goals and goal-setting processes for a cross-functional team.)

Empowered Teams Engage Key Stakeholders

Although empowered teams are free to act, they do so in concert with key stakeholders in the organizations. Cross-functional teams need, first and foremost, the support of the functional department managers. As survey respondent Barbara Bennett of The Stanley Works put it, "While cross-functional teams have the responsibility to solve problems and implement solutions, they must get the right stakeholders involved." Bill Hines of Bellcore (now Telcordia Technologies) believes strongly that "cross-functional teams will fail if they don't (1) have all interested parties involved and (2) do the 'stakeholdering' up front to gain agreement that this is an issue we need to work on and that we will all be part of the solution" (interview with the author, January 1993).

Because so much of the work done by cross-functional teams involves coordination with other teams in the organization, their support is critical. Empowerment does not mean ramming your decisions through the organization. For example, the Clark County (Nevada) Major Projects Review Team works closely with the functional departments. "In areas where we have experience, we make empowered decisions, but where we don't have experience, we go to the departments for direction" (group interview with the author, October 2001).

Empowered Teams Are Committed to Something

The members of the team all care deeply about something and are ready to work hard to achieve the purpose. This is especially true for cross-functional teams because the members come from different organizations, each with his or her set of prior commitments. Members need to put aside these often-conflicting commitments and get behind an overarching team challenge. As an exercise, ask team members to recall a team they thought was successful and to describe what made it successful. More often than not, deep commitment will be on the list of success factors. It really doesn't matter what team members rally around. It can be, as Northern Telecom's Jim Kochanski points out, "a common enemy, like a competitor" (interview with the author, January 1993).

In the case of cross-functional teams in the Technical Operations unit of Parke-Davis, nothing less than the future viability of the organization was at stake. As Karen Soskin told me, "Things took entirely too long and we didn't have much process. We were on a 'mission from God'" (interview with the author, December 2001). Paul Allaire, former CEO of Xerox, put it another way: "You can't get people to focus on the bottom line. You have to give them an objective like 'satisfy the customer' that everybody can relate to. *It's the only way to break down those barriers and get people from different functions working together*" (Dumaine, 1991, emphasis added).

Empowered Teams Communicate with Key Stakeholders

For senior management and functional department heads, "no news is *not* good news." Effective cross-functional teams provide stakeholders with meeting minutes, periodic progress reports, and informal updates as a way of maintaining their credibility in the eyes of these stakeholders and continuing the confidence that initially led to the empowerment of the team. Stakeholders will intervene or withdraw power when they do not have a good idea of what's going on. Gerwin (1999) reported that, in his study of fifty-three new-product development teams, *recentralization*—his term for the withdrawal of power from the team—took place when stakeholders and the team did not have a shared understanding of the process. When there is no shared understanding and little communication about the direction of the project, managers are more likely to be uncomfortable with the team's ability to complete the task. (There is more about how to communicate with key stakeholders in the next chapter.)

Empowerment: Why It's Important

Empowerment has a number of direct and obvious benefits, as well as many ancillary and subtle advantages for a cross-functional team.

Speed

Whether it is getting a new drug application filed faster, processing an insurance claim in record time, or responding rapidly to a customer query, empowering the team to act is at the heart of the process. Consider this: if a customer calls with a complaint about poor service and a member of the customer service team says, "We'll have to check with our boss on this," the customer will end up being more dissatisfied. If, however, the team is empowered to respond on the spot with a way to correct the situation, the customer's dissatisfaction will diminish. "It allows us to move faster," says Helena Gordon of Penn National Insurance, "when we don't have to get approvals for everything" (interview with the author, October 2001).

Ownership

When the team is empowered and it is aware that it is empowered, "it creates a sense of ownership and accountability for the team. When the team knows they're accountable, they will try to help rather than pointing fingers" (Dave Prochaska, manager of training and development, Delta Faucet, interview with the author, October 2001). Empowerment creates ownership that, in turn, creates commitment. And there is no limit to what a committed cross-functional team can do when they feel they "own" the project or the problem and it is up to them to get it done. However, it is very important, as Michael Poole of Parke-Davis stresses, "to make the team accountable but not tell them how to do it. Empowerment is critical because 'ownership' is the Holy Grail of this stuff" (interview with the author, October 2001).

Creativity

Empowerment sends a clear message to the team that encourages members to think independently and, as team leader Mary Sylvain of Parke-Davis says, "to take risks and look for creative, 'out of the box' solutions" (interview with the author, October 2001). If the team is empowered, members feel trusted and get the sense that management believes in their ability to make well-reasoned decisions that will further the best interests of the organization. As a result, the team is less likely to look for solutions just because they think management will accept them.

Respect

"You respect people when you empower them" is the message of a recent study by Harvard sociologist, Sara Lawrence-Lightfoot (1999). Managers empower teams in their area by both encouraging and supporting their efforts to make decisions about key aspects of their work. It sends a powerful message that says, "I value you." When the team feels respected, they will work hard to be successful. As someone once said, "When I believe in you, you believe in yourself." When a team believes in itself, the possibilities are limitless.

Motivation

Empowerment has the effect of liberating people to grow and use all of their strengths in the context of the team's mission (Vogt and Murrell, 1990). When team members have a sense of their worthiness, they will grow and develop, with the net result that the quality and quantity of their contributions to the team increase.

The Foundation of Team Empowerment: Member Empowerment

We spend so much time and effort addressing the issue of team empowerment that it is easy to overlook the necessary empowerment of each member of a cross-functional team. Many of the advantages discussed earlier such as speed, creativity, and motivation also require member empowerment to make them come alive in the context of the team. It is an interactive, synergistic process. Member empowerment supports team empowerment that, in turn, facilitates member empowerment. They are bound together and are key factors in the success of the team. As Dr. Katherine Erlick of Boeing said while reflecting on the work of her project team, "If we constantly got redirected, we would not have been successful" (interview with the author, October 2001). If the empowerment mandate is shaky and the team or its members get mixed or changing messages, it will be difficult for the team to succeed.

Member empowerment involves six critical factors:

1. *Freedom to make decisions.* Members must be able to actively participate in the team discussions up to and including the making of a decision. In order for the team to move forward rapidly, and that usually means making decisions, members must be empowered to act. Nothing is more frustrating than to sit in on a team meeting when a decision is on the agenda and no action is taken because a number of members say, "I'll have to check with my boss first."

2. *Freedom to make commitments.* Members must be able to commit their functional area to work projects or other activities that are needed by the cross-functional team. In much the same way, they should also have the freedom to say, "No, we are unable to do it." A cross-functional team member must be able to fully represent his or her department on the team.

3. *Freedom to accept work assignments.* Members must be able to take on action items needed by the team, whether that action item is as simple as getting the latest regulatory requirements or as complex as a needs assessment. If the team is to move forward rapidly, then members must be empowered to decide if they should do the work and when they can get it done. When certain team members always have to "get approval" before they can accept a work task needed by the team, overall morale of the team decreases because

other team members equate lack of member empowerment with a lack of commitment on the part of that department.

4. *Communication of department information.* Team members must be able to bring current information about relevant activities in their department that has an impact on the work of the cross-functional team. The department head should trust (empower) the team member to be a responsible spokesperson for the function. Unfortunately, many team members are often sent to a cross-functional team meeting simply to be "the eyes and ears" of the department at the meeting. They also need to be "the mouth."

5. *Communication of team information.* Communication goes both ways; therefore, team members also need to communicate relevant team actions back to their functional area. Functional stakeholders usually want and always need information about team goals, decisions, and actions. Functional heads should see the team member from the department as a trusted communicator of team information. And as was pointed out earlier, sharing information with functional stakeholders is an important way to maintain and sometimes to expand the overall empowerment of the team.

6. *Orientation of substitutes and new members.* How many times have you heard this at a cross-functional team meeting: "I'm not sure what's going on. I was just told to show up at this meeting today." Lack of orientation of new and substitute members is extremely frustrating for both the team and the member. It means having a so-called warm body but not much else. A member cannot participate as an empowered, effective contributor unless he or she is given the relevant background information and authority to act as a fully functioning team member.

A Process for Team Empowerment

Here is a simple but effective five-step process for empowering a team.

1. Senior management provides the team with an overarching goal, for example: *create a Web-based course for training managers to manage remote employees.*
2. The cross-functional team prepares a plan that includes performance objectives, specific tasks, milestones, outcomes, success measures, and costs.

3. Senior management and the team meet to review the draft plan and come to an agreement on the final plan. The agreement includes an understanding that the team is empowered to implement the plan.
4. The team provides senior management with periodic progress reports.
5. Senior management is available to coach and support.

Is Your Team Empowered?

Figure 5.1 offers a quick way to assess your team's level of empowerment.

Figure 5.1. Are We Empowered?

Directions: Please read each of the following statements and respond by selecting the number that most represents the degree to which the statement is characteristic of your team according to the following scale:

1. Not at All
2. To Some Extent
3. To a Moderate Extent
4. To a Great Extent
5. To a Very Great Extent

_____   1. Our team has significant influence over the development of our goals and plans.

_____   2. Our team is empowered to make all decisions that affect our work.

_____   3. Our team is empowered to identify and solve all problems that arise within the scope of our goals.

_____   4. Our team is responsible for obtaining all the resources needed to accomplish our goals.

_____   5. Our team plays a major role in selecting and changing team membership.

_____   6. Functional department managers do not interfere with our decision making.

_____   7. People outside our team are unable to influence our work assignments.

_____ 8. We set our own objectives, deliverables, timelines, measures, and budget.

_____ 9. Senior management demonstrates a strong commitment to our success.

_____ 10. External stakeholders do not unduly influence or second-guess our decisions.

_____ 11. Our team has control over our work assignments.

_____ 12. Team members are empowered to action on behalf of their functional area without checking with their manager.

_____ 13. Team members can select the way they will perform their team tasks.

_____ 14. The team is empowered to do whatever it takes to accomplish the goals and carry out the plan.

_____ 15. Our team can change plans as long as the new plans do not conflict with those of other teams.

_____TOTAL

SCORING:

15–30 Dependent: Teams that score in this range have little authority or freedom to act in an independent manner. They look to management to tell them what to do and often how to do it as well. Becoming empowered will require management to delegate increasing degrees of authority to the team. The team will need coaching in goal setting, decision making, and maintaining good relations with stakeholders.

31–59 Participative: Teams in this range are moving toward self-direction by using a variety of participative tools that involve members in the setting of goals, the development of plans, and the making of decisions with minimal management involvement. However, all plans and major decisions must be approved by management. Moving toward empowerment will require management to agree to setting the overall direction and then allowing the team the freedom to develop and implement the plans.

60–75 Empowered. Teams that fall in this range are highly self-directed, which is reflected in their freedom to develop goals and plans and develop ways to carry out those plans with minimal control by management.

The Empowerment Continuum:
Where Is Your Team?

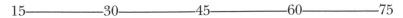

15————————30———————45————————60—————————75

Looking Back: Some Issues to Consider

1. Peter Block (1987) says that to feel empowered means three things: (1) we feel our survival is in our hands, (2) we have an underlying purpose, (3) we commit ourselves to achieving that purpose.

   Do you agree? Are all three factors necessary?

   Which one of the three factors is the most important? Why?

   Based on that definition, is your team empowered?

2. Team empowerment at IBM is based on a set of expectations and parameters set out in a Statement of Work agreed to by the team and the management sponsor.

   How do you feel about that approach?

   Would it work for teams in your organization?

3. The chapter states that if a team finds its authority unclear, members should just act as if they are empowered as long as their actions are legal and ethical. Do you agree?

4. In your organization, what decisions are cross-functional teams typically empowered to make, what decisions are made jointly with management, and what decisions are made by management but with input from the team?

5. Based on your experience, would you say that it is more important for the *team* to be empowered or for the *team leader* to be empowered?

6. A section of the chapter discusses the importance of team member empowerment. In your experience, how important is member empowerment for the success of the team?

7. The chapter makes the point that the level of team empowerment may change over time. Should team empowerment be flexible and open to change, or should it remain consistent during the life of the team?

Chapter Six

Setting Goals for
Shared Commitments

The best teams invest a tremendous amount of time and
effort exploring, shaping, and agreeing on a purpose that
belongs to them both collectively and individually.
JON KATZENBACH AND DOUGLAS K. SMITH, COAUTHORS,
THE WISDOM OF TEAMS[1]

Only a few things about teams are sure, and one is this: *successful teams have clear goals.* It is that simple. However, if it is true that all high-performance teams have a clear purpose, what's so special about cross-functional teams? All teams need to have a clear mission and a set of goals that everyone on the team supports. But cross-functional teams are different, and goal setting is even more critical to their success. After observing many project meetings and surveying hundreds of team members in the pharmaceutical industry, management consultant Ira Asherman pointed out that having "clear goals, specific objectives, and a detailed project plan is one of the most important factors that distinguish the high-performing (cross-functional) drug development teams from average, run-of-the-mill teams" (interview with the author, January 2002).

In their fascinating three-year study of a wide variety of primarily cross-functional teams, Larson and LaFasto (1989) found that "two insights about teams emerged early, consistently and very

---

[1]Katzenbach and Smith, (1993b), p. 50.

emphatically. . . . First, high performance teams have both a clear understanding of the goal to be achieved and a belief that the goal embodies a worthwhile or important result. Second, when an ineffectively functioning team was identified and described, the explanation for the team's ineffectiveness involved, in one sense or another, the goal" (p. 27). Members may come to the team as total strangers, knowing each other only informally or with some past negative experiences on teams. However, a solid goal-setting process that culminates in a clear mission and goals can reduce conflicts, build positive relationships, and create a sense of ownership.

Goals Reduce Conflict

One of the most important roles that clear goals play on a cross-functional team is to reduce the potential for conflicts and minimize past differences among the various disciplines represented on the team. Even without any past differences, people often come to a team with a belief that the contribution of their function is most important and should take precedence over the other areas or have more clout in the decision-making process or resource allocation. Sometimes the assumed rank order of the various disciplines is embedded in the existing culture of the organization, as in "around here, marketing calls the tune," or "on this team, engineering is the major player." However, when the goals are clear, differences are resolved by looking at the issue or proposed decision in the context of the goals and plan. For example, at a meeting I observed, a product development team was debating the value of additional testing. The conflict was resolved by looking at the impact of each alternative on the goal and, more specifically, the plan's milestones.

The resolution of these differences is facilitated by the development of a common goal that all members of the team accept and are willing to support. Team goals and the implementation plan have to go beyond the general (for example, "improve quality" or "reduce costs") to more specific outcomes, deliverables, and milestones. Although cross-functional teams often start out with general goals such as "develop a water-based product," "increase customer satisfaction," "improve market share," or "decrease turnaround time," they must move quickly to something more specific and operational. Many teams are given a broad charter by senior management. The team then must come up with a clear goal and set of objectives that are transmitted to senior management and the functional department heads. As Maira Rieger of Parke-Davis pointed out, "Teams were simply given an end goal and then had to develop a plan to reach that goal" (interview with the author, October 2001).

Clear goals help team members discuss differences, evaluate alternatives, resolve conflicts, and decide the best course of action. Mushy goals encourage mushy thinking and little productive action.

Goals Build Partnerships

Goals help cross-functional teams resolve intragroup conflicts, but they also help maintain positive relationships with the functional departments and senior management. At the *Reader's Digest,* top management scopes out an issue and then hands it off to a cross-functional team to "work out the details," according to Naomi Morrow, the company's director of human resources (interview with the author, January 1993). Team members have to buy into the overall goal (for example, "reducing customer complaints" or "globalizing the business"), help fashion a team goal that is more specific, and then get the support of their functional organization. In turn, the functional departments have to blend the team goal into their overall department goals. In this way, the teams at *Reader's Digest* address one of the major barriers to the success of a cross-functional team: lack of support by the functional departments.

A similar approach was used at U.S. West by Jose Varga, a product manager who worked with cross-functional teams responsible for the development of major new telecommunications products and services. "You have to be clear about your vision," Varga said, "and then communicate that vision to the team" (interview with the author, January 1993). The team, with Varga playing facilitator, assessed the degree of a problem's complexity and then developed a series of objectives and, ultimately, a very specific timeline of milestones. This process built support for Varga's vision because functional department managers were clear about the team's priorities. Later, when a department balked at supplying the assistance they had promised, he could refer to the team's goals and milestones. Goals break down barriers between enemies and strangers and help build positive relationships.

Goals Provide an Incentive

Challenging goals spur a team to action. Karen Soskin of Parke-Davis put it in no uncertain terms: "We were on a mission from God!" (interview with the author, December 2001). Whether it is forging a river in a team-building exercise, putting a man on the moon, or beating the competition to the market with a new product, a compelling goal motivates team members to give their best effort. Although not all teams can be given a goal with monumental implications or global reach, a compelling goal can serve as a motivator for a cross-functional team working on a basic business issue. For example, the IBM team working on a new training course for remote managers felt that the challenge of their goal "created the sense that this was an important project," and, as a result, "we had a real sense of pride and a real passion for the project" (team interview with the author, December 2001).

Goals Establish a Scoreboard

People like games, especially games that have an ongoing score. In a soccer game, if the other team is leading 1 to 0 at the end of the first period, you know you have to work harder and play better if you want to be ahead by the end of the game. In much the same way, goals and the plan to achieve the goals serve as your scoreboard.

The team can conduct a "plan versus actual" assessment at various times. For example, the team compares the list of tasks to be accomplished by the end of the first quarter with the actual tasks completed to obtain their first-quarter "score." If the assessment shows they have not completed certain tasks, team members know that they will have to work harder and smarter to improve their score at the next review period. At a team meeting that I observed, a team leader posted the goals and timeline on the screen. Then when members proposed additional tasks, she referred them to the timeline and asked them to consider the impact on the team's "scoreboard." At IBM, Fred Stevens said that at meetings of the new professional development and training team, "goals spelled out in the Statement of Work are tracked weekly" (interview with the author, November 2001).

Goals Must Be SMART

Xerox, which make heavy use of cross-functional teams to solve all sorts of problems, begins with a broad problem, often emanating from a customer, and then turns it over to a team.

Goals Must Be Specific

For example, several years ago, customers told the company that what they really wanted to know was when their new copier would arrive and be installed and up and running (Dumaine, 1991). Unfortunately, Xerox could not answer this question with any degree of accuracy. CEO Paul Allaire turned the problem over to an experienced middle manager who put together a cross-functional team from distribution, accounting, and sales. The team set its objective as satisfying the customer's need to have this question answered and, as a result, developed a tracking system that follows each copier through the distribution process.

Motorola's Communications Sector provides another example of the value of a clear mission followed by the articulation of specific objectives and plans by the team. A cross-functional team, composed of representatives from industrial engineering, robotics, process engineering, procurement, product design, human resources, finance, and a vendor representative from Hewlett-Packard, were charged with developing "an automated, on-shore, profitable production operation for its high-volume Bravo pager line" (Clark and Wheelwright, 1992, p. 14). Known as the Bandit Team (they "took" ideas from anywhere), they began by preparing clear objectives and a work plan for the project and performance expectations, which each member and senior management approved. It worked. The team met its time schedule, quality standards, cost objectives, and product-reliability goals. Again, an overarching mission and clear objectives drove the process.

Goals Must Be Measurable or Observable

The use of goals as a factor in creating a successful cross-functional team seems to work best when some development of the problem or issue has been done prior to the hand-off to the team. In the pharmaceutical industry, so-called discovery teams conduct preliminary research on the feasibility of a potential compound. If potential exists, the product is turned over to a cross-functional project team to carry the ball. In some telecommunications companies, a product line team identifies products to be developed and then turns over the promising ideas to a product development team for further development. In other industries, a senior management team or key leader develops ideas or identifies potential opportunities that are, in turn, handed off to a cross-functional team in the specific area. These teams should then take the broad charter and turn it into a set of measurable performance objectives. Taking the broad charter to the next level of specificity is critical to success because, as Barbara Bennett, vice president of human resources at The Stanley Works, pointed out in her response to our survey, "Many teams have been slowed down with goals that were too broad." Goals become the measures of success because you can tell if you have achieved your objective when it is possible to count it or see it.

Goals Must Be Attainable

Although achieving the outcome may be a challenge, it is possible with the current team and its resources. However, it is important to point out that success may come in the form of a team coming to the conclusion that the project, product, or process is simply not feasible or profitable for the company. For example, one product development team concluded that "the cost of producing this product is such that the company is unable to make a reasonable profit, given the current pricing patterns for similar products on the market." A "smart" goal is also attainable, even if it is difficult and may involve a degree of reasonable risk taking. There is no joy in participating in a frustrating, impossible task.

There is no gain, and there may even be a loss, to a cross-functional team experience that involves hours of valuable staff time devoted to unrealizable project goals.

Goals Must Be Relevant

Cross-functional team goals must be consistent with overall direction provided by senior management and aligned with the strategy of the organization. At Xerox, for example, Pat Pendell reported that "initial goals come from outside the team, usually systems engineering, via a flow-down process, but the final goals and plan are negotiated with the team" (interview with the author, December 2001). This "negotiated process" ensures that the goals are aligned with other goals and the overall strategic plan of the organization. Although senior management wants this alignment, it is also important for the cross-functional team. Team members need to have a sense that their goals are important. It is a source of both pride and motivation for team members to conclude that "we had a clear goal and it was a business imperative" (interview with Karen Soskin, Parke-Davis, October 2001).

Goals Must Be Time-Bound

An effective objective must be achieved within a particular time period such as by the end of the quarter or by a specific date. Time creates a sense of urgency and realism for a team. If there are no time limits, then it really doesn't matter how long it takes members to complete subgoals and tasks. As a result, the motivation to achieve is lacking and team morale declines. For the company, time is a critical ingredient in the strategic planning process. For example, the plan incorporates a pipeline of new products with expected launch dates. The pipeline sits on a foundation of cross-functional project teams that are driving the product development process.

A summary of the main ideas discussed in this section appears in Figure 6.1.

Figure 6.1. Goals Must Be SMART.

GOALS MUST BE *S M A R T*

S   *Specific:* The outcome or the end result is very clear to everyone.
M   *Measurable:* You can tell if you have achieved your objective because you can count it or see it.
A   *Attainable:* Although achieving the outcome may be a challenge, it is possible with the current team and its resources.
R   *Relevant:* The objective is in line with the direction provided by senior management and is aligned with the strategy of the business.
T   *Time-Bound:* The objective will be achieved within a specific time period such as by the end of the quarter or by a specific date.

Typical Team Goals

Here are some examples of goals:

- Develop a plan to reduce cycle time for ABXY product from eighty-nine days to thirty-five days by June 30.
- Reduce the December reject rate by 25 percent, with no increase in standard costs.
- Increase the customer satisfaction rating for the year by 10 percent.
- Commercialize a new product with the following specifications by the end of the third quarter of Year 2.
- Reduce the average waiting time for patients in the emergency room to ten minutes.
- Respond to all customer inquiries within twenty-four hours by October 1.

Team Goals Must Be Integrated into Department Goals

The process of developing clear goals and an action plan only carry the process so far. It will only work if there are no problems or there is a senior management sponsor who is vitally interested in the project. These so-called high-profile projects will get whatever they want, regardless of the process. However, for other teams one more step helps make the goal-setting and implementation process work effectively.

Team goals must be incorporated into the goals of each functional department and, where feasible, into the goals of each team member. In other words, both the department and the individual team member should have their contributions to the team effort included in their performance plan. This approach helps with time and resource allocation within the department and increases the likelihood that the team will get what it needs from the team member and the department. It also means that both the person and the department will be evaluated against those objectives, which, once again, will reinforce the importance of the cross-functional team's objectives. Jim Kochanski, human resources director at the Northern Telcom's Research Triangle Park, North Carolina, reported that the fact that "team goals are folded in with functional department goals is one of the critical success factors for our cross-functional teams" (interview with the author, January 1993).

Why Teams Don't Set Goals

One obvious question is this: If we all agree that goal setting is important for the success of a cross-functional team, why don't more teams set effective goals? Here are some of the reasons I've encountered:

"We don't have time; we have a lot of work to do."

"This place is always in a state of crisis, so why bother?"

"We might look bad if we don't achieve our goals."

"Nobody looks at those things anyway."

"Nobody follows those things anyway."

"Our boss should set the goals; our job is to carry them out."

"The last team that did it lost their funding."

"I heard there's a big reorganization coming soon; let's wait until then."

Goals Provide the Glue

A clear set of goals is critical to the success of a cross-functional team. Because the team is often composed of people with little experience in working together, goals can be the glue that holds this band of allies, enemies, and other strangers together. However, goals by themselves cannot do the trick. A cross-functional team needs the help and support of others to achieve their goals. In the next chapter, I discuss how to effectively manage the boundary with other key stakeholders in the organization.

Looking Back: Some Issues to Consider

1. Review the list of reasons that teams do not set goals. Which ones apply to teams in your organization? Which reasons apply to your team?

2. Some people believe that goals should be general because setting specific objectives limits a team's flexibility to respond to opportunities during the course of a project. Do you agree? Why or why not?

3. What conditions need to be in place for a team to have an effective goal-setting process?

4. What role should the following people play in a team's goal-setting process:
     Senior management sponsor?
     Team leader?
     Functional department manager?
     Team member?
     Facilitator or coach?

Chapter Seven

Building Bridges Outside the Team

You can't just sit inside your own silo and expect to be successful.
PAUL HARTLEY, VICE PRESIDENT, XEROX[1]

To coin a phrase, no cross-functional team is an island. Although much of the research and thinking about teams has focused on their internal dynamics, experts are only now coming to realize the importance of external relations. British researchers Hastings, Bixby, and Chaudhry-Lawton (1987) were among the first to note that successful teams give a good deal of attention to what they call managing the outside. But the importance of building bridges for cross-functional teams should be obvious by now. Cross-functional teams are linked in many ways to many different people and organizations and, in fact, are dependent on others for their success. Some of these people may know your work and be supporters; some may have worked with you in the past and be potential barriers; others may not be aware of your work and may need to be convinced of its value.

If the proliferation of cross-functional teams is to be successful, there must be an emphasis on what is sometimes called boundary management—the process by which a team manages its "borders" and the flow of information and resources to and from

---

[1]Interview with the author, December 2001.

its key stakeholders. The flow may be vertical (to senior management) or horizontal (to the functional department) and interactive in the sense that the team both sends and receives information or resources to and from the stakeholders. A recent study of cross-functional new-product teams seems to indicate that effective boundary management can make a real difference.

> High-performing product development teams carry out more external activity than low-performing teams. . . . High performers interacted more frequently with manufacturing, marketing, R&D, and top division management during all phases of activity. Members of high-performing teams did not simply react to communications from others; they were more likely to be the initiators of communication with outsiders than those individuals on low-performing teams [Ancona and Caldwell, 1990b, p. 28].

More succinctly, Xerox's Paul Hartley said that his experience tells him, "You can't just sit in your silo and expect to be successful" (interview with the author, December 2001).

As others have noted, cross-functional teams differ from functional teams in the way they emphasize effective boundary management. The unique nature of cross-functional teams makes it essential that they develop positive relationships with key stakeholders in the organization. It is important that the cross-functional team maintain an appropriate balance between external relations and internal team development. This drive toward interaction with the outside world, coupled with the equally strong drive toward positive internal dynamics, can provide the team with certain tension points. Properly managed, this tension can be helpful when it requires the team to look at two sometimes competing but always important success factors. At this point, the emphasis needs to be on the external side because so little attention is usually paid to building effective stakeholder relations.

The Key Stakeholders

Most cross-functional teams have the same kinds of important stakeholders, although the number and identity of stakeholders varies, of course, by organization. Therefore, each team must do its own stakeholder analysis and develop a plan to effectively manage the boundary.

Functional Department Managers

The department managers of the cross-functional team members are often in a make-or-break role in regard to the success of the team. They can freely give a resource—their employee—or they can keep the person on a tight leash. For the team to be successful, the functional department managers must

- Understand the purpose and priorities of the cross-functional team
- Allow and even encourage the team member to complete team assignments
- Clarify the team member's authority as the department's representative on the team and then allow the team member to exercise that authority
- Regularly communicate with the team member about the work of the team
- Periodically communicate with the team leader about the team's progress and the nature of the team member's work
- Obtain feedback from the team leader about the team member's performance

"The most important factor for a cross-functional team is building effective relationships with functional managers by doing your best to help them succeed" (Paul Hartley, interview with the author, December 2001). Although in a different context, John Dew of the University of Alabama agrees. "We focused on their needs. In the case of the chairman of the math department, we showed him the student data and he immediately got on board" (interview with the author, September 2001).

Customers and Clients

No team should exist without customers for its output; the customers may be internal or external to the organization, and they may have varying levels of needs. The team's success depends on how well it interacts with its customers; it must continually obtain information from them about their needs and desires. Some teams designate specific team members as the client liaison responsible for ongoing contact with the customer. Often this person is the project manager, but the client liaison can be the product manager, client interface manager, or a systems analyst. One of my clients (an automobile industry supplier) has designated customer representatives who are responsible for communication and plant visits with their automobile assembly customers. The Office Systems Group (OSG) at Xerox has a formal process to ensure effective relationships with their key customer groups—the operating companies. As Xerox Vice President Mark Waxenberg pointed out, "Operating companies come in at key decision points with the opportunity to kill the program" (interview with the author, December 2001).

Having a single point of contact is an efficient and often effective way of working with clients because it (1) makes it easier for clients to give feedback, (2) allows the team to designate, train, and develop one person skilled in client interface, and (3) eliminates the confusion that occurs when many team members talk to the same client. Some teams have reduced the stakeholder communication problem by having customers serve as members of the cross-functional team. The customers attend all meetings and provide their input throughout the process.

Senior Management

One of the key internal stakeholders is senior management or, more specifically, the senior manager who sponsored the cross-functional team. It is critical that the team keep management informed about the team's progress, successes, need for resources, potential problems (especially problems with clients), and changes in the timetable. Geri Weber, a leader and member of many cross-functional teams at Bellcore (now Telcordia Technologies, Inc.), recommended that the team and particularly the team leader take responsibility for establishing a structure to ensure systematic feedback to management, even in those cases where no formal structure currently exists (interview with the author, January 1993).

Senior management does not like surprises such as complaints from customers, delays in the project timetable, and unforeseen, last-minute problems. One cross-functional team in a major pharmaceutical company spent a great deal of time preparing a plan and developing internal communication processes but neglected to sell the concept sufficiently to senior management. Despite much good work and good intentions, the team and its concept were cancelled. In another company, a team prepared a careful market analysis of a potential product, but the boss refused to fund the continuation of the project. Team members agreed that they had not brought him in early enough to gain his support.

In some situations, senior management is an ongoing member of the team. This can prove beneficial to the team. At Motorola's plant in Austin, Texas, a senior manager serves as a team sponsor who helps the team get the resources it needs (Kumar and Gupta, 1991). In this case, "resources" can mean anything from an expert whom the team needs to help solve a problem to the money to procure a piece of equipment.

Support Groups and Service Departments

At various stages in its cycle, a cross-functional team needs assistance from other groups in the organization. Service and support stakeholders include information technology, computer centers, research groups, purchasing, prototyping, customer service, and government or regulatory affairs, among others. The effective team builds and maintains positive relationships with these groups because their support is often in the form of tangible aid. The task here can be difficult because people from these functions are often adjunct or ad hoc members or simply part of the extended team network. Therefore, they usually do not feel the same level of commitment as other permanent part-time or full-time members. In addition, they are often overlooked when it comes time for recognition and team celebrations.

Suppliers, Vendors, and Consultants

Many stakeholders are not found on the standard organization chart because they are not company employees. And yet they are often key members of the cross-functional team, on either an ad hoc or a permanent basis. The Deepwater project team of the U.S.

Coast Guard (USCG), charged with developing a plan to renew and replace all of the USCG's assets (for example, cutters), includes a number of naval architects and related experts from a consulting firm. A reorganization project at BOC Gases included many full- and part-time change management consultants. Many pharmaceutical companies use contract research organizations (CROs) to conduct clinical studies in conjunction with cross-functional drug development teams. At CyLogix, a Princeton, New Jersey–based software solutions company, a team of their experts integrates with a team at the client organization to complete project tasks. According to Helena Gordon, software vendors always work in close collaboration with internal programmers and business analysts on corporate project teams at Penn National Insurance in Harrisburg, Pennsylvania (interview with the author, October 2001). Building and maintaining a positive relationship with these stakeholders can be challenging, if only because they are not full-time employees of the internal organization.

The Needs of Cross-Functional Teams

Ongoing, empowered teams constantly need accurate and current information for daily decision making, along with resources and support.

Information

Project teams of various levels of empowerment usually have a great need for information at the outset of a project. They need customer and market data about the potential need for the product, system, or service. Quality action teams need data about the nature and extent of the problem. All cross-functional teams have to draw data from the political winds in the organization to see whether there is support for the team's project.

Resources

At some point, the team will need some "stuff." The types of resources that teams often need from support and service groups include

- *People*—from experts to offer advice and do real work to extra hands to pitch in and get the work done
- *Product*—from the production of a prototype to the supply of test samples for a field trial
- *Research*—from statistical studies or laboratory experiments to focus groups or field tests

Support

When it comes to tangible needs, external groups can truly support the team by helping the team get its needs met. They can do this in an easy, no-hassle manner and in a professional and timely fashion. If the team has to fight to get the support it needs, to get the work done quickly, and to get it done correctly, then the whole process breaks down. Intangible support involves expressing interest in the project, asking questions, talking the project up, providing publicity, and responding rapidly.

Awareness of Impact

Cross-functional teams need to be aware of the impact of their work on other groups in the organization. For example, a team may come up with a wonderful new procedure that reduces the time it takes to get the job done, but this new procedure may cause problems for another group. At one plant, the team on the C shift came up with a way to speed up their work by eliminating setup for the next job; their time improved, but the A shift was left with extra work. Effective teamwork requires collaboration among teams. A lack of awareness can cause a severe breakdown in stakeholder relationships and, eventually, derail a team.

Barriers to Bridge Building

Despite all the good reasons for effective interteam relationships, groups in organizations often do not work well together. Cross-functional teams do not manage their boundaries well, do not get the support they need, do not get the resources they require, and fail as a result. Before looking at methods for achieving positive external relations, let's look at the causes of breakdowns in the process.

Stereotyping

Yes, plain old-fashioned prejudice can be a cause of process break-down. Team members come to a relationship with preconceived ideas about how certain groups behave. These stereotypes stand in the way of building positive relationships. Think about the stakeholder groups we identified. How are they perceived by cross-functional teams in your organization? Figure 7.1 gives examples of some typical stereotypes about these stakeholders. Feel free to add some perceptions of your own.

Figure 7.1. Stereotypes About Stakeholders.

Senior Management. "All they care about is the bottom line. They don't know what it's like out here in the real world."

Functional Department Managers. "All they care about is meeting their personal objectives so they can get their bonus. They love our help but don't like to give anything back."

Customers and Clients. "All they want is more for less. They can't tell us their needs up front but they sure have a lot of complaints about the finished product."

Support Groups. "Ask those market research folks for some help and they dump a stack of useless data on you." "Ever try to get a *fast* answer out of an engineer?"

Vendors, Suppliers, and Consultants. "It's all about the bottom line—*their* bottom line. They just want to sell us a prepackaged solution and not take the time to see if it fits our needs."

Competition

Groups in organizations are in competition. There is nothing wrong with some healthy competition between teams in an organization; competition to be the best team, to get to the market faster, to solve a complex problem, to bring in the most sales are all examples of positive competitive goals. But if a team tries to achieve a goal at another's expense, for example, by not sharing resources or information, it is negative competition. Unhealthy competition can stand in the way of healthy collaboration, which is a key to successful cross-functional teamwork.

Teams compete for all sorts of things, including

- Recognition for their efforts
- Budget to continue or expand their project
- Tangible rewards and compensation
- Opportunities to work on high-visibility, interesting projects
- Use of internal resources

Differentiation

Depending on the degree of certainty in the environment, groups in an organization need to be differentiated (Lawrence and Lorsch, 1967). For example, all accountants work together in the finance department. As groups become more differentiated in their work styles, practices, and orientations, the challenge of integrating them increases. Although this differentiation helps units in an organization pull together to get the work done, it can be a barrier when they have to work collaboratively on a cross-functional team. Each group in the organization develops its own culture and work practices that can make it difficult for the group to network with other groups in a team setting. Tension ensues because the need to maintain differentiation is at odds with the need to integrate multiple functions for the benefit of the project.

Lack of Information

Often a barrier is created because of a lack of basic information about a stakeholder. Team members simply do not take the time to learn what the other organization does and how it goes about getting a job done. Cross-functional teams often need information about such things as

- *Goals.* What are the organization's goals? What are the high-priority goals of the organization?

- *Procedures.* How does the organization function? More important, why does the organization insist that you follow certain procedures in dealing with them?
- *Orientation.* What is the fundamental orientation of the organization? Long term? Short term? Who is its customer? What is the customer's definition of quality?
- *Work style.* What is the organization's primary style? Analytical? Collaborative? Perfectionist? Consensus?
- *Fun factor.* What is the organization's definition of fun? What types of celebrations are well liked?

It is important to get to know the inner workings of your key stakeholders if you expect to have any success in building an effective relationship with them.

Strategies for Bridge Building

Cross-functional teams need to recognize the importance of managing the outside. Beyond this recognition is the necessity of taking action—planning to work effectively with the key stakeholders. Certain actions can help. The Ancona and Caldwell (1992) study of forty-five cross-functional product development teams found that team members engage in three different types of interactions with external stakeholders:

- *Being an ambassador.* These activities involve representing the team to outsiders and protecting the team from interference.
- *Coordinating tasks.* Activities designed to coordinate the team's work with others are included in this type of interaction.
- *Scouting.* Activities in this category involve seeking out information about markets, technology, and competition.

More specifically, ambassador activities include (1) building support for the team and its work, (2) reporting the team's progress to sponsors and other senior managers, (3) understanding the company's strategy and its impact on the team, and (4) protecting the team from outside influences that might have a negative impact on the team.

Identify the Key Stakeholders

Begin by making a list of the people and groups you need to ensure your team's success. Include the things you need from these stakeholders. Make up another list of people and groups who have something to gain and something to lose from the work of your team. For example, if you come up with some cost-saving ideas or quality improvements, will some people stand to lose their jobs as a result? As Bill Baker, a team leader at BOC Gases put it, "It was critical for us to identify the key 'influencers' who, in our case, were the departments that had to implement the model we were developing—in other words, our ultimate customer" (interview with the author, October 2001).

Look for Commonalities

Look beyond what you need from the identified stakeholders to see what you can do for them. In what ways do they need your ideas, your help, or other things they might get from you? The net result of this analysis should be a set of *common* objectives—outcomes you both share. Is there an umbrella you can both get under? "It helps to have a clear end goal that is checked with the key stakeholders and approved . . . and then reviewed periodically" (Paul Hartley, vice president, Xerox; interview with the author, December 2001).

Communicate Information

Find ways to tell others about your team. Use reports, meeting minutes, newsletters, company publications, and other written methods to communicate with your key stakeholders. But in most cases, verbal communication still works best. Look for opportunities to make formal presentations as well as have informal chats (at lunch, in the hallways, at the copy machine, and other places where you can report to groups of managers, customers, and others in the organization). For example, each team member representing a functional department should have the ongoing responsibility of keeping his or her manager informed and "sold" on the team's project. Some teams also ask key stakeholders to come to team meetings to hear firsthand how the team is doing.

Select Boundary Managers

The best cross-functional teams carefully select the "ambassadors" who will handle the key interfaces. They do not assume that the team leader will do all of this work. They ask, What needs to be done? and Who is the best person to do it? We need some help from the people in the computer center. Who has worked successfully with them in the past? We need to get budget approval for some additional field studies. Let's ask Arlene to talk with them because she used to work over there. One of our customers has a complaint about the product. Why not ask Ming to handle it? She helped develop the prototype.

Identify Potential Barriers

An important aspect of building relationships with key stakeholders is looking at potential barriers. For example, ask,

- Are there any past problems that need to be resolved or overcome?
- Are you in competition with this group?
- Does this group stand to lose as a result of your team's project?
- Does this group support the concept of cross-functional teamwork?
- Do you respect this group?
- Does this group respect you?

Once the team has identified the actual barriers, it can prepare a plan for overcoming them and achieving successful relationships with stakeholders.

Prepare an Analysis and a Plan

You can use Figure 7.2 as a planning tool for building bridges to key stakeholders for your cross-functional team. If you identify several stakeholders, divide the task by asking individual members or groups of members to each do an analysis of one of the stakeholders.

Figure 7.2. Building Bridges Worksheet.

1. Identify a person, department, team, or other stakeholder that your team needs to develop a successful relationship with in order to be successful.

2. What specific types of help do you need from this stakeholder?

3. What kinds of assistance or input does this stakeholder need from your team?

4. Identify common objectives you share with this stakeholder

5. What potential barriers may prevent this stakeholder and your team from working together effectively?

6. Which member of your team would be the best person to work with this stakeholder?

7. What specific steps can you take to develop a positive relationship and obtain the necessary assistance from this stakeholder?

Effective Stakeholder Management

The following guidelines are designed to help cross-functional team leaders and other stakeholders build effective stakeholder relationships.

• *Walk around.* It's "stakeholdering" by walking around. As team leader Mary Sylvain of Parke-Davis said, "I spend most of my time walking around asking 'What do you want from us?' and saying to them, 'Here's what I want from you'" (interview with the author, October 2001). The leader, the boundary manager, and team members must get around to the stakeholders to do their "ambassador" duties. And Penn National Insurance's Helena Gordon does much the same thing. "I drop by for informal chats with stakeholders to keep them up to date on their project" (interview with the author, October 2001).

• *Be accessible.* Make yourself easy to find and easy to relate to. There are two aspects to this. First, it's the physical aspect of being where stakeholders can easily locate you when they have a question or comment for the team. The second is being interpersonally accessible so that stakeholders find you easy to talk to.

• *Focus on their needs.* Resist the tendency to always be asking for things that meet *your* team's needs. As the University of Alabama's John Dew pointed out, one of the most important success factors was the team's ability to address the needs of key stakeholders (interview with the author, September 2001). Recognize that the stakeholder also has needs and that your team may either make it more difficult for him or her to get those needs met or your team may be in a position to help the stakeholder get those needs met. In one case, a department head facing a challenging deadline on an important business opportunity came to the team leader with a request. She asked that the cross-functional team member from her department be temporarily relieved of some team action items in order to have the person put some extra time into preparing a proposal.

• *Be responsive.* When a request comes in from a stakeholder, respond quickly and completely. You want the team to be seen as caring about the stakeholder's issues, as well as the overall relationship with the stakeholder. As Karen Soskin, a senior manager at Parke-Davis said, "Team leaders drove effective relationships with stakeholders, they 'hustled,' they were responsive. They were relationship-oriented" (interview with the author, December 2001).

• *Tailor your message.* Sue Whitt, vice president of technical operations at Parke-Davis, reported that team leaders in her organization "had a lot of one-on-ones with stakeholders 'packaged' in the language of the customer" (interview with the author, October 2001). The message has to be tailored to the issues and concerns and even the language of the stakeholder. For example, the folks in marketing are going to be more concerned about the product's packaging than the people in clinical research who want to know about the number of patients in the trial at a site.

• *Manage expectations.* It is important that the team be clear about what they can and cannot do; it is equally significant that the team knows what to expect from the stakeholders. As Toni Hoover, a Parke-Davis vice president in drug development correctly noted, "While the team leader has to respond to the needs of the key stakeholders, she also has to be honest in managing their expectations" (interview with the author, October 2001).

• *Be credible.* All these strategies work only if you and your team members are credible—only if other people can depend on you and your word. Assess yourself and your team. Do other people trust you? Can they count on you to deliver on promises, to tell the truth? In developing positive relationships with key stakeholders

- Don't ask for more than you need.
- Don't promise more than you plan to deliver.
- Don't set a due date you can't possibly meet.
- Don't exaggerate project benefits or results.

Once you have completed a thorough analysis of your key stakeholders and have a plan for building positive relationships, move on to the next chapter where the focus is on a subject of vital importance to every team member: performance appraisal. All your good work in developing clear goals and boundary management will evaporate if team members do not feel that their work on the cross-functional team is valued and incorporated into their regular performance appraisal.

Looking Back: Some Issues to Consider

1. Some research on cross-functional new-product teams seems to indicate that external relations are more important than internal team dynamics. Do you agree? Why or why not?

2. Given a limited amount of time to devote to stakeholder relationships, to which stakeholder would you devote the most effort?
   Senior management?
   Functional managers?
   Customers?
   Support and service groups?
   Suppliers, vendors, and consultants?

3. How do you feel about the recommendation to identify one member of the team as the boundary manager? Would it work in your organization? Why or why not?

4. In your world, which stakeholders give your team the most problems? Why? What have you done to improve relationships with them?

5. In your experience, what are the three most important things a cross-functional team can do to develop effective stakeholder relationships?

Chapter Eight

Appraising Teamwork and Team Members

Why should I knock myself out doing work for this team when none of what I do here gets included in my annual performance appraisal?
CROSS-FUNCTIONAL TEAM MEMBER

Why should I knock myself out trying to be a good team player when all that really counts around here is your technical expertise?
CROSS-FUNCTIONAL TEAM MEMBER

Cross-functional team members can only be expected to work so hard and for so long in response to the leader's charisma and general calls for commitment. Eventually, team members are going to ask how they personally will benefit from their participation on the team. In fact, most people's favorite station is WIFM—What's in It for Me. Performance appraisal is one of the most important avenues for obtaining credit for work on a cross-functional team, especially because appraisals are often used to determine salary increases, promotions, and new assignments.

Performance Appraisal and Teamwork

Do performance appraisal and teamwork represent irreconcilable differences? Deming seems to think so (Deming, 1987). Deming's famous fourteen points for achieving continuous quality improvement include the elimination of the annual employee evaluation process because it diminishes or destroys the importance of teamwork. The traditional (and up to now typical) performance appraisal focuses on individual performance as assessed by the employee's supervisor. In this process, the emphasis is on technical excellence, assignments completed, objectives reached, and individual productivity. Even when general factors such as cooperation and teamwork are included, the assessment is still based only on the supervisor's view of his or her immediate team. Performance on cross-functional teams is rarely considered.

The problem intensifies when the appraisal process is combined with a competitive rating system. In this system, a pool of money is budgeted for raises and is distributed, based on the ranking of all employees in a unit. Although employees are usually not told their ranking, they know they are in competition with their colleagues in the ranking process. The result is that people are more likely to be competitive than collaborative with their teammates. I have interviewed employees in companies with this system who will say flat out, "Why should I help my teammates or teach them something I know when, at the end of the year, we'll be competing with each other in the ranking process for a bigger share of the pie?" Even when team members want to be collaborative, the system does not allow it.

> Two employees who had to work together throughout the year and enjoyed being team players tried an experiment. During the year, all of their reports, programs, and memos were published under joint authorship. They accomplished a great deal and were satisfied with their effort as a team. However, in preparation for the annual division appraisal meeting, their manager asked that they indicate specifically who prepared each document. The system required that there be some way of differentiating them! [Parker, 1996, p. 146].

The situation is exaggerated when employees spend a great deal of their time serving on cross-functional teams. If their manager is solely responsible for their appraisal, and the manager does not have a clear view of the employees' work, then an assessment of their performance on these teams will not be included in the total appraisal. And if teamwork is not a valued behavior in the organization, then the manager is not likely to make the effort to include performance on teams in the appraisal.

All these factors tend to have a negative impact on the success of cross-functional teams. I have talked with many cross-functional team members who are unhappy with the situation because they believe all their efforts on behalf of the team are not considered in their appraisal. Other team members interviewed said they simply make tactical choices between their functional department work and their cross-functional team assignments. Clearly, when there is any doubt, they choose to complete their department assignments first. Team leaders are frustrated by this situation because it limits their ability to get their projects completed.

Pressures on Performance Appraisal

Fortunately, not all is lost. The performance appraisal process is beginning to change in response to pressures in the work environment. These changes will have a positive effect on cross-functional teams.

Emphasis on Cross-Functional Teams as a Business Strategy

As organizations make greater and greater use of cross-functional teams, there will be increased pressure to include feedback from team leaders and team members in the appraisal process. Increasingly, functional unit managers do not see much of the work of the people in their department because most will be off at project team meetings or doing work for submission to the team. Therefore, managers must get input from cross-functional team leaders and others in order to obtain a fair and complete assessment of the person's performance.

Quality Initiatives

Most serious quality efforts are team-based because they often involve process improvements that cut across organization lines. Many employees have lost interest in quality initiatives because, in the past, they have worked hard and produced significant cost savings due to such changes as cycle-time reductions that have led to corporate gains. And yet, although the company benefited, team members did not feel their efforts were recognized. Performance on these quality teams was not considered when time came for the annual appraisal and corresponding rewards. Therefore, as companies search for factors that will support their quality teams, they are seeing the importance of including teamwork in the appraisal process.

Downsizing

The flattening of organizations in the last twenty years has resulted in a reduction in the number of middle managers, which has naturally increased the responsibilities of the remaining managers. Because they have so many employees to supervise, they can't possibly see everyone's work; as a result, they have to rely on the input of others, including peers, team leaders, and other managers.

Credibility

Employees are less and less satisfied with the performance feedback they receive from their supervisors. At one company, for example, less than 50 percent of the employees agreed with the statement, "My immediate supervisor provides feedback about my performance that is helpful to me in performing my job." As a consequence, performance feedback as a motivator of employees is less effective. Employees are more responsive to feedback from colleagues, team leaders, and customers who, they believe, have a more accurate perception of their performance.

Cultural Diversity

As global business organizations change dramatically to include increasing numbers of employees from a wide variety of cultural groups, the pressures to more accurately assess their performance increase. The traditional white male supervisor is often less able to understand the behavior of women employees and employees of Asian, African, or Latin American descent. For these employees, obtaining feedback from multiple sources is on the rise. "Studies show compelling evidence that multirater systems yield, for example, higher performance measures for women than do traditional supervisor-only measures" (Edwards, 1991, p. 96).

Changes in the Appraisal Process

All the pressures just discussed have resulted in some changes in the performance appraisal process and, specifically, in its application to cross-functional teams.

Changing Performance Criteria

Performance criteria are changing to incorporate teamwork behaviors in employee evaluations. Phrases such as "shares information with others," "negotiates differences effectively," and "encourages cooperation and teamwork among people in his or her group and people in other groups in the company" are increasingly showing up on appraisal forms. The net effect is to send a message to employees that performance as a team member and team leader will be considered in the overall appraisal. Yes, we are still looking at individual performance, but we are now considering how well the individual works in the team context. It's working. I am aware of certain technically talented individuals at one company who received lower ratings because they were perceived to be uncooperative team players. At another company, Bull HN Information Systems (the North American arm of France's Groupe Bull), David Dotlich says, "Your ability to work in teams, to get things done through people, and to build teams, is a critical criterion around which we are now ranking people" (McClenahen, 1990, p. 23).

Incorporating Team Participation

Companies are no longer relying on one manager's evaluation for an assessment of employees' performance on teams. Increasingly, managers are asking team leaders for data on the performance of their employees who spend considerable time on cross-functional teams. At Hewlett-Packard, Stuart Winby reported, "You [project managers] get e-mail from functional managers all the time asking for input on people who are on your teams. They know they can't write an effective evaluation without going to team leaders, customers, and others who have a more objective view of how the employee works in a team setting" (interview with the author, February 1993).

Hewlett-Packard has no formal procedure that requires including these data; it is just done because it makes sense. Even an informal approach can have the desired effect on employee behavior when it becomes a visible part of the culture. For example, at Intel's plant in Hillsboro, Oregon, "the managers of all departments regularly exchange information about how well their subordinates have served on project teams. That tends to keep everyone on their toes . . . ready to do the extras like coming in early to call the East Coast for information" (Dowst and Raia, 1988, p. 85).

International Flavors and Fragrances (IFF) quickly found that in order to solidify its quality effort, team members had to get credit for their participation. IFF's Michael D'Aromando reported that participation on cross-functional quality teams is included in the performance appraisal form; as a result, "people know we are serious" (interview with the author, February 1993). D'Aromando said that supervisors find out about the performance of their employees on teams by (1) chatting informally with team leaders, (2) getting feedback from facilitators, and (3) occasionally sitting in on meetings. Similarly, Sue Whitt, vice president at Parke-Davis, reports that in the technical operations organization, "with 50 percent of your performance appraisal based on your team performance, it let team members know that we were really serious." She goes on to say that "previously there were no consequences for lack of team performance. I really believe you should be rewarded for doing the right thing" (interview with the author, October 2001).

The Parke-Davis performance evaluation criteria are significant because they send a strong message about the importance of teamwork to the success of the organization. For nonsupervisory technical people, half of their evaluation is based on technical performance in five areas: (1) project work (quality, quantity, and timeliness), (2) technical expertise, (3) professional development, (4) SOP (standard operating procedure) compliance, and (5) innovation. The other half is derived from the team component, which is based on the degree to which employees demonstrate the shared values of the organization: (1) participation, (2) shared power, and (3) truth telling.

Keeping It Informal

Members of cross-functional teams will continue to be appraised by their functional managers, with input provided by team leaders and other key team stakeholders. At the moment, organizations are struggling to develop a process that incorporates performance data from people who have important information to share with the functional manager about the team member. Thus far, a simple informal process seems to have worked best. The functional manager simply asks for feedback on the person, and the information is included in the overall assessment. In some cases, team leaders actually fill out the company appraisal form as if a person were their official subordinate. As Bill Hines of Bellcore (now Telcordia Technologies, Inc.) pointed out, "I follow the basic approach of our PMP for each of these people" (interview with the author, January 1993). However, the company has no formal policy that requires a manager to complete a PMP form; it just seems like a good idea to some managers because it means that they've considered all the important factors.

In some cases, performance feedback for participation on cross-functional teams is part of the formal evaluation process. For example, at the Robert Wood Johnson Pharmaceutical Research Institute (a Johnson & Johnson company), team leaders and members are evaluated on an annual basis with a link to a compensation bonus (as a response to my survey indicated).

Introducing Team Appraisals

As cross-functional teams move to the high-performing stage, the opportunity for team-member appraisals conducted by other team members increases. Studies of self-directed teams have shown that as a team becomes fully functioning and empowered, it takes on such former management responsibilities as hiring, firing, exacting discipline, appraising performance, and awarding compensation (Wellins, Byham, and Wilson, 1991). There were earlier experiments with team appraisals.

Procter & Gamble is tossing out the old supervisor-only performance appraisal process, as the company makes the transition to a culture dotted with many cross-functional teams. Similar to other programs, the person being assessed sits down with his or her boss to select a group of people who can provide input on the person's performance. "The appraisers receive detailed surveys that ask them to answer open-ended questions about the employee's performance: What does the candidate do well? What could be improved? This unique database is consolidated and used as the centerpiece of the formal performance appraisal discussion" (Austin, 1992, pp. 32, 34).

In much the same way, Eastman Chemical, a subsidiary of Eastman Kodak, is moving toward a total team-based organization. In the process, it is creating a team appraisal system that puts a different spin on the peer review concept operating at Procter & Gamble. It is reminiscent of the old sensitivity exercise, "Hot Spot," in which each member of the group takes a turn receiving feedback from everyone else. At Eastman Chemical, team member appraisals are conducted at a team meeting. Each team member in turn goes to the flip chart and writes a list of personal strengths and weaknesses. Other team members add to the list in the course of an open discussion. The company reports that this is not easy to pull off. The process requires lots of trust and collaboration, and management is providing the teams with training in these areas (Austin, 1992).

Perhaps sensing a potential growth market here, a consultant has stepped in and created a computer-based team appraisal process. The system incorporates survey feedback data from a supervisor and four colleagues. This multirater system, called the Team Evaluation and Management System (TEAMS), was developed by Mark R. Edwards, director of the Laboratory for Innovation and Decision Research at Arizona State University in Tempe (Edwards, 1989).

Although still in the minority, team appraisal systems are increasing in number, as organizations make greater use of teams, especially cross-functional and self-directed teams. In the meantime, organizations that do not use the team appraisal systems must align the performance appraisal system with the new emphasis on cross-functional teams. The factors used to assess performance must reflect team player characteristics, and the process must ensure that observed performance on teams is included in the appraisal.

Cross-Functional Team Performance Behaviors

The following list of behaviors is a resource to help you incorporate performance on teams in the total appraisal process.

- When necessary, works outside defined job area or function to help the team achieve its goal
- Encourages and supports the participation of other team members in discussions and decisions
- Listens attentively, using paraphrasing and similar listening techniques; considers all views
- Actively seeks and communicates customer needs to the team
- Is open to new ideas, different points of view, and feedback from team members
- Raises questions and concerns about the team's goals, methods, and other issues
- Backs off when his or her views have been adequately considered and lets the team move forward
- Gives feedback to teammates that is specific, descriptive, and helpful
- Supports and actively works to implement all team decisions, even those with which he or she disagrees
- When necessary, works effectively with little or no direction
- Makes honest and reasonable commitments to the team and honors all commitments made to the team
- Collaborates with other team members in subgroups and all activities in support of the team's goals

Techniques for Appraising Performance on Cross-Functional Teams

Although not the result of a research study, my observation from numerous conversations with cross-functional team members is that performance appraisal is a critical factor for success. Team members want to be sure that their performance on cross-functional teams is included in their appraisal. It affects their performance because it is linked to their motivation. Fortunately, it is not terribly complicated to alter the performance appraisal process to include assessment of cross-functional teams.

Incorporate Team Participation in the Appraisal

Whether you do it formally or informally, you simply must make sure that the managers responsible for employee appraisals reach out to cross-functional team leaders for their input on team members. I recently worked with a department manager who told me that all her people worked on cross-functional teams. She managed a group of technical experts whose primary job was to serve as resources to a variety of teams. In fact, she rarely saw them. The only way she could prepare a fair evaluation of their performance was to obtain feedback from project team leaders.

Include Team Player Behaviors in the Appraisal

If we believe that performance on cross-functional teams should be included in the appraisal process, then we must revise the appraisal form to include specific behaviors associated with the success of these teams. Earlier in this chapter, there is a list of team-player behaviors that can be used as a basis for revising the performance appraisal form. In Chapter Twelve, you will find a description of the characteristics of team members required for effective participation on cross-functional teams.

Use a Peer Appraisal System

As McGee (1998, p. 311) points out, "Peer evaluation is not for the faint of heart." The process is not easy to design and implement. It calls for a great deal of patience and a trusting environment. At the core of peer appraisal is a performance evaluation process that involves the input of teammates in the assessment of a person's performance on a team and the incorporation of that assessment in the formal evaluation. Peer appraisal should only be attempted by a mature, high-performing team and only after the team has progressed through a series of preliminary steps. McGee (1998) suggests a three-phase development:

1. Manager or team leader conducts a series of individual interviews with team peers to collect data on the person's performance. He

or she prepares the evaluation and holds the performance discussion with the team member.

2. The manager or team leader facilitates a group session with team members to collect information on the person's team performance. He or she still retains responsibility for preparing the evaluation form and holding the meeting with the team member.

3. The manager or team leader conducts group sessions with team peers to collect feedback data and reach a consensus on the performance assessment of the person. A team member, called a performance coach, is responsible for preparing a draft evaluation and reviewing it with the leader or manager and the team. At a team meeting, the person is present and has the opportunity to hear the feedback and discuss it with the members.

A Cross-Functional Team Peer Review form can be found in Parker (1997).

The appraisal process in most organizations sets the foundation for decisions about compensation, promotions, and assignments. Appraisals are important because we want effective team players to be acknowledged by the organization. However, our research indicates that salary treatment, promotions, and new assignments are necessary but not sufficient for the development of a team-based organization. An effective reward and recognition program must be part of the package. In the next chapter, a variety of options are presented, followed by some specific conclusions about the design of a positive rewards system.

Looking Back: Some Issues to Consider

1. How do you feel about peer review as a performance evaluation tool for cross-functional teams? How would it be received in your organization?

2. How do you react to Deming's conclusion that performance appraisals destroy teamwork?

3. If you were trying to convince your organization to include performance on cross-functional teams in the employee evaluation process, what principal arguments would you use?

4. Some organizations prefer an informal process in which managers gather input from team leaders on their own; others feel that only by formalizing the process can you ensure that everyone is treated fairly. How do you feel? How does it work in your organization?

5. Among the pressures on performance appraisals mentioned in the chapter (pp. 114–115), which ones are having the most impact on organizations in general? On your organization in particular? Why?

Chapter Nine

Team Pay for Team Play

The growing use of cross-functional project teams . . .
contributes to the need for more innovative approaches
to the reward system.
MICHAEL WHITE, COMPENSATION EXPERT,
TOWERS PERRIN[1]

The drive for successful cross-functional teamwork is years ahead of the systems needed to support these teams. Although training and technology systems are moving rapidly to fill the development and support needs of cross-functional teams, performance appraisal and reward systems are lagging behind. A recent survey by compensation consultants in Sibson and Company showed that "many companies reported a need to 'catch up' when it comes to implementing team reward systems. Only 33 percent of respondents reported that they use group incentives while nearly 50 percent said they are considering such incentives" ("Non-Financial Rewards Motivate and Drive Performance," 1996). The situation is much the same in Europe. A report by the London-based Institute of Personnel and Development found that only 24 percent of the ninety-four public and private organizations had already established team pay systems ("Pulling Together Can Pay Off," 1996). This situation needs to change and change fast. Charismatic leadership and calls for commitment can go only so far with team members. Already teams and team players want to be rewarded for

---

[1]White (1991), p. 5.

accomplishing their goals, saving the company money, and doing the right thing.

In an earlier work, my colleagues Jerry McAdams and Dave Zeilinski and I presented a detailed examination of twenty-seven team reward and recognition plans (Parker, McAdams, and Zeilinski, 2000). Therefore, in this chapter, which draws heavily on that work, I only touch on the highlights of various team reward and recognition plans that are relevant to cross-functional teams.

Three Types of Plans

Three approaches to team rewards and recognition can be used by cross-functional teams. By the way, it should be noted that we distinguish between *reward* and *recognition* and see them as different, even though they are often used as interchangeable terms. Each approach has certain advantages and disadvantages. In addition, each type is designed to seek achieve specific objectives.

Team Recognition

Recognition is *after-the-fact* acknowledgment of the performance of a team or team member. In the vernacular, it goes something like this: "I caught you doing something right." It is a way of saying thank you for the special or extra effort. Recognition has two fundamental goals: (1) to encourage the person or team to repeat or continue the behavior and (2) to encourage others to do the same.

Most team recognition plans fall into one of the following categories:

• *Celebrating organizational objectives.* Usually, these sessions are group events, designed to acknowledge the successful completion of important company goals or remind people of the importance of the goals. For example, one company changed the traditional summer picnic into the customer-focus picnic. A division of a large telecommunications company held an "all-hands" meeting at an off-site facility to celebrate the accomplishment of their goals, despite a major downturn in the industry. Although the celebration may honor the contributions of cross-functional teams, a cross-functional team always does the planning of the event. Celebrations need not be expensive but they should always be fun and take place as often as possible.

• *Reinforce outstanding teams and team players.* Some organizations are experimenting with more direct payments to teams for specific results. These so-called spot bonuses vary in format. They are typically given at the discretion of management and often through a nomination process, with a committee making the final determination. Spot bonuses can be given out on a regular basis, but in some organizations they are based on events as they happen. Bonus plans tend to be tailored to the type of work done by the team or to a specific organizational goal such as reduced costs or time to market or quality improvement. Not all programs provide cash awards; many reward team members with merchandise or services that have substantial value.

Temporary teams that come together for a specific purpose and for a defined period of time (usually short) can be offered a team bonus for achieving various objectives. Objectives such as on-time, ahead-of-schedule, or under-budget delivery or cost-saving ideas can be clearly spelled out and tied directly to team awards. For example, Honeywell's Space Systems Group had a chance to win a major contract with the U.S. Air Force for highly specialized computer chips if the group could design the best chip first (O'Dell, 1989). The objective was to turn out perfect chips and cut down the design time. Honeywell's project manager came up with what might be called a bounty system. He offered to pay each engineer $150 when a chip passed the first design step on target and up to $1,200 when three chips passed in one design cycle; the team could receive up to $4,000 for similar passes. It worked. The team designed two chips perfectly in the first cycle, which put Honeywell some nine months ahead of IBM, its nearest competitor.

General Electric also used a bonus plan to motivate a cross-functional team of engineers, technicians, and plant layout specialists responsible for the start-up of a new plant in Mexico. There were three milestones for each phase of the plant's development, in addition to a quality milestone linked to the failure of any new product during the initial warranty period after the plant began production.

Team Recognition Case: Ralston Purina

The Customer Development Group (CDG) of Ralston Purina (the pet food company) designed an array of recognition plans for teams and individual accomplishments (Parker, McAdams, and Zeilinski, 2000). The goal of the plans is to support a key organizational objective: the sharing of information, including best practices, among the sales teams in the western region. The awards include

- *Best of Breed.* The CDG West's highest award is given to a team or individual for "business excellence results that reflect consistent and sustainable improvement contributing to the overall success of CDG West." A committee reviews all nominations and makes the decision. Although the payment is modest ($500), it is highly coveted. The award also includes a commemorative item so the person or team remembers the event long after the money is spent.
- *Top Dog.* This team-based peer award, designed to foster intrateam cooperation, is given by an account team to one of its members for "outstanding accomplishments that assist in meeting the team's goals." The team leader picks the winner for the first quarter; then that winner works with the team leader to select the winners for the next three quarters. The award is $50 and includes a commemorative award item.
- *The Bulldog Award.* This team-based award is given semiannually to team members who "through perseverance and tenacity" overcome a major obstacle. Nominations can be submitted by anyone to the appropriate team leader, who makes the decision. The award is a denim shirt featuring a bulldog's face, surrounded by the words "For Tenacity and Perseverance."
- *Thanks Notes.* This program uses notepads that say "Thanks" across the top and "for going the extra mile" along the bottom. The notes are used by team members to recognize each other for efforts above and beyond the norm, although no specific rules govern the use of the notepads. The notes are intended to supplement but not replace verbal recognition.

An Employee-Based Recognition Program

The Common Language® Products unit of Telcordia Technologies, Inc., in Piscataway, New Jersey—a 120-person group of computer scientists, engineers, and support personnel—operates a very successful, homegrown recognition program. Although the reward criteria are quite general (for example, "creativity," "promotes teamwork," "assists others," "has positive impact on clients"), the nomination form insists that the nominator provide specific examples of how the criteria were met and what benefits were achieved. The selection committee includes the department director, one other manager, and five nonmanagement people, as well as the permanent volunteer secretary-facilitator. Thus the selection is made by both peers and senior management, and the management and nonmanagement members of the committee change each quarter. In this way, over time everyone has a chance to participate in the selection process. Awards, which are presented quarterly, may be given to both teams and individuals. The value of the award is approximately $150 per person; each person has a choice of gifts, such as dinner for two (up to $150), a gift certificate, desk accessories, or a leather attaché case. Recipients also receive a certificate. In addition, their photo, along with a detailed description of their accomplishments, is posted on a prominent department bulletin board until the end of the quarter. The program includes a number of effective components:

- It allows the department to encourage and reward behavior that is consistent with its overall strategy, such as customer satisfaction and teamwork.
- Individuals and teams receive recognition from their peers and from management.
- Everyone is eligible to receive an award and to participate in the selection process.
- Everyone knows why the person or team was selected and therefore learns what behavior is valued in the department.
- The award is a noncash award of sufficient value to be coveted.
- The award provides the recipient with a choice of items and the chance to share the award with family and friends.
- The award has staying power because the pictures and descriptions of accomplishments remain on the bulletin board for three months.

Informal Team Recognition

Not every department, branch, division, or company can establish a program for rewarding cross-functional teams, but every organization *can* recognize effective teams and positive team players. Recognition can take place every day and neither cost a great deal of money nor require the establishment of a rewards program. Recognition is free or at least low-cost. In workshops, I often ask managers or team leaders to come up with a list of ways they can recognize teams or team players now, within their current budget and without violating company policy. Participants are often amazed at how empowered they actually are, even though they rarely use all the authority they have. And they do not use all their creativity. A great deal of recognition can be accomplished without a formal program.

One simple but effective effort I especially liked was a regular column titled "In Appreciation," which appeared in a company newspaper. Each month, employees submitted items thanking other employees for those little extras. Here are some samples:

To Dottie and D'Juana: Thank you for the blood, sweat, and tears (not to mention Saturdays and Sunday nights!) in helping to complete the report on time. Don, Dave, Dean, Mary, and Mary Margaret

To the Maintenance Department: Many thanks for your ongoing help in setting up the training room for the leadership classes. Your responsiveness and cheerfulness are greatly appreciated. Terry

To Gene and his staff: Our efforts could not have been so successful without the help you and your department cheerfully and willingly gave us. Thanks much. Research-Project CHAMPION

To the laboratory staff: Thanks for your continuous high-quality efforts. Stan

Getting your name in the paper may appeal to you but not to someone else. Some teams prefer rewards that are external, that is, they appeal to what psychologists call extrinsic motivation. Other teams tend to be motivated by intrinsic rewards—those that appeal to the "inner self" of the team. In my experience, teams develop a character or style that is usually apparent, which makes it easy to determine the right type of recognition. But when in doubt, do some of both; provide rewards that appeal to both types of motivation.

Ideas for Team Recognition

The following lists present some ideas developed in brainstorming sessions with team leaders and managers in organizations. These lists provide a repertoire of recognition ideas that are available in most organizations. The first are *extrinsic* awards.

- Give verbal recognition at a staff meeting.
- Ask the team to give a presentation at a staff meeting or company conference.
- In a prominent location, display a poster with pictures, letters of commendation, and a description of team accomplishments.
- Send the team on an outing (to a ball game or on a boat ride or other recreational activity).
- Invite the team to your home for a barbecue.
- Place a picture and story about the team in the company or community newspaper.
- Encourage the team to speak at a professional conference.
- Ask your boss to come to a team meeting to personally praise the team.
- Send a letter to your boss about the work of the team.
- Give each team member a T-shirt, hat, or mug with his or her name on it.

Here are some ideas for *intrinsic* recognition:

- Ask the team to take on a tough problem or new challenge.
- Provide timely, handwritten comments in the margin of documents prepared by the team.
- Give the team the opportunity to work flexible hours, work at home, or have periodic off-site meetings.
- Give the team new tools and other resources.
- Ask the team for its opinion on a tough problem or new business opportunity.
- Give the team the opportunity to learn a new system, operate some new equipment, or in other ways increase skills and knowledge.
- Ask the team to help another team get started or solve a problem.
- Make it clear you are implementing a team solution or in other ways using the results of the team's efforts.
- Offer to pitch in and help the team directly, either by picking up some of the load, sharing your expertise, or helping to obtain outside assistance.
- Empower the team to act in ways that will further its objectives.

In the end, the team itself is best able to decide how it would like its members to be recognized. I often tell teams that if they wait for the organization to provide recognition, they may be very disappointed. Rather, they should plan and implement their own rewards program. If they have just launched a new product or program, deployed a new system, reduced turnaround time, decreased the number of customer complaints, or just had a good month, they should celebrate. Why not share a pizza for lunch, buy buttons or hats for everyone, or make up their own award certificate? How about a team awards meeting where "Oscars" are presented to team members? Here are some examples:

- The Most Valuable Player in a Supporting Role
- The Ralph Nader Award for Challenging the System (and living to tell about it)
- The U.S. Air On Time Every Time Award (for showing up on time to every meeting)
- The BFMA (Best Functional Manager Award) to the department manager who fully supported the work of the cross-functional team

The best recognition comes from being part of a successful effort and enjoying the work and the interaction with your colleagues. The daily forms of recognition that come from your teammates seem to be the most powerful and lasting. Here are some comments from cross-functional team members at a feedback meeting:

"I know you'll give me a straight answer."

"I respect your knowledge of computers."

"I like using you as a sounding board for my ideas."

"You have integrity."

"We need your sense of humor."

There are few more powerful forms of recognition than (1) really listening to what a person says and (2) asking another person for an opinion. When team members do these things with each other, everyone feels valued and rewarded for his or her participation on the team.

Project Team Rewards

Team rewards are always based on a *pre-announced* formula that is tied to specific targets; in the vernacular it is something like, "Do this, get that." In other words, if the team achieves certain objectives, everyone on the team will get the promised award. The assumption of this type of plan is that knowing the reward in advance will encourage team members to work hard and collaborate with each other to accomplish the objectives and get the award. Project team rewards are usually based on several measures:

- *Project milestones.* If the team hits a milestone, on budget and on time, all team members receive a defined amount. This measure can be tricky because milestones can change for reasons beyond the control of the team.
- *Project completion.* All team members receive the predetermined award if they complete the project within the limits of the budget—on time or according to some fixed standard.
- *Value added.* Teams receive an award if they achieve some value measure such as reduced turnaround time, improved cycle time, cost savings, or sales.

One problem with team rewards is the difficulty of acknowledging people who are not members of the team but who make significant contributions to the accomplishment of the team's objectives. One way to overcome these objections is to reward team members and recognize the peripheral players who support the team.

Project Team Reward Case: Lotus Development Corporation

To oversee the worldwide deployment of new SAP enterprise resource planning systems, Lotus created a cross-functional core team of twenty-three people who were assigned to the project on a full-time basis. Small teams in Lotus locations around the world, charged with preparing the site to receive the new SAP systems, supported the core team. The project team rewards were two bonus payments that were tied to key milestones. The first bonus, described as being "in the thousands" of dollars, was awarded when all the new systems were up and running by a specific date in all North and South American locations. However, the bonus was "vested" in the sense that it was not actually paid out until two months later, so team members did not see the first deadline as the end point. The second bonus—half the amount of the first payment—was paid when full, worldwide deployment took place on schedule. Other key aspects of the plan were:

- Local support teams attended a celebratory party, and team members received cash bonuses based on their contribution to the local installation. In this way the project team recognized the contributions of peripheral players who supported the team.
- Additional bonuses were given to core team members to reward their individual performance on the team. There were three levels of performance bonuses based on their contribution to the overall core team effort. The size of the payment varied by level. Only five of the twenty-three core team members received no additional cash bonus.

Other Team Reward Plans

Some organizations are experimenting with less complicated incentive programs for teams. These programs are attempts to bring the awards down to the team level in an effort to improve the "line of sight" between team performance and the payoff. In a very interesting effort with a team of knowledge workers, a biotechnology company has developed a program that provides a bonus to cross-functional teams that shorten the time it takes to bring new products to the Food and Drug Administration (FDA) for approval.

> The plan they designed rewards the research and development group for developing viable concepts, testing them adequately and preparing the necessary documentation for the FDA. It emphasizes speeding up the process but only pays out if the quality remains high. For example, no awards are paid if the FDA returns the submissions for additional data that should have been included in the original package [Huret, 1991, p. 40].

In another experiment, team awards are combined with individual bonuses at a local bank in New Jersey (Eisman, 1990). Branch employees each have a quarterly quota for things such as cross-selling and referrals, and they receive cash awards for each successful action. Each branch also has a quota for the total number of deposits per quarter. However, in order for an employee to receive a commission, both the branch and the employee must meet their quotas. As the branch results increase, so do the bonuses received by each branch employee. Cross-functional teamwork is emphasized because the branch must succeed before employees can receive their individual awards. However, individual effort is also recognized; the top salesperson of the quarter receives a bonus, and managers of the top branches are given additional rewards.

In another bank, an incentive program directly encourages more cross-functional branch teamwork among all personnel, including tellers, teller supervisors, customer service representatives, assistant managers, and branch managers (Elliott, 1991). The bank established goals in three areas: product sales, customer service, and profitability. In each area, measurable goals were defined (for example, the number of credit card applications), and each received a point value weighted in accordance with the bank's overall goals. Incentive dollars are paid to a branch, based on the extent to which it reaches its quarterly goals. Cross-functional collaboration in the form of sharing ideas, pitching in, and helping each other out is fostered because no one employee gains anything unless the total team succeeds.

Organizational Unit Incentives

Group incentives cover a defined organizational unit such as a plant, a division, or a department. The award is based on a preannounced formula so that team members know how much they can expect to get if the whole group meets the objectives. The measures are usually business goals such as revenue growth, safety, or customer satisfaction. Most plans have goals and payouts for a year, with the option to be revised and renewed for another year. Good plans publish progress reports throughout the year so employees can see how they are doing. These plans have the advantage of giving everyone a chance to participate and benefit equally, the reward is based on tangible results, it provides the basis for educating employees about the business, and it can be changed as conditions change. One critical factor is that employees rarely understand all of the measures, so they have difficulty seeing how their team's effort can contribute to the reach for goals. In other words, there is a long line of sight between individual and work team performance and the reward. "These long line-of-sight organizational unit incentive plans can be effective if management understands what 'effective' means. These plans are for communication of critical objectives, the opportunity to educate employees about the measures, and to reinforce the vision and mission" (Parker, McAdams, and Zeilinski, 2000, p. 43).

Organizational Unit Incentive Case: Merck Pharmaceuticals

The Merck plant in Wilson, North Carolina, has a so-called Pay for Performance plan that provides payments to all employees if the plant hits targets in four key performance areas:

1. *Product quality:* Reducing product-related complaints and improving cycle time
2. *Customer service:* Meeting promised delivery dates and reducing the number of complaints tied to delivery or service-related problems
3. *Employee safety:* Improving lost-time injury and "recordable injury ratio"
4. *Financial performance:* Meeting revenue targets and profit budget for the year

In 1998, the per-employee payout was 30 percent of an $800 maximum if product quality goals were achieved, 25 percent of $800 for customer service, and a similar amount for safety and financial performance. The maximum possible payout per employee per year was $800. The incentive was paid shortly after the end of the year. A key component of the Merck program is educating employees about the measures and how their efforts could influence the outcomes.

Rewards for Cross-Functional Teamwork

Relatively few rewards programs are designed specifically for cross-functional teams. To design such a program, we must look to the work done in other areas with standard work teams and broader group-incentive systems. It is clear that a program must encourage, support, and reward successful cross-functional teamwork. We must focus the rewards on such things as the coordination of all functions toward the achievement of team goals, the reduction of conflicts among departments, leadership that brings team members together, and results that come from the integration of diverse priorities. It is also important to recognize the work by teams and individuals that provide the support required by the cross-functional team to be successful.

Guidelines for Cross-Functional Team Rewards

As the Lotus Development case makes clear, the award should be based on the notion that "none of us can win unless we all win." A true team award requires the combined effort of team members representing all the related functions. In fact, the purpose of a project team award should be to encourage cross-functional collaboration.

Reinforce the Cross-Functional Team Concept

Employees must get a consistent message that cross-functional teamwork is valued in the organization and will be rewarded. This message must be heard, especially by the managers of functional departments who are sending people to these teams and by the service and support departments that the cross-functional teams often rely on to reach their goals.

As compensation experts Combs and Gomez-Meija (1991) point out, "The single most important factor contributing to the relative integration of functional areas is the way rewards are allocated across these units. The compensation system and the particular mix of pay components used can send powerful signals to employees as to the organization's goals. If different signals are sent to the various functions . . . coordination will suffer" (p. 45).

Bring the Reward Down to the Team Level

Most experts agree with the line-of-sight concept, in which the reward is clearly related to the team's performance. In other words, team members can see the relationship between their effort and the reward. In large organizations, gain-sharing and profit-sharing programs are too far removed from the work of individual cross-functional teams. In most cases, the organization must include an educational component to the incentive plan that helps team members understand how their performance affects the overall team and organizational results. The Merck Pharmaceuticals Pay for Performance Plan is a good example of an organizational unit incentive that encourages cross-functional collaboration.

Reward Individual Team Players, Too

We still need to recognize individual team members who are outstanding team players—people who go beyond what is required and those who make an outstanding individual contribution to a team that is less than completely successful. For example, the Morris Savings Bank team incentive program described earlier in this chapter includes payoffs for employees who meet their individual quota, even when their branch does not receive a team award (Eisman, 1990). The Lotus Development project team award program provided supplemental bonuses to team members who made extraordinary contributions.

In addition, we also need to reward the "coordinating" cross-functional teams that rarely engage in any real interdependent teamwork. These teams simply coordinate the efforts of individuals and departments. As team rewards experts Mower and Wilemon (1989) point out, "When the degree of interdependency among team members is low, team success depends mainly on each member's individual effort and ability. In such a situation, rewards may be most effective if they are distributed competitively and unequally, provided the basis for differentiation among members is perceived as fair" (p. 27). I am not sure I would use the word *competitively* to describe what is required, but I do agree that it is important to recognize individual team members who make important contributions to the total team effort.

Use Noncash Rewards

Many successful team incentive and recognition programs use merchandise and services as rewards in lieu of money. There is some disagreement about the value of noncash incentives. However, as my colleague and rewards program expert Jerry McAdams says, "Everyone wants more money, but studies continually show that people also want recognition for their contribution to the company" (Miller, 1991, p. 5).

McAdams sees a trend toward an increase in the use of noncash awards by companies (letter to the author, June 1993). With the current focus on quality, there is a need for awards that generate attention. Cash tends to get lost in the compensation process, but merchandise provides additional recognition. Noncash rewards last longer and are not perceived as compensation. The motivational value has a longer "shelf life" because each time employees use the briefcase, for example, they are reminded of how they obtained it. The item can also serve as a motivator to other people. Some noncash awards, such as dinner for two, a clock, or a lawn mower, can be shared with family and friends. Most experts suggest including some other form of acknowledgment, such as a certificate or plaque, that is a permanent reminder of the accomplishment. The certificate, for example, can be displayed in an office or meeting room for others to see; perhaps it will motivate them as well. And, finally, everyone agrees that one size does not fit all. In other words, do not give every team member the same item. I like the use of a catalogue or a list of items having the same value. Then each team member can select the item that appeals.

Use Your Arsenal of Informal Methods

Do not wait for your company to establish a formal team incentive system or other program. As we indicated, much can be done on an informal, low-cost basis to recognize teams and team players. And when a formal program exists, use your insight into the needs of the teams to tailor your recognition efforts to them.

Align Rewards with Business Goals

Most successful plans reinforce the business objectives of the organization. Rewards are more than just a "nice thing to do." The plans can focus on general goals such as customer satisfaction or quality or specific objectives such as cycle time reduction or revenue growth. For project teams, the rewards can reinforce milestones and specific program targets, as in the case of Lotus Development.

Create Many Winners and Few Losers

Companies are getting the message that the "winner-take-all" programs such as "employee of the month" are just not effective. Such competitive plans result in one winner and many losers, or they migrate to a rotational plan where eventually every person gets the award. The goal should be to give out lots of little awards rather than a few big ones. Recognition is free or at least cheap, so spread it around.

Involve Employees in the Selection Process

Many organizations are coming to see the value of a peer review process in which employees develop the guidelines and administer the award program. The Telecordia Technologies program is a good example of a process that employees have come to see as open, honest, and fair because they are deeply involved from start to finish.

Communicate and Then Communicate Some More

It is extremely important to communicate about your rewards program. Team members need to know what the measures are, how they work, and how they can contribute to their achievement. Everyone needs to know why an individual or team received an award and how the performance helped the organization. In general, communication about the rewards should be reinforcing the organization's goals and values.

Rewards and Team Strategy

Rewarding cross-functional teamwork is an important part of the overall team strategy. Although there are many rewards programs past and present to look to for models, it is clear that each organization must design a system that meets its unique needs. This chapter has presented examples from a variety of organizations to draw some specific conclusions about applications for cross-functional teams. The next chapter focuses on a potential benefit of cross-functional teamwork: team learning.

Looking Back: Some Issues to Consider

1. Many organizations are afraid of project team rewards because of the potential backlash from people in the organization who do a great deal of work to support the team but are not rewarded. How do you react to this point? How would you overcome this objection?

2. Given a choice, would team members in your organization choose a cash or noncash award?

3. Some organizations take the position that team members should not be rewarded for just doing their job. How do you respond to this position?

4. There is an ongoing debate about whether peer-based recognition is a more powerful motivator than recognition by management. What are the advantages and disadvantages of each? How do you feel about it?

5. Assume you had a very limited budget for recognition (for example, $100 per person per year). What are some forms of recognition that team members in your organization would covet?

Chapter Ten

Learning as a Team Event

Training is one of the things that makes a cross-functional team work well. You come to a meeting and you know what the process will be. It makes things easier. It's the glue that holds the team together.
MARK WAXENBERG, VICE PRESIDENT, XEROX[1]

Cross-functional teams provide an exciting opportunity for the creation of a learning community. As teams bring together scientists from different disciplines, craftspeople with different skills, employees from different functions, technical people with different specialties, and professionals from different countries, the learning possibilities are almost limitless. A community of self-directed learners and teachers, with everyone playing both roles, is established.

A Learning Community

Colleagues and strangers can learn from each other in both formal and informal settings.

Technical Learning

On the surface, the learning appears to be exclusively focused on technical or subject-matter learning. In other words,

---

[1]Interview with the author, December 2001.

As an electrical engineer, how can I learn about the tools of market research?

As a machinist, how can I learn more about electrical wiring?

As a geologist, how can I learn more about computer modeling?

As a billing clerk, how can I learn more about processing claims?

As a toxicologist, how can I learn about dealing with regulatory agencies?

There are great opportunities for cross-functional learning in the team setting. During team workshops, I ask participants to brainstorm a list of advantages of cross-functional teams for the individual team member. Without fail, "opportunities to learn" is high on the list. Many people view the opportunity to learn new things as a real benefit of team membership. People no longer want to be stuck in the same job, doing the same thing for their whole career. It is not only boring, it is not a smart career move. As we move into the twenty-first century, the survivors will be employees with a broad-based technical background coupled with excellent problem-solving tools, interpersonal skills, and an open mind. In a reflective piece on the future of work in America, published some ten years ago but still applicable today, *Fortune* concludes:

> Specialization is out, a new-style generalism is in. The most employable people will be flexible folk who can move easily from one function to another, integrating diverse disciplines and perspectives. Similarly, people who can operate comfortably in a variety of environments will fare better than those stuck in the mind-set of a particular corporate or even national culture. People will need the ability not only to learn fundamentally new skills but also to *unlearn* outdated ways [Sherman, 1993, p. 52, emphasis added].

More recently I wrote, "Going forward, a team player will be a more complex person. The effective team player will be adaptive, creative, visionary, supportive, flexible, and candid. More will be expected and the people who thrive in this new world will both work and think 'outside of the box'" (Parker, 2000b, p. 25).

Interpersonal Learning

Team learning goes much beyond the exchange of technical knowledge and the ability to understand the jargon of other disciplines. Cross-functional teams provide the opportunity to learn to work with a variety of different people. You can learn to understand the needs, values, and working styles of other people and, in the process, learn to work effectively with them. Team learning, therefore, involves the development of interpersonal skills and the establishment of a level of comfort in working with a diverse group of colleagues, strangers, and even your old enemies. Adaptable interpersonal skills will be valued in the future, as organizations make increasing use of cross-functional teams. The most prized employees will be people who can easily move from one team to the next and hit the ground running.

Cross-Cultural Learning

Cross-functional teams are now often cross-cultural as well. As the workforce in the United States becomes more culturally diverse and as business "goes global," teams are reflecting this diversity. In some cases, cultural diversity is consciously baked into the membership of the team. For example, in a recent team-building experience with a scientific team, it became clear that interpersonal conflict was the key issue. Although this was an American company, four of the six members of the team were born outside the United States. As a result, one of the underlying causes of the conflict was a lack of understanding and appreciation of the cultural differences among team members. Team-building exercises brought out these differences as team members learned about each other and how their cultures influenced their teamwork styles.

In another team-building session, the cross-functional team was composed of people based in different countries. The two primary countries, the United States and France, have very different business cultures. Americans tend to be informal, direct, and fast; the French tend to be formal and like to take time to build relationships and arrive at a decision. In the process of participating on this team, members learned the nuances of the other culture and how to work most effectively in this cross-cultural environment.

Beyond the immediate situation, team members are learning how to be effective in any transnational team. Once again, this ability to work with a diverse group of people will be valued, and the cross-functional team provides that learning community. The effective team leader and member learns the basic elements of cultural differences and then continually updates this knowledge base as a result of cross-cultural team experiences.

Cultural Considerations in Learning

Hofstede's five dimensions of national culture (1993) are especially useful for people working on cross-cultural teams.

Reverence for Hierarchy

Team members from countries that revere hierarchy are less likely to speak up and especially to disagree with the team leader and other team members who hold a higher rank in the organization. Latin Americans, as well as people from China, Russia, and India, revere hierarchy, whereas Israel scores low; the United States falls somewhere in the middle. Achieving a true consensus in a multicultural team can be problematic unless you are aware of the different views of hierarchy.

Individualism Versus Collectivism

American team members are highly individualistic and, therefore, value independence and are primarily concerned with their own achievements, whereas people from collectivist countries see themselves as part of the team first and strive for team harmony and team success. When harmony is highly valued by some team members, they will not communicate their honest opinions during a disagreement, causing problems for individualistic members who openly communicate their ideas.

Task Versus Relationships

Team members from "all-business" cultures such as Japan, Germany, and the United States value hard work and dedication over relationships among members, concern for others, and work-life balance that are hallmarks of the cultures of Sweden and the

Netherlands. Understanding these differences can help plan team meetings and team-building events.

Risk Avoidance

Team members from countries such as Denmark think outside the box, embrace change, and encourage innovation, whereas team members from risk-avoidance cultures such as Japan value stability and control. Understanding these differences can be important on new-product development teams.

Long-Term Versus Short-Term Orientation

This dimension most clearly differentiates Eastern and Western cultures. China and Japan, for example, emphasize persistence, patience, and a long-term view, whereas Germany, France, and the United States value the present, the here-and-now, and the need to get it done today. For cross-functional teams, this orientation toward time can have an impact on the team's willingness and interest in developing a plan and sticking to it.

Context and Culture

Hall's formulation of high-context and low-context cultures (1976) is also useful to members of cross-cultural, cross-functional teams (see Chapter Twelve for more discussion of this topic). *Context* refers to the situation in which communication takes place such as the relationship, the social environment, and the background. The context determines the communication among team members. Team members from low-context countries such as Germany, Sweden, and the United States communicate directly, care little for developing relationships, and like to "get down to business." Team members from high-context countries in Latin America, East Asia, and the Arab world like to take the time to build relationships, develop trust, and socialize with their teammates. Once again, the implications for team training and team building are obvious. For example, Tim Miller heads a cross-cultural virtual team at BakBone Software that includes members from San Diego, California, Lanham, Maryland, Poole, England, and Tokyo, Japan. Miller finds that communication with the Japanese members during teleconference meetings has to be carefully managed because "in Japan, a yes-or-no question almost always results in a 'yes' answer, even if it shouldn't" (Alexander, 2000, p. 55).

Cultural Considerations

Although these models and categories are helpful in reminding us of the existence of culture and its potential impact on the success of a cross-functional team, it is also important to be cautious in applying them without careful assessment of your specific team. Here are some additional thoughts about culture and cross-functional team success to consider.

Professional Culture Supercedes National Culture

Many people believe that the cultural norms of a profession are more important in developing relationships on a team than the norms of a country. For example, the engineering subculture, the software developer subculture, and the scientific subculture all provide the basis for bonds that reach across national differences. In other words, an engineer in Prague has no trouble teaming with an engineer in Pittsburgh because they speak the same (technical) language.

Not All Cross-Cultural, Cross-Functional Teams Are Global

Many cross-functional teams are composed of people representing a variety of national cultures that are based in one country. In fact, many of these teams are also located in the same facility, often in the same building.

People Often Adopt the Norms of the Local Culture

Many team members live, work, and participate on teams in another country for years. During that time, they may leave behind the norms of their country of origin and adopt the norms of the current country. Therefore, the models and categories discussed earlier do not apply to them.

Corporate Culture Can Be More Powerful Than National Culture

The cultural norms of the organization are powerful drivers of team-member behavior. Often these norms are more controlling of the actions of team members than the culture of their country.

Check Your Prejudices at the Door

The best advice is to do your homework. Do not presume to know how the team will function, based on the cultural makeup of the group. Get to know the team, including the members, the type of work, the goals, the relationships, and yes, the culture of the team.

Problem-Solving Learning

There is also something magical about the learning that can result from the interplay among the members of an *effective* cross-functional team. Viewing a problem or an opportunity from many angles can provide some exciting payoffs for the organization. The team is able to see possible changes on the horizon that may cause problems or provide opportunities for new products, systems, or services. Cross-functional teams can be in the vanguard of the so-called adaptive organization. The adaptive organization is especially necessary in fast-changing markets, such as computers, where speed and flexibility are necessary for survival. Because cross-functional teams counter the rigidity of the bureaucratic functional organization, they can lead a change effort or at least respond quickly to opportunities.

Cross-functional teams can also be important in the movement toward what Peter Senge calls generative learning organizations (Senge, 1990). Although adaptive organizations are reactive to cues from the environment, generative organizations rely on imagining and dreaming about entirely new possibilities. It means going beyond asking customers what they want to creating something customers *might* want if they knew it was possible. By bringing together people from a variety of disciplines with diverse backgrounds and thinking styles, the cross-functional team increases the possibilities for generative learning, that is, for creating new ideas, not by reshaping old ones but by fashioning a whole new cloth.

Creating the Learning Community

How does all of this happen? Learning does not always take place in an organized educational environment. There are often no classes, textbooks, or lectures. Rather there is the creation of a learning environment—a culture that encourages exploring, taking risks, and being open to new ideas. Initially, the leader is critical to successful team learning. One of my favorite leaders talks a great deal about vision and encourages those on his leadership team to join with him in creating a vision of the organization of the future. He also challenges the team with the need to look at the realities of the present that can either help or hinder the team's journey toward the future. He is open to a variety of possibilities and encourages others on the team to think and act in creative new ways. He is also constantly exposing the team to new views of the world as seen by people outside of the company and the industry. As someone said about him, "He is not afraid of new ideas." As a consequence, the team is a good example of a cross-functional team that is engaged in team learning—a place where people are continually learning and growing and using that learning to shape their future.

A recent study of ten cross-functional teams confirms the nature of the team as an informal learning community (Kettley and Hirsh, 2000). The data suggest that cross-functional team members learn via four different routes:

1. Directing knowledge or skills transfer from other members
2. Observing other members in action
3. Engaging in team problem solving
4. Expanding prior experience and reframing new insights

It is important to note that members come to the team with little or no expectation that it will be a learning experience. Three different types of learning emerge from participation on a cross-functional team:

1. *Interpersonal learning.* Developing communications competencies such as influencing others, handling conflict, and listening, as well as enhancing their self-awareness in terms of their motivation, preferences, and style

2. *Organizational learning.* Increasing the member's knowledge of the various parts of the organization and other internal processes, as well as external issues such as customer requirements and dealing with suppliers and regulatory bodies
3. *Functional learning.* Acquiring the knowledge, tools, and techniques of other technical specialists

Kettley and Hirsh (2000) also point out that organizations that value knowledge management as a goal can do some things to support and enhance the informal learning that takes place on a cross-functional team. Suggested strategies include formal team training to develop problem-solving techniques, realigning human resource systems (for example, rewards, performance appraisal), and direct intervention to capture team learning for transfer to the rest of the organization.

Organized Team Learning

Learning and development for cross-functional teams can be approached with two different but related strategies.

Team Training

Teamwork does not come naturally. Working together in a team environment is a learned behavior; there are skills to be developed and knowledge to be acquired. As Alfie Kohn (1986) has shown, competition is as American as apple pie. And competition often comes down to winning and losing, with much of it focused on individual effort. We value individual excellence: the high scorer in the basketball game, the winning pitcher in the baseball game, the halfback who scores the winning touchdown. Even so-called team sports put a premium on individual performance. Little children, especially little boys, are encouraged to be the stars of the team. The school system reinforces this behavior, as students are pitted against each other for grades and other forms of recognition. There is little emphasis on team learning. In fact, collaboration is often viewed as cheating. When groups of students are asked to work together on a school project, there is often bickering among teammates over who did the most work and, therefore, should get the best grade. And, of course, things do not get much better in the business world where performance appraisal is often a competitive exercise.

The net result of this scenario is that people need to learn how to be an effective team player and how to create effective teamwork. Therefore, team training includes opportunities for team leaders, members, sponsors, and others to learn both skills and knowledge. A coordinated and integrated approach to team learning includes the same fundamental content but with adaptations to the specific role played by each category. In the following sections, I describe the content and the various applications to different groups.

Being a Team Player

In all programs, people learn what it means to be a team player and how they can increase their personal effectiveness as a team player. We start with the premise that effective teamwork comes from effective team players. Our research shows that there are many ways you can be an effective team player, just as there are many ways you can be an ineffective team player. I have identified four team player styles (Parker, 1996):

1. *Contributor:* a task-oriented person who is good with details and enjoys supplying the team with technical data
2. *Collaborator:* a goal-oriented member who pushes the team to fulfill its mission and is open to new ideas or methods for achievement
3. *Communicator:* a process-oriented individual who is an effective listener and consensus builder
4. *Challenger:* a person who questions the goals, methods, and ethics of the team and encourages the team to take well-conceived risks

These style differences can be a valuable resource for a cross-functional team (see Chapter Twelve for more discussion). And because a cross-functional team is composed of people from different backgrounds, it is likely that there will be a diversity of styles on the team. As a result, it is important that team members and leaders learn

- The strengths and weaknesses of each style
- The strengths and weaknesses of their personal team player style
- How to increase their personal effectiveness as a team player
- How to work effectively with team members who have different styles

Because *style* refers to how a person carries out his or her role, team leader training focuses on the person's leadership style and ways to increase the usefulness of each person's style. Members learn how to use their style to be an effective team member. Sponsors or managers learn how to increase the impact of their style on their role as nurturers of a team-based organization. A self-assessment survey instrument, the *Parker Team Player Survey* (Parker, 1991; also see the Resources section), is used in this session.

With an intact team, a companion instrument, the Parker Team Player Survey: Styles of Another Person, is also used to provide each person with feedback from teammates. In this design, members complete the self-assessment and one feedback instrument for each of their teammates. At the team-building meeting, each person receives a report that contains his or her self-assessment, along with the scores of his or her teammates. These data are used to create discussion exercises and develop improvement plans.

Developing an Open Climate and Avoiding Groupthink

In this unit, the focus is on developing open communication and trust and avoiding the pitfalls of groupthink. Using the Challenger disaster as a case study, the session focuses on ways of developing, creating, and maintaining a climate of openness. The team leader learns what he or she can to promote an open climate; the team member learns how individuals often "self-censor" their thoughts, and managers learn how the total organizational culture affects open communication.

Resolving Conflicts

By its very nature, a cross-functional team will have conflicts. Because the team is composed of people representing different styles, goals, priorities, expertise, and other factors, differences are endemic to cross-functional teams. There is nothing wrong with the existence of conflicts, only with the failure to satisfactorily resolve them. Teams need to (1) understand that differences are to be expected and even encouraged and (2) learn how to resolve differences in an effective manner.

Here is an approach from my program that seems to work. Each person identifies a recent conflict that did not turn out well and a conflict that was resolved successfully. They discuss the approaches that were used and the results. Each person completes the *Thomas Kilmann Conflict Mode* (Thomas and Kilmann, 1971), which identifies a person's tendency to use five conflict resolution approaches: (1) avoiding, (2) accommodating, (3) competing, (4) compromising, and (5) collaborating. The *Dealing with Conflict* video (CRM Learning, 1992) is shown. The video depicts the five conflict styles in a series of vignettes.

Each person returns to the conflicts he or she identified and looks at them in light of the conflict modes identified in the survey and demonstrated in the video. When members of an intact team participate in the training together, they are encouraged to identify and discuss actual conflicts on their team. The outcomes include ways the team member can increase his or her effectiveness in resolving interpersonal conflicts with teammates and the development of norms for conflict resolution on the cross-functional team.

Training in Meeting Management

Team leaders need training in designing, planning, and facilitating meetings, whereas member training should focus on ways to be an effective meeting participant. I often start a training program with a brief assessment of current team meetings. The assessment can include an informal brainstorming exercise that lists the positives and negatives of meetings. For a more formal evaluation, I use the Team Meeting Assessment (TMA), a thirty-six-item survey that yields results in four different but related areas: (1) meeting planning, (2) mechanics and procedures, (3) meeting process, and (4) closing and follow-up (Parker, 1998). Leaders or teams use the TMA results to plan interventions that target the areas in need of improvement. I also use a brief video, *Be Prepared for Meetings* (1991), which demonstrates in a positive manner the techniques of running an effective meeting. It helps that the video follows a cross-functional team through an entire meeting as the various tools are demonstrated. Using the video as a starting point the sessions cover the following:

- Understanding the types of meetings
- Choosing the right location for the meeting
- Using an agenda
- Stating the purpose of the meeting
- Establishing the climate
- Starting on time
- Beginning with an attention-getter
- Getting participation
- Staying on track
- Providing meeting leadership
- Learning closing techniques

Another good training video is *Meeting Robbers* (CRM Learning, 1995), which presents, with some good humor, the types of behaviors that can derail a meeting, along with tools for getting a meeting back on track.

Meeting planning always includes preparing an agenda. Using the sample meeting notice (see Figure 10.1), the unit covers the importance of having an agenda that covers premeeting preparation, specific topic descriptions, the action required on the topic, the person responsible for the topic, and an estimate of how much time we expect to devote to the topic. It is important to make clear that it is an "estimate" that can be adjusted if, for example, the initial discussion indicates that more time is necessary to resolve the issue. Agenda planning also requires that the topic be listed in descending order of importance so that the most significant issues are addressed early in the meeting, thus guaranteeing they will be considered and discussed when the members are fresh and alert. The session closes with a plan to increase meeting effectiveness by using the tools from the unit.

Figure 10.1. Sample Meeting Notice.

Meeting Name: RAM   MEETING NOTICE

Project Team Meeting   Meeting Date: June 25, 2002

Starting Time: 2:02 p.m.   Ending Time: 3:17 p.m.

Location: Conference Room B

Pre-Work: Read 1st Quarter Report; Read Customer Survey
Executive Summary; Review May Meeting Notes (proposal for
a new district).

AGENDA

Topic	Action	Responsibility	Time
Status of '99 Budget: Plan v. Actual	Decision on Overruns	J. Kaplan	30 min.
Creation of New District	Decision	V. Ku	20 min.
Feedback from Customers	F.Y.I.	S. Edwards	15 min.
Presentation at ACM Conference.	Who Will Prepare?	A. Carlin	10 min.

Team Building

The most successful development opportunity for a cross-functional
team is usually team building. In other words, the intact team goes
through the experience together. For example, I offer a course at a
company titled "Increasing the Effectiveness of Cross-Functional
Teams." Employees sign up for that course as individuals who are interested in learning about the subject. The hope is that they will go back
to their teams and apply the new information. However, that can be
a stretch, as other team members have not had the same experience.
Therefore, attending the program remains an educational experience
("I now know what makes a cross-functional team successful").

The course is also offered to cross-functional teams who want to attend the program as an intact group. In this format, they learn and apply the new information to their team at the same time. For example, they learn the success factors for cross-functional teams and then see how their team stacks up against these criteria. Based on this exercise, the team then devises an action plan to increase their effectiveness. The net result of the program is powerful: the team leaves with increased knowledge about cross-functional teams and a shared plan for growth and development of their team.

However, the approach that has the most impact is a data-based team-building intervention tailored to and based on the team's unique experience. The approach follows the classic team-building process. Data are collected via interviews, surveys, and meeting observation. These data are used to identify the team's strengths and weaknesses and then design a team meeting. The facilitator presents a summary of the data as a springboard for a series of problem-solving and planning activities that focus on action designed to improve team behaviors and team processes. The team walks away with plans to increase the effectiveness of their team that are accepted by all members of the team. Checkpoints for monitoring and evaluating progress are built into the plans.

Technical Training

One of the assumed benefits of cross-functional teams is the opportunity for cross-training. Thus far, successful cross-training has been limited to shop-floor teams and client service positions in offices. One of the best-known experiments is taking place at Aid Association for Lutherans (AAL)—a company that sells life and health insurance to a mainly Lutheran customer base (Kaeter, 1993). Several years ago, the company shifted the focus of the staff serving the field sales representatives from functional management to a team-based, cross-functional organization. In essence, that meant going from a situation in which one person handled only one function, such as new applications, to a team approach in which every team member could handle any request from a sales rep. There are many benefits of this approach, but the most significant are that the salesperson does not get bumped from one person to the next, requests are handled faster, and there are fewer mistakes.

Obviously, the only way to make this system work is to train each team member in how to handle all the required functions. AAL relied primarily on one-on-one training; team members taught each other but later found that some formal classroom instruction was necessary to fill in knowledge gaps. However, what made the whole thing work was a pay-for-knowledge system that rewarded team members with additional compensation as they learned and *applied* the new information on the job.

At the shop-floor level, many companies are creating self-directed cross-functional teams. Where it makes sense, the company is reducing the number of classifications and cross-training team members. Cross-training gives the organization the flexibility to speed up the existing process ("we don't have to wait for an electrician to show up") and move quickly to shift to another product line in response to an order. Motorola, Corning, and General Motors are among the many companies using the flexibility of cross-trained teams to improve their business.

Cross-training on scientific and technical cross-functional teams has been limited to presentations at team meetings and informal one-on-one learning that is self-directed. And yet, according to Pearson (1983), "One of the prime requirements for effective interdisciplinary interaction is that all members should have an understanding and appreciation of the contributions from other disciplines. This includes understanding their attitudes and values, as well as their technical skills" (p. 391). It is true that some professionals do not want to share their knowledge. Some professionals are fearful that if they share their expertise with others, this will decrease their value to the organization. We must help people get beyond this, perhaps by rewarding them for sharing their expertise, to help them understand the value of their knowledge to the success of the team. In the future, the training of cross-functional teams must include cross-training in technical knowledge and skills. It's important to understand what this type of technical training is and is not.

A market research specialist will never become a fully trained toxicologist but can learn enough to ask intelligent questions about the product, which may help with the formulation of the overall team strategy. An engineer may never fully grasp the psychological implications of a proposed product enhancement, but she could learn enough to help tailor the specifications to the targeted consumer. If these teams are to be successful, cross-training will be synonymous with cross-functional teamwork.

Cross-Functional Team Learning Strategies

In this section you will find several different approaches to providing effective learning opportunities for cross-functional team members.

Facilitate Informal Team Learning

Team leaders can encourage the informal learning that should be so much a part of the natural dynamics of a cross-functional team. In discussions at team meetings, the leader can seek a wide range of opinions about a topic. Too often, members feel they can only speak about an agenda topic that falls within their recognized area of expertise. In other words, scientists can only discuss the scientific issues, whereas the marketing representative should restrict her remarks to the market potential of a product. Leaders need to take a broad view of the potential for learning in a team setting. Approaches that often help break down these rigid barriers and open up learning possibilities include

- Off-site team meetings where the climate is more relaxed
- Informal sessions before and after team meetings (for example, over coffee or a casual lunch)
- Brief presentations at team meetings by technical experts using nontechnical language

Provide Blended Solutions

Recent experience with organizations under pressure to move quickly to get teams up and running has necessitated a more flexible approach to team learning and development. There is a need to unbundle services to fit the needs of a variety of organizations. Some organizations, with limited time and resources, opt for one or two interventions; others need more assistance. Here are some approaches that have proven beneficial.

• *Leader training.* In some large organizations with a large cadre of team leaders, all of the learning focuses on developing team leaders. The assumption is that the leaders have the most influence on the success of the team. In addition, the leader is able to transfer the learning to the team via informal coaching.

• *Leader training plus coaching.* In this model, the leader participates in leader development workshops that include assessment, feedback, and development plans. The training is supplemented by one-on-coaching that builds on the development plans.

• *Leader training plus member training.* This dual-track approach includes a leader-development program and a member-development program that have parallel curricula. For example, leaders learn how to set a climate for open communication while members learn the importance of expressing their views at a team meeting.

• *Leader training plus follow-up workshops.* Intensive leader training is followed by short, targeted workshops tailored to their needs in specific areas such as facilitation skills.

• *Member training plus Web-based learning.* Because the number of team members is often large, the logistics and cost of extensive classroom learning can be prohibitive. Therefore, some organizations are using Web-based or other individual learning options such as CD-ROMs to provide additional training to team members (Parker, 2000b).

Recommend Team Building and Training for Intact Teams

If we have learned one thing about the development of teams, it is that providing training or team building for intact teams is clearly the most effective strategy. When the team goes through the experience together, they are able to apply the learnings on the spot. The outcomes are more likely to be sustained.

Support Technical Training

I see team members asking, pleading, and demanding to know more about the work of others. They see technical training both as a personal benefit and an enhancement of the team process. The best way to institute team-based technical training is to have team members teach each other. Each team member is better able to tailor the training to the needs of their teammates than a person from the training department. In addition, team members also will see each other as valued resources.

The development of a team learning community works best in a small group and an informal environment. Large teams make it difficult to obtain the benefits of the team training described in this chapter. The next chapter tackles the issue of team size and suggests methods of dealing with large teams.

Looking Back: Some Issues to Consider

1. How realistic is it to assume that you can teach someone to be an effective team leader or team member? Aren't some people just born leaders?

2. What is the best team training program you ever attended? What made it memorable?

3. Assume you are the leader of a global new-product team that has just started up. What is more important—technical training, interpersonal training, or cross-functional team training?

4. What are the advantages and disadvantages of cross-functional team training?

5. Given a limited budget and assuming you can't do everything, in what type of team learning would you invest most of your budget?

Chapter Eleven

Team Size
Small Is Beautiful

*Team effectiveness breaks down when you get beyond
ten members.*
MICHAEL POOLE, SENIOR DIRECTOR, CLINICAL
RESEARCH, PARKE-DAVIS[1]

Bigger isn't always better, especially when it comes to cross-functional teams. In the drive for participation and involvement, many organizations have sought to demonstrate their commitment by searching out every last person with some connection to the task and putting them on the team. It's a high price to pay for trying to make sure people do not feel left out. The net result is that teams have grown in size but experienced a decrease in productivity, with members having no real sense of involvement beyond having their names on the team roster. I have seen cross-functional project teams in the telecommunications and pharmaceutical industries with twenty, thirty—even as high as fifty members, even though we know that groups that large are just not effective.

THE ALLURE OF LARGE TEAMS

For some organizations, bigger does indeed seem to at least feel better. Why? The answers vary:

- More team members mean more ideas.
- The bigger the team, the more important the project.

---

[1]Interview with the author, October 2001.

- A big team means my job as team leader must be big and important.
- We can't leave anyone out.
- Team meetings are good educational forums. They provide a good opportunity to orient and train junior staffers.
- Having large teams means having fewer teams, which translates into a reduced need for coordination and lower administrative overhead costs.

Despite the allure of bigness, none of these rationalizations stands up to closer examination and the test of research data.

More Team Members Mean More Ideas

Although having more team members does provide the *potential* for more ideas, we emphasize potential because it does not often translate into reality. Of six studies that examined the effects of group size on idea generation, only one found larger groups to generate more ideas than smaller groups (Hackman and Vidmar, 1970; Bouchard and Hare, 1970; Bouchard, Draden, and Barasaloux, 1974; Renzulli, Owen, and Callahan, 1974; Lewis, Sadosky, and Connolly, 1975; Fern, 1982).

The clear conclusion is that although large groups bring more minds to bear on a problem, not all of the minds actually contribute ideas. Small groups encourage participation because more people feel free to speak up. The net result is that more ideas come out in small groups; in a large team, most members do not feel comfortable expressing their ideas. As Paul Hartley of Xerox pointed out, "We had stifled creativity with large teams. So we slimmed down to the right-sized groups" (interview with the author, December 2001).

The Bigger the Team, the More Important the Project

It is true that people often associate the relative importance of a project with the size of the team. In other words, if it's big it must be important. And one way an important project team gets bigger is that more people want to be on the team. A hot, visible project tends to draw people who want to be where the action is. Unfortunately, one of the best ways to ensure the failure of an important project team is to allow the membership to grow beyond a small, solid working group. All research studies on group size show that as the size of the group increases, per-person productivity decreases. For example, in a study of eighty teams at Allstate Insurance Company, team size was a characteristic that was highly correlated with team effectiveness, as measured by productivity, employee satisfaction, and manager judgment. In other words, smaller teams were more effective than larger teams (Champion, Medsker, and Higgs, 1993).

A Big Team Means My Job as Team Leader Must Be Important

Some team leaders think that if they have a big team with a big budget, they themselves must be big. Imagine how good it must sound to say, "I head the Polymers Team, which has forty-five members from across the division." Although that can be a major ego trip for some team leaders, it will be short-lived if the team produces little of real value to the organization. And unless the team uses some effective subgrouping, they are not likely to produce anything of value. The team leader would be better advised to reduce the size of the team, thereby increasing their chances of being successful. In the end, it will sound a great deal more impressive to say, "I was leader of the Polymers Project Team that brought that new heavy-duty adhesive to the market in less than twenty-four months." Although it may look good on paper to lead a large team of thirty-five scientists or engineers, that makes the team leader's job extremely difficult. "If a team has more than six to eight people, it's unwieldy. Anything more than ten becomes counterproductive" (Mike Waters, Xerox vice president; interview with the author, December 2001).

We Can't Leave Anyone Out

This can be one of the most seductive arguments. Aren't we looking for more participation and involvement? Don't we want various departments to support the team? Shouldn't anyone who wants to participate be allowed to participate? Although we do want involvement and support, it does not require the direct participation of every last person to achieve that end. In fact, as a cross-functional team increases in size beyond ten members, an individual's opportunity to participate effectively in the operation of the team decreases dramatically. So although you have not been "left out," you are not really "in." You are included on the team's roster of members and meeting distribution list, but your opportunity to be an active team player is more symbolic than substantive. "As the number increases, misunderstandings increase, decisions are more difficult, and changes are cumbersome" (Mary Black, executive director, Parke-Davis; interview with the author, October 2001).

However, in some situations it is just not possible or even desirable to have a small team, despite the well-documented risks. For example, John Dew of the University of Alabama noted, "The team was a little big. But we needed all the pieces of the puzzle. Yes, it slowed things down a bit but in the end the overall quality increased. Most importantly, managers would not have understood all of the details if they had not been involved" (interview with the author, September 2001).

Team Meetings Are Good Educational Forums

Many managers use project team meetings as an opportunity to orient new employees and provide a broadening educational experience for junior staffers. Employees are sent to team meetings, not to participate but to observe, learn, and often to take notes and report back to the department.

There is no question that team meetings are educational. Members can learn about the topic being explored as well as how cross-functional teams operate. However, there are many problems with this approach. First, let's be honest. Some managers and senior staff members simply do not want to go to team meetings. In these cases, sending junior people to the meetings for the "educational value" is suspect. Second, making team meetings a positive educational experience requires that (1) the person attend meetings on a regular basis, not just when a senior person does not feel like going, (2) the person have some background on the subject or be briefed before the meeting, and (3) the person have an opportunity to ask questions and clarify issues that come up at the meeting. Unfortunately, these criteria are rarely met. Third and perhaps more important, the cross-functional team does not benefit from their attendance. In fact, their presence may detract from team effectiveness by simply increasing the number of noncontributing bodies in the room.

Having Large Teams Means Having Fewer Teams

In organizations that place a high value on employee involvement, just about every person is on a problem-solving or process-improvement team. In these environments, teams tend to be quite large. However, employees are usually on just one team. As a result, there is a decreased need for

- Qualified team leaders
- Management coaches and sponsors
- Team skills training and team building
- Support services

Although the cost savings are potentially substantial, the issue remains one of good news and bad news. The good news: the company saves a lot of money. The bad news: a high percentage of the teams fail to meet their goals (Magjuka and Baldwin, 1991).

An Increase in Team Size

Researchers who have studied team productivity have concluded that increasing team size means (1) decreasing team productivity, (2) decreasing team member involvement, and (3) decreasing participation and trust.

Decreasing Productivity

Researchers who study team productivity have concluded that as numbers of team members increase, the individual productivity of team members decreases because they are spending more of their time communicating about the task to others. Louis Fried, vice president of information technology for SRI International, who has studied project teams, found that "in groups of five members or less, such task oriented communication can consume from 10 percent to 30 percent of each member's time. As the number of people in the group increases beyond five, members must spend more of their time communicating and may eventually reach an upper limit of approximately 90 percent" (Fried, 1991, p. 28). Fried concludes that "with every team member added, the communication load increases and the net productivity of each team member decreases" (p. 29).

Decreasing Team Member Involvement

Just about every study of team size shows that as the number of team members increases, participation, trust, and accountability decrease. *Social loafing* is a term psychologists use to describe the reduction in individual effort as the size of the team increases (Zaccaro, 1984). So-called loafing occurs because as the size of the team increases beyond eight, each team member feels less responsible for the team's success; other people are around to pick up the slack. Individual accountability declines. When the team counts on you to deliver on your commitments and you feel your performance is being closely monitored by your teammates, you are more likely to be concerned that they are evaluating you. As a result, you are more likely to produce than on larger teams where you can get lost in the crowd. In general, the larger the team, the more you feel that your responsibilities can be diffused; the smaller the size of the team, the greater the individual accountability.

Decreasing Participation and Trust

Two additional concerns with large teams are participation and trust. The more members a team has, the more likely it will be that a few strong personality types will dominate discussions and the decision-making process. Many potentially good team players will remain passive, hesitant to voice their good ideas and opinions in front of a large group. This phenomenon is likely to kick in as the team exceeds eight or nine members.

The level of trust on a team, always a key issue, tends to decrease as group size increases (Sato, 1988). As the size of the team increases, members are less likely to

- Be open and honest in their comments
- Be willing to disagree with the leader
- Feel confident they can depend on each other
- Give each other honest feedback

OPTIMAL TEAM SIZE

It is not surprising that managers' perceptions support the results of studies by empirical researchers. Although optimal size depends on the specific team mission, in general, the optimal team size is four to six members, with ten being the maximum for effectiveness. It is important to remember that many team tools in decision making, problem solving, and communicating were created to take advantage of small-group dynamics. Consensus, for example, just does not work as a decision-making method in a team of twenty members.

The following are some typical views on the size of cross-functional teams:

"Team effectiveness breaks down when you get beyond ten members. For example, one team was so large we had to go to an off-site facility to get a room large enough to hold us. It was hopeless until we decided to have a core group of seven." (Mike Poole, Parke-Davis; interview with the author, October 2001)

"Our goal is to get all interested parties involved. If fifteen parties are users, I invite a representative sample of those parties to work on the team but then give everyone a chance to review the recommendations. We call the small group a core team." (Bill Hines, executive director, Bell Communications Research [now Telcordia Technologies, Inc.]; interview with the author, January 1993)

"The size of the team is based on the issue, but it is typically in the range of six to eight people." (Naomi Marrow, director, human resources, *Reader's Digest*; interview with the author, January 1993)

"Our teams are large, sometimes as large as eighty people. The total team meets periodically to review status reports. However, the working group is a core team of about eight people who are usually also the chairs of the various subgroups of the team. In subgroups is where most of the real work gets done." (Jose Verga, product manager, Pacific Bell; interview with the author, January 1993)

"Eight to ten is the best size." (Jim Kochanski, director, human resources, Northern Telecom; interview with the author, January 1993)

"One of the key success factors is team size. In my view, four to six is optimal." (Larry Sherrill, human resources manager, Abbott Laboratories, Diagnostics Division; interview with the author, February 1993)

"For work teams, that is, teams doing real work such as process re-engineering, team size is first determined by the required inter-dependence of the task. Team effectiveness is then considered and eight to twelve people is the usual size." (Stuart Winby, director, Hewlett-Packard; interview with the author, February 1993)

"Large teams are broken down into subteams. I recommend eight per team." (Alf Higginbotham, Maritime Life Assurance Company; survey response)

"Teams should be limited to no more than a dozen people. Beyond that you begin to lose the ability to communicate and work closely as a team." (Mike McGrath, managing director, Pittiglio, Rabin, Todd & McGrath; Whiting, 1991, p. 51)

TEAM SIZE STRATEGIES

What should you do? There is simply no getting around the fact that small teams work best. Here are some ideas that are being used successfully in a variety of organizations.

Play Hardball: Limit the Size of Your Team

Do the right thing. You know that large teams do not work well. When new teams are formed, insist that they include fewer than ten members or use subgroups or the core team concept. Reorganize existing teams into smaller units. One major pharmaceutical company slashed the size of its large project (drug development) teams into small, working teams. Team leaders were free to invite other subject-matter experts to assist the team as the need arose. It was not easy to eliminate people from some teams, but the long-term impact on the teams and the development process was salutary.

Use the Core Team Approach

A core team is a cross-functional team consisting of representatives of the functions critical to the achievement of the team's goals. Typical core teams include from five to eight members. For example, a core team at Sun MicroSystems responsible for the development of a new workstation included representatives from software engineering, hardware engineering, operations, customer service and support, and marketing and finance, along with the team leader. The core team provided the leadership and made the key decisions for the project. Sometimes they did much of the real work. More often, however, they met regularly with people in their functional area who supported (did the work for) the team to ensure that the work required by the core team conformed to quality standards and was done on time.

In some organizations, core team members also serve as leaders of the functional teams. Another variation was reported by Toni Hoover, vice president of drug development at Parke-Davis (interview with the author, October 2001). "We use a core team of ten to twelve, composed of the key functions who handle the strategic direction plus subteams who handle the tactical issues." In a slightly different variation, Govindarajan and Gupta (1996) recommended a core team of under ten members but "if the core team requires input from others, those individuals could be brought in on an ad hoc basis. Thus the extended team could include all relevant stakeholders both within the organization and outside" (p. 65).

Divide into Subgroups

An old group-dynamics tactic is to break up large teams into small working groups. Many leaders of cross-functional teams, faced with the political necessity of having a large team, have skillfully used subgroups to achieve the advantages of small groups. In this model, the full team meets monthly or even quarterly to review the status reports of the subgroups. The subgroups provide a real opportunity for team members to use their expertise and have an impact on the outcome. Participation is limited to technical work because decisions on the mission and critical project direction are usually made by the leader and a small cadre of influential members.

Small Is Beautiful and Better

Cross-functional teams seem to be particularly prone to the problem of being too large to be effective. In an effort to avoid offending both allies and enemies alike, team sponsors simply add people from the various functional areas to the team. And they do this, despite the fact that both common sense and research data tell us that smaller is better. A major study of fifty teams in a variety of industries concluded that "large numbers of people usually cannot develop the common purpose, goals, approach, and mutual accountability of a real team. And when they do so, they usually produce only superficial 'missions' and well-meaning intentions" (Katzenbach and Smith, 1993b, p. 47).

In this chapter, I have provided some techniques for dealing with the size problem. In the next, I explore a variety of techniques for shaping the positive internal dynamics of a successful cross-functional team.

Looking Back: Some Issues to Consider

1. In your experience, what is the most compelling reason for a cross-functional team to be composed of fewer than ten members?

2. If you agree that having more members means more ideas, how do you keep your team small but still get the benefit of more ideas?

3. Assuming your team is already large enough, if someone with expertise you need wants to join your team, how do you handle the situation?

4. Let's assume your team has been operating for six months with minimal success. It has also become clear that one of the team's problems is that it is just too large. What are your options in regard to the size issue at this point? What would you do?

5. How do you react to the proposal to use a core team to handle the strategic direction and make the key decisions buttressed by subgroups that work on specific team tasks? How would that approach work in your organization?

Chapter Twelve

The Team Working Together

Talent wins games but teamwork wins championships.
MICHAEL JORDAN[1]

A number of internal issues affect the success of cross-functional teams:

- *Conflict resolution:* the ability of the team to discuss and resolve differences
- *Openness:* the degree to which team members feel free to express their views
- *Meeting management:* the tcam's ability to plan and conduct effective meetings
- *Characteristics of team members:* the capabilities and styles of team members
- *Customers and suppliers:* the degree to which the team effectively partners with suppliers and customers
- *Virtual teamwork:* the degree to which the team effectively collaborates across distance, time, and organizational boundaries and uses technology to enhance team communications

It is possible to look at these issues and think that they apply equally to any type of team. And, of course, the ability to effectively manage the internal dynamics is important to the success of all teams. However, each of these areas presents special problems for

---

[1]Karvelas, 1998.

cross-functional teams, and each requires a solution tailored to the unique characteristics of a team composed of people from a variety of functions in the organization with a myriad of past relationships.

Conflict Management

As the traditional hierarchical organization gives way to a horizontal division of labor dominated by technical specialists, conflicts on teams will be endemic. In fact, if we define *conflicts* as simply differences of opinion, this is exactly what we want to happen. In bringing together a diverse group of experts, we expect and want these differences to surface because, in the end, we expect a better outcome to result. As McCorcle has pointed out, for cross-functional teams "a prime advantage over other types of groups is their diversity of members. Ideally, each person brings a specific set of skills and a unique perspective to the problem at hand" (McCorcle, 1982, p. 296). However, he goes on to note that this diversity can become a barrier to success. "Though such a group may have the potential to bring expertise to bear on a wide range of problems . . . it might also face serious difficulty in working as a unit. It is not because group members might refuse to work together, but because in such a group each person (or represented discipline) could have different ideas about the best way to solve a given problem" (McCorcle, p. 296). If the team is composed of people with different priorities, various team player styles, and some past negative experiences in working together, conflicts will arise.

Conflicts and Performance

These built-in conflicts can lead to poor performance. Ancona and Caldwell's study of cross-functional new-product teams suggests that "high levels of functional diversity are directly associated with lower levels of performance, particularly for management ratings of innovation and for teams' ratings of their own performance" (Ancona and Caldwell, 1991, p. 14). Assessments of performance can be deceptive. Because the use of cross-functional teams is relatively new, expectations can be high and standards of success can lack uniformity. In many situations, it was assumed that simply bringing together experts from a variety of disciplines would produce tangible, high-quality results in less time. The power of the idea of cross-functional teamwork obscured the conflicts inherent in the design of the team. As a result, expectations were, in many cases, unrealistic. Management expected cycle time to be reduced, product quality to improve rapidly, and customer service to be upgraded immediately. And members expected a smooth-running team to happen from the very beginning. "But functional diversity does not always have positive effects on performance . . . because the advantages provided by multiple perspectives are often offset by problems generating consensus . . . and result in teams that have less flexibility, less capacity for teamwork, [and are] more open to political and goal conflicts between functions" (Lovelace, Shapiro, and Weingart, 2001, p. 2). But not all hope is lost. The key to success for cross-functional new-product teams "seems to depend on how effectively members from different functional areas integrate information and perspectives" (Sethi, 2000, p. 11).

Cross-functional teams do produce conflicts among members; we expect it and we want it. But these differences take time and skill to resolve. And rarely are teams warned about the potential for conflict and given the training to resolve the differences. There-fore, when management and team members are asked to assess performance, they are dissatisfied because their expectations are not met. They see team conflict and the time it takes to resolve it as a negative feature of the team; as a result, they are less than com-pletely satisfied with the results. They fail to understand that con-flicts are to be expected and valued, and they do not appreciate the fact that time invested up-front in exploring differences can lead to time savings and quality improvements down the line. As Elizabeth Culotta has noted in her report on cross-functional sci-entific teams, conflicts are seen as positive because disagreements among team members point to problems in the research that need to be fixed (Culotta, 1993).

How to Deal with Team Conflict

The unique nature of cross-functional teams requires that some actions responding to the conflict be central to the existence of any such team:

• *Team training, as suggested in Chapter Ten, must include sessions on conflict resolution.* Team members and leaders must learn that conflicts are to be expected and even valued. However, they must also learn to be open to new ideas and develop skills in listening, questioning, and consensus building.

• *Top management, as well as functional department managers, must be oriented to the characteristics of cross-functional teams.* These managers must also be helped to accept realistic expectations about the potential outcomes of cross-functional teams.

• *It is very important to create opportunities for members in conflict to work together on team projects.* In a study that looked at reducing conflict between engineers and marketing people, it was found that the most effective strategies for reducing the rivalry were working together on cross-functional teams and visiting customers together in the field (Yu, 2001). The study reported that when you work together on a team over a long period of time, you stop thinking of each other as "engineers" and "marketers" and start to see each other as simply teammates who have something useful to offer.

• *In some cases, teams may need expert help in team process facilitation.* Some companies use human resource professionals; other organizations use coleaders who have been trained in group process. For example, TRW in Cleveland, taps high-potential people, gives them training in facilitation skills, and then has them help facilitate teams in other areas.

OPENNESS AND TRUST

On some cross-functional teams, conflicts exist but do not surface. The culture of the team is such that members do not feel free to express their opinions and share their expertise. In some situations, the teams not only represent different functions but different management levels as well. When the corporate culture makes people "level conscious," open communication may be limited when team members include different management levels as well as nonmanagement employees. Lower-level employees are afraid to speak up because, as one person told me, "If you say the wrong thing, it is used against you." Or in another case, when I asked a cross-functional team member why she didn't disagree with a particular point, she said, "Oh, I wouldn't disagree with him; he's got too many Hay points."

Trust creates the pathway to open communication. Lack of trust can be high in cross-functional teams that are also cross-level. In her study of a cross-functional project team, Linda Loehr found that "the lack of trust among team members constrained their individual and collective voices, restricting the sharing of knowledge, experience, and opinions. . . . Indications of mistrust among non-managerial team members ranged from mistrust of the worth of their ideas to mistrust of the system that required their generation" (Loehr, 1991, p. 53).

Lack of communication also occurs on teams that do not have significant differences in levels. Strangers do not immediately trust each other. Antagonists from past team wars may feel they have reason not to be trusting. Others may simply take a wait-and-see attitude.

Communication Barriers

Some of the factors that lead to poor communication among cross-functional team members include

- *Lack of appreciation of the contributions of other functions.* For example, in telecommunications projects, some engineers do not value the input provided by human factors psychologists.
- *Plain old-fashioned turf battles.* Some departments play out their competitive games on the field provided by the cross-functional team.
- *Some functions simply talking a different language.* For example, line department users often do not understand the terminology and technology employed by computer programmers.
- *Members of different functions not sharing similar work orientations.* For example, researchers tend to take a long-term view and have an informal work climate; operations people are more short term and formal; salespeople are usually informal and have a short-term focus. Although one may argue with these generalizations, it is clear that each department or function develops a work style that often clashes with the styles of people from other functions.
- *Some members simply having more interest in the team's purpose and more to gain from a successful outcome.* In one government

agency, team members from one bureau have more interest in the outcome of the team because it affects their client group more than it does the other bureaus represented on the team.

- *Some members mistakenly seeing harmony as the goal of cross-functional teamwork.* As a result, they are afraid to express a contrary point of view for fear that it will destroy the positive feelings among team members. The net result is a false consensus and a less-than-satisfactory outcome.

Although these factors explain the lack of trust and communication on cross-functional teams, they do not excuse it. Members of cross-functional teams are there because they have something to contribute. They must be allowed and even encouraged to share their ideas, information, and opinions without restrictions. Open communication is an absolute requirement for successful cross-functional teamwork. The concept of the team is that the outcome—the product, the system, the service—will be better because it has been created by the combined sharing of expertise from people representing a variety of functions. It is this viewing of the problem or issue from many vantage points that is the strength of the cross-functional team. However, the value of divergent views can only be realized when there is a free flow of information. As Helena Gordon of Penn National Insurance points out, "This is a major issue for our team. As a team leader, it's important that I allow people to bring up issues, even if I don't think they're issues" (interview with the author, October 2001).

Communication Norms

Team norms are usually associated with members' perceptions of a highly successful team (Cohen, Ledford, and Spreitzer, 1996). In addition, Jehn (1995) found that norms that encourage open communication enhanced the positive effect of task-based conflict because members felt they were able to express their ideas freely. When working with cross-functional teams, we encourage the establishment of norms or guidelines on communication and trust. A team's list of norms often includes, for example, "all ideas are given a fair hearing," "everyone will have an opportunity to contribute information and opinions," "open and honest opinions are welcome," "members are expected to actively listen to each other," and "rank does not have its privilege."

In Figure 12.1, you will find communication norms developed by a cross-functional team at a major telecommunications company.

Figure 12.1. Communication Norms.

- Communicate with my teammates as if their ideas, suggestions, and opinions are valued.

- Communicate with my teammates that I understand their message.

- Allow my teammates to express their ideas freely.

- Disagree with my teammates without putting the person down.

- Avoid doing things that inhibit others from contributing.

- Do not interrupt teammates while they are expressing an idea, suggestion, or opinion.

- Do not make remarks that are demeaning to the ethnic or cultural background of anyone.

- Keep teammates fully informed of relevant issues.

- Listen openly and carefully to teammates' ideas, even if I have a different opinion.

- Ask questions if I do not understand something presented by a teammate.

- Respond to all requests from teammates within twenty-four hours.

- Respond with an explanation if a prompt response is not possible.

- Do not push my ideas after a consensus has been reached.

- Do not work behind the scenes to undermine a decision after a consensus has been reached.

Meeting Management

As noted in Chapter Ten, effective meetings are especially important for cross-functional teams. When you bring together a group of people who have different skills, diverse experiences, a variety of work styles, and conflicting priorities, the process of managing the interactions can be tricky at best. As much as we hate meetings, they are still the principle vehicle for team actions and the most visible aspect of a team's operation. Meetings are where the conflicts and communication discussed in the previous sections of this chapter get played out.

Meeting Malpractice

Cross-functional team meetings seem to be susceptible to what might be called unprofessional behavior or malpractice.

Too Many Meetings

There is an erroneous belief that the only place to get teamwork done is in a meeting. Wrong! This belief is the chief contributor to the anti-teamwork backlash that exists in some organizations. Because many meetings are poorly conducted and people associate bad meetings with teamwork, they are quick to conclude that teamwork isn't working. The best way to eliminate this form of malpractice is simply to eliminate those unnecessary meetings. Here's how:

- Adopt the view that not everything requires a face-to-face meeting or a meeting of the full team. Successful teams use small task groups that are subsets of the full team.
- Only meet if there is a clear purpose for the meeting. The regular weekly team meeting may not be necessary this Monday if there is no reason to meet. The simple rule is: no purpose, no meeting!
- Only meet when the time is right. Although you may have a clear purpose, the time may not be right because
  Not all of the required information or equipment is available.
  Not all of the key players are available.
  An appropriate meeting facility is not available.
  An important organizational change is about to be announced.

- Consider other possible alternatives. If the purpose of your meeting is to communicate information, why not consider other alternatives such as voice mail, e-mail, fax, or even one-on-one meetings with each team member.
- Ask yourself, What if the meeting is not held? If the answer is "no problem" or "there would be a loud cheer throughout the organization," then you may have your answer.

Meetings Too Long

There are several reasons meetings last too long:

- The agenda contains too many items.
- We don't include time allocations for each agenda item.
- We don't follow the agenda and the time limits.

The best way to keep the length of the meeting reasonable is good, solid premeeting planning. Begin by clarifying the purpose of the meeting and then include only those items that pertain to the purpose. Delete other items by using nonmeeting methods to communicate progress reports and similar information that requires no discussion. Then add time limitations to each agenda item. During the meeting, remind team members about the time limits and try to stay within the limits. If you are going over the limits, either refer the item to a subgroup or ask the team if they want to take more time and eliminate other agenda items.

Too Many People at Meetings

Cross-functional teams seem particularly susceptible to this malpractice. Many of the teams are either just too large or they allow too many visitors and observers to attend team meetings. One way to reduce the number is to have the meeting notice designate "required" attendees and "optional" attendees. At the meeting, seat the required or core team members around the table to facilitate discussion and decision making. Ask the other people to sit around the perimeter.

Not Enough Gets Done at Meetings

This is the most frustrating problem of cross-functional team management. Because expectations are high and so much seems to be riding on the meeting, lack of action is especially detrimental to team morale. The management of the meeting requires good group process skills, which many cross-functional team leaders do not possess. As we have said, good process skills are needed because a cross-functional team brings together people with little experience in working together and with different working styles. We have suggested providing either training for team leaders or an experienced facilitator to assist the leader. In the absence of either approach, here are some useful tips for conducting a team meeting:

- Start on time. Need we say more?
- Open the meeting with brief statement of purpose and a review of the agenda and time limits.
- Follow the agenda. Begin the discussion with, "We've allocated thirty minutes to this item." Intervene during the discussion with, "Let's move on; we only have ten minutes more for this subject." If someone wants to bring up another subject, ask that it be held until the item is discussed later in the meeting, made an agenda item at the next meeting, or given to a subgroup for consideration.
- Manage the discussion. Use facilitative comments or questions that move the team along:
  Ask for opinions: "How do you react to . . . ?"
  Involve participants: "Can marketing live with this new approach?"
  Clarify ideas: "In other words, you feel we should talk directly to the customer."
  Explore differences: "At this point, the operations folks feel that . . . while engineering can only do . . . "
  Stay focused: "We were discussing data collection. What other approaches can we use?"
  Summarize: "OK, it looks like the feedback is telling us that . . . "
  Test for consensus: "We seem to be saying that we want to."
  Take action: "We have agreed to . . . What steps do we need to take to get started?"
- Summarize the meeting. When the agenda has been completed, the leader should close the meeting by briefly summarizing the key decisions and next steps.

- Confirm action items. As part of the meeting, the action items should be confirmed. Each action item should specify the (1) action required, (2) person responsible, and (3) due date.

CHARACTERISTICS OF TEAM MEMBERS

Teamwork starts with you and me. It begins with the individual—the team player. You cannot have effective teamwork without effective team players and, more important, a *diverse* group of effective team players. As many organizations reorganize into permanent cross-functional teams and make greater use of ad hoc project teams, the opportunity to select the best mix of team players is presented. What characteristics of team members are especially relevant to cross-functional teams?

Has Technical Expertise

There is no getting around the need for people who "know their cookies." The team needs information, skill, and expertise to solve problems and make decisions. However, there is more to the story. Technical expertise must be coupled with the willingness and ability to share the expertise. This is the key characteristic of the team player type I call the Contributor (Parker, 1996; see also Chapter Four for a discussion of team player characteristics). Although the willingness to share expertise may seem obvious, it is not universally practiced. Some experts see their knowledge as a source of power and a factor that differentiates them in the organization. As a result, they either withhold information or make it difficult for others to use it. The effective Contributor, however, freely shares the information in a form easily understood by others and is willing to serve as a mentor and trainer of team members from other areas.

Technical expertise should be linked with an ability to communicate with team members in other disciplines and those who lack the same technical background. It is not enough to know your subject; effective teamwork requires an ability to communicate it in a form that can be easily understood by other team members.

I recently overheard a team member say, "I didn't realize that you were not 'technical.'" This was a not-so-subtle put-down delivered to another team member who had asked questions during a presentation. My reaction to that comment is that it's the presenter's responsibility to communicate effectively with nontechnical team members. I know some very good technical experts who are able to communicate with just about anyone because they understand the audience and can translate their ideas into analogies and other forms that are easily understood.

Is Open to New Ideas

Cross-functional teams bring people from a variety of disciplines together. As a team member, you must be able to do more than just share your ideas; you must be willing to listen to and consider the views of others, even when those views differ from yours. The willingness to be open to new and different ideas is critical because it is the behavior that allows the team to take advantage of the unique nature of the cross-functional team. In other words, there is no sense bringing together all these people with different ideas if we are not going to give adequate consideration to their ideas.

I refer to this type of team player as the Communicator (Parker, 1996). This person should also have the ability to help the team synthesize the various points of view.

Is Willing to Ask Tough Questions

Because we value the need for open communication on a cross-functional team, we need to have team members who will raise questions about the team's work and disagree with other team members, including the team leader. I call this team player style Challenger (Parker, 1996). In Loehr's study of a cross-functional project team, the failure of team members to disagree in a constructive manner during team meetings greatly diminished the team's effectiveness (Loehr, 1991). Team members had opinions, which they shared with the researcher in private interviews, but were reluctant to express them during team meetings. Although the team has to establish and enforce norms about open communication, it is helpful to stock the team with effective Challengers.

Can See the Big Picture

Because the cross-functional team can get bogged down in the details of data, studies, field trials, and other day-to-day things, the team needs someone who can provide the vision: a Collaborator. This is the team-player style of a person who helps the team set overarching goals and put its work into the proper organizational context (Parker, 1996). Periodically, the team needs to remember why it exists and where it is heading.

Is Aware of Cultural Diversity

Increasingly, team members have to able to work with people from other cultures. Cross-functional teams are increasingly cross-cultural, too. As the population of the United States changes such that women and people from other cultures become a larger percentage of the workforce, the composition of cross-functional teams reflects these changes. In addition, global companies are, of course, using global teams composed of members from many countries around the world. In Chapter Ten, I described a recent team-building intervention with a scientific team of six team members; four were born outside the United States. Many of the conflicts on the team stemmed from members' lack of knowledge of each other's culture and its impact on team participation. As team members discussed their family and cultural background, it helped explain their current behavior on the team and led to improved interpersonal communication.

In another organization, the new-product development teams include representatives from at least three different countries. The language barriers are among the easiest hurdles to overcome; cultural differences present the biggest challenges. Team members from France come from what are called high-context cultures, whereas members from the United States typically represent low-context cultures (Halverson, 1992). Americans like to move quickly to get down to work, move things along fast, and make decisions in the meeting. The French like to take time to build relationships and trust before proceeding to the business at hand. Therefore, cross-functional, cross-cultural teams need to adjust some of their meeting-management techniques to accommodate the needs of all team members. For example, earlier in this chapter we recommended starting meetings on time, getting right down to business, and sticking to the agenda. This approach favors people from low-context cultures but does not meet the needs of high-context team members who might want to spend time at the beginning of the meeting (or over coffee prior to the meeting) socializing with their colleagues.

Customers and Suppliers

As organizations begin to see work as a process with suppliers at one end and customers at the other, teamwork with suppliers and customers becomes the most natural thing to do. In addition, as companies experiment with the certification of suppliers, reduce the number of suppliers, and go to single-source suppliers, it makes sense to include supplier representatives as cross-functional team members. And as companies define *quality* as satisfying the customer, the next most logical step is to include customer representatives on your cross-functional quality improvement and product development teams.

There is a practical payoff to the involvement of suppliers and customers in the work of cross-functional teams: it can result in more creative and innovative solutions. For example, a study of the factors that contribute to higher levels of creativity in new-product development concluded, "Leading customers, technology suppliers, and other contributors to environmental uncertainty are defined as insiders, interdependent with the organization and capable of being trusted and engaged in the new product development processes. New ideas emerging from marketing or production groups, or directly from customers, receive as much credence and support as those that emerge from R&D" (Jassawalla and Sashittal, 1999, p. 8).

Involving Suppliers

Once companies woke up to the fact that supplier quality is inextricably linked with their product and service quality, they jumped to involving (some might say pressuring) suppliers to conform to certain quality standards. Motorola shook things up a bit by telling its six thousand suppliers that they had to apply for the Malcolm

Baldrige National Quality Award if they wanted to keep doing business with Motorola. Ford, Xerox, and Florida Power and Light Company also brought suppliers into their quest for quality: "Common elements of these new relationships include cross-functional vendor review and development teams, which often include personnel from purchasing, quality assurance, and end-user organizations. They work so closely with suppliers that they often come to seem like a part of the suppliers' own organizations" ("Vendor Certification Improves Buyer/Supplier Relationships," 1990, p. 2).

As suppliers join the cross-functional team, they have to be seen as true partners in the overall team process. Once a supplier has been certified or is on a "preferred" list, it should not be used to simply leverage a lower price. The focus should be on performance and on how the suppliers' input on the team can improve product quality, service quality, and overall project performance. And the goal should be to build a long-term relationship that leads to cost savings, performance excellence, improved quality, and more business for everyone. For example, one of the key goals of the U.S. Coast Guard's Deepwater Program is to "leverage partnerships" both internally and externally with a so-called system integrator—a major industry supplier who will provide the expertise necessary to guide this multibillion-dollar effort to replace or renew all Coast Guard assets.

Gaining Customer Participation

Every cross-functional team should have a customer for its output, whether it is a tangible product such as a part, a service such as generating data, a new computer system, or even a report recommending a corporate reorganization.

As organizations come to see the customer as a partner and not an adversary, customers are becoming regular members of the team. As described in Chapter One, systems development teams almost always include user representatives on the team to ensure that the system meets their needs and is user-friendly. Car manufacturers are even including dealers on their cross-functional design teams to get instant data about how the customer likes the product instead of waiting for formal survey results. Car rental companies are involving customers on process improvement teams to solve key customer complaints. And the rest of us who rent cars are reaping the benefits. For example, one of the biggest customer complaints concerns the time between getting off the plane and actually getting on the road in a rental car. Customers complain that it takes too long to wait in line, fill out the forms, get to the car, and get out of the parking lot. At one major car rental company, a cross-functional team, which included customers, came up with a system that reduced the transaction time dramatically. As you might suspect, these changes not only result in satisfied customers but also increase employee satisfaction; employees have to deal with fewer unhappy customers.

Virtual Teamwork

As the number of quality and teamwork initiatives increases, the number of meetings also increases. And with the increasing number of meetings, we can expect a backlash against more and more meetings. Once more we will hear, "I can't get my work done; I'm always in a meeting." The backlash against meetings will turn to a backlash against the quality and teamwork efforts. What to do? First, we need to improve the productivity of meetings using the methods described earlier in this chapter. Second, we need to carefully assess the value of a face-to-face meeting for accomplishing certain goals. We need to look at the costs versus the benefits of a team meeting. For example, we recently calculated the cost of a one-hour team meeting at approximately $1,000. The question for the team is, Did we get $1,000 in benefits from the meeting, or could the time have been better spent elsewhere?

Certain team activities seem to require a face-to-face meeting such as developing a team vision, mission or goal, or debating strategy or making a key decision. However, other activities can be accomplished electronically. In addition, the increasing globalization of business, the consolidation brought about through mergers and acquisitions, and the improvements in communications technology have all contributed to the significant increase in the number of so-called virtual teams (Lipnack and Stamps, 1997; Duarte and Snyder, 1999). Virtual cross-functional teams are similar to traditional cross-functional teams except that they must reach their goals "by working across distance, time and/or organizational boundaries and by using technology to facilitate communication and collaboration" (Duarte and Snyder, pp. 4–5).

One of the best ways of looking at communications technology support for virtual teams comes out of the literature of groupware (Ciborra, 1996). The model involves the interaction of time and place. Various teamwork tools fit into one or more of the boxes (see Figure 12.2). In the following section I describe each of the tools, including an analysis of their advantages and disadvantages.

Same Time, Different Place

In this category, you find typical synchronous tools such as video teleconferencing, desktop video teleconferencing, audio teleconferencing, electronic whiteboard, and electronic chat. Although many companies are using video teleconferencing for cross-functional team meetings, the results are, at best, mixed. Although it does save travel time and expense, it does not eliminate team meetings. In most cases, some team members are in a company meeting room in one location while others are in a similar room in another location. The technology usually allows team members to view the same documents in both rooms on the video screen. The medium received a big push during the Gulf War and again after the terrorists' attacks on 9/11 when all business travel was severely restricted. However, many of the limitations of the technology became more apparent during these periods. For example, it is often difficult to hear comments from anyone but the few people

Figure 12.2. Teamwork Technologies Spanning Time and Place.

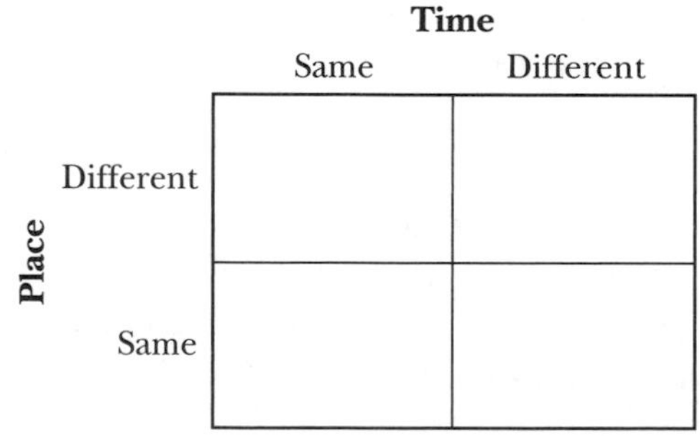

seated near the head table. It is also hard to see everyone. In general, the discussions lack an easy, informal flow.

More recently, with the advent of desktop videoconferencing systems, it's become possible for team members to have face-to-face interactions with their teammates located in multiple locations throughout the organization while each person is sitting in his or her own office. The value of this technology is that not everybody has to go to a dedicated videoconferencing meeting room. These special videoconferencing rooms are quite expensive to set up and maintain. However, a typical desktop workstation system costs less than $1,000 per station (Townsend, DeMarie, and Hendrickson, 1998). For example, with Microsoft's NetMeeting, coupled with their Whiteboard and Chat capability, team members can send messages, including graphics, video clips, and real-time video images and voice to other members around the building or around the world. Members of a new-product team can look simultaneously at an engineering drawing, test results charts, or marketing data and then comment and even edit the document on-line. *Chat* even allows members to have classic "side conversations" because they can send text messages to one person or a subgroup during the meeting.

Another product that often works in conjunction with *NetMeeting* is Lotus *Sametime,* which fosters informal communication outside of formal team meetings. This communication system includes three components:

1. *Awareness.* Members are aware when other members are on-line.
2. *Conversation.* Once a member is aware that another member is on-line, he or she can send an instant message or launch a chat session.
3. *Sharing of objects.* The use of application sharing or whiteboard sessions allows members to share word files, spreadsheets, drawings, and other text material designed to enhance conversations.

Different Time, Different Place

In this category, you find typical asynchronous tools such as e-mail, voice mail, discussion lists, and calendars or program schedules. In our experience, e-mail is still the communication medium of choice for virtual teams. It is fast, efficient, and cheap. When combined with audio teleconferencing for synchronous communication, a team can be extremely successful, as evidenced by the IBM PdxT Team, as described in the Case Study Two. However, as many observers have pointed out, "You must have agreed upon procedures for communicating via e-mail. It may appear informal, but it must not be used thoughtlessly. Otherwise, with a single press of a button, a person can wreak organizational havoc" (Merrick, 1996, p. 40). Katzenbach and Smith (2000) agree that every virtual team should develop their own "netiquette" by discussing how they expect to apply technology to help complete their task and, when possible, agree on the selection of the groupware that the team will employ. Lotus Notes and other groupware platforms provide teams with a shared space where members can engage in synchronous text chats related to team issues. Groupware platforms such as Xerox's proprietary *DocuShare* software allow a geographically dispersed team to establish a secure, shared space where members can post documents relevant to a project that can be viewed and even edited by all members of the team at different times and in different locations. Calendar programs allow team facilitators to plan formal team meetings and team members to schedule ad hoc subgroup meetings. Calendar programs help virtual teams with information about different holidays, local events, time zone differences, and site meetings that affect meeting planning. In the automobile industry, for example, design and communication technologies are minimizing delays in new-model design due to differences in geographical location among design team members (Lockwood, 2001).

> Programs such as CAD/CAM permit global data sharing among designers, engineers, suppliers, partners, and even customers. . . . The better and faster the engineers' access to design ideas, the sooner they can suggest necessary adjustments and the more time they will have to figure out how to work within the proposed design. Chrysler's CATIA systems allowed engineers to identify and resolve more than 1,500 interference, fit and design issues prior to the building of the first prototype vehicles for the Intrepid and the Concorde. This was a major contributor in the reduction of cycle times for design and engineering form 39 to 31 months [pp. 3–4].

Same Time, Same Place

Included in this category are face-to-face meetings of the team where all members are together at the same time in the same conference room. Hybrid same-time-same-place meetings include sessions in which most members are in a conference room and a few members are in remote locations connected to the room via technology. The most typical scenario uses audio teleconferencing capability, with the telephone speaker set up on the table in the conference room. In the best of all possible worlds, the members in remote locations have copies (in hand or on-line) of all documents being discussed so they can fully participate in the discussions and decisions. Desktop videoconferencing also supports this situation because members in remote locations can simultaneously work on documents with their colleagues in the conference room. Figure 12.3 lists some considerations when planning a teleconferencing meeting.

Same Place, Different Time

Very few situations fall into this category. A common meeting room where members working on different shifts can interact via in-room communication is one variation. For example, a permanent team collaboration facility allows team members to leave messages, files, and documents for review by members using the same place at a different time.

Issues for Virtual Cross-Functional Teams

Hardware and Software Are Not Substitutes for Peopleware

Although the systems described here can support a virtual team, "proficiency in groupware is not the critical factor in virtual team performance. In fact, it is clearly secondary to the basics of team discipline. If the people in your group get this wrong, they will e-mail themselves straight into a nonperformance booby trap: relying on technology to elevate performance when the real problem is undisciplined behavior" (Katzenbach and Smith, 2000, p. 17).

Figure 12.3. Guidelines for Audio Teleconference Meetings.

- Prior to the meeting, send each person a copy of the agenda and the reading material.

- Ask for volunteers for the roles of scribe and timekeeper.

- Begin by asking each person to identify him- or herself.

- If time permits, ask each to indicate where he or she is calling from, what the weather is there, and other brief icebreakers. Asking team members to say a few words at the beginning makes it easier to identify them when they speak.

- Refer to the agenda, review the items, and state the overall purpose of the meeting.

- Review the norms, especially the one about no multitasking (doing other work during the meeting).

- At the beginning, ask members to identify themselves before they speak and, if necessary, to specify to whom their remarks are directed.

- If some people do not speak on an issue, call their name and ask if they have an opinion.

- Summarize all decisions and action items as they are completed during the meeting.

- When conflicts arise, carefully state or get the members to state both sides of the issue. Recognize that it is more difficult to resolve conflicts during a teleconference meeting. Resolution may require some off-line discussions.

- Because not all members can see a flip chart or projector, be careful to summarize key items at the end of the meeting.

Building Trust Is More Difficult But Essential

In a virtual team, there is only one way to build trust and that is through delivering on your commitments. The first step is a willingness by members to take on tasks or action items, followed by the more important step of completing the assignment in a timely fashion. More specifically, trust is built on a foundation of responses to queries from other members of the team. Because electronic communication does not involve nonverbal cues as to interest or involvement, a rapid and complete response is all the more critical for the development of trust.

Interesting and useful is the concept of so-called "swift trust" (Myerson, Weick, and Kramer, 1996). Swift trust occurs when team members assume all team members have been screened for competence and therefore they are willing to forgo much of the "testing" that takes place in the normal forming stage of a team. We assume these are good folks who can be trusted to do a good job and deliver on their commitments. For example, to record the onscreen narration for a video with CRM Films, *Team Building II*, a crew showed up at the studio for the taping in the morning. Although a few of the people knew each other from past projects, the full team had never worked together. However, each person arrived at 8 A.M., ready to do whatever it took to complete the taping in the time allocated, with the assumption that their teammates were willing and able to do the same. Swift trust took place within minutes, as each person knew his or her role and just did it. One additional factor is the importance of the first actions taken at the first few meetings of a team. Or as I often say to a team, "The way you start is a good predictor of how you will finish." This factor is akin to making a good first impression. If members volunteer for assignments and respond to requests and honor those early commitments, the team has a good chance of building trust in a virtual environment.

Team Size Is Very Important

Keeping the team small (under ten) helps facilitate the building of trust and clear communication. Although developing an effective team in a large organization is very difficult, a large virtual team makes the task even more daunting. The trade-off here is that although you add expertise to the talent bank of the team, you also have the difficulty of tapping into that talent in a virtual environment. "Having more and more skilled and expert contributors can provide the talent you need, but the need is to put that talent to work. Integrating larger and larger numbers of people can be costly. Too many contributors can create communication and integration nightmares" (Katzenbach and Smith, 2000).

Face-to-Face Meetings Are Needed

When possible, hold an in-person kickoff meeting in which members can get to know each other and put a face with the name. Then have periodic milestone meetings—celebrations or project reviews where members can interact in person with their teammates.

Create a Common Team Culture

If face-to-face meetings are not possible, create symbols of a team culture (Carmel, 1999). Some possible ideas:

- Create a real name with input from team members to replace the bureaucratic name given to the team (for example, Release 4.2 team or R287 Project Team).
- Create a team logo, saying, or slogan.
- Develop team norms.
- On the shared space, scan in photos of team members, including a picture of them outside of work, with family or engaged in their hobby.
- On the shared space, post short biographies of each team member that include work experience as well as nonwork activities.
- Have a virtual party to celebrate milestones.
- Create a place on the shared space for funny stories, unusual events, or situations that other members may find interesting.

Select the Right People

Some people are better suited than others for work on virtual teams. Some characteristics to look for include

- *Dependable:* has a track record of delivering on commitments.
- *Independent:* is a self-starter who does not need a lot of direction.
- *Empowered:* is willing to get things done without being told.

- *Strong communicator:* works hard to deliver a clear message and understand the messages of others.
- *Technically adept:* can use communication technology with ease.

There is an ongoing debate about the comparative advantages of face-to-face meetings and so-called virtual meetings (Schmidt, Montoya-Weiss, and Massey, 2001). It is also important to distinguish between meetings using synchronous versus asynchronous communications technology. In synchronous meetings using same-time-different-place technology, for example, the frequency of communication among members is less than in same-time-same-place technology, but the messages are more task-focused. In other words, there is not a lot "shmoozing." In addition, some studies have shown that the use of communication technology in these meetings tends to equalize participation and lessen status differences because inhibitions among members decrease; research also shows that it reduces cultural differences among members. In an even more fascinating conclusion, it was found that "dispersed, asynchronous teams generated more diverse perspectives, conducted more in-depth analysis, and produced higher quality decisions than face-to-face groups. However, due to coordination challenges, asynchronous teams may need more time to reach a decision and have more difficulty achieving a consensus" (Schmidt, Montoya-Weiss, and Massey, 2001, p. 5).

The Importance of Internal Team Dynamics

Group dynamics has always been an important ingredient in the success of a team. However, as the new organizations of the future create flat, more horizontal team structures, internal dynamics will still be important but with a different focus. Teams will need adaptable members and flexible leaders who can come together quickly to learn how to value and incorporate the contributions of people from different functions and cultures and use their expertise to gain a competitive advantage. Teams will need to get better at quickly establishing trust, creating open communication, resolving conflicts, and making better use of meeting time and communications technology.

Even though all these internal team factors are necessary, they are not sufficient for the sustaining of effective cross-functional teamwork. The leadership of the organization must work to create a culture that encourages and supports cross-functional collaboration. Chapter Thirteen provides specific advice for senior-level managers who are serious about creating a team-based organization.

Looking Back: Some Issues to Consider

1. There is some evidence that cross-functional teams produce too much conflict that may, in fact, derail a team. What are some ways a team can gain the benefits of functional diversity without the downside of debilitating conflict?

2. As a leader of a cross-functional team, what is the first thing you should do to establish a climate of trust among team members?

3. In your experience, what is the biggest cause of a breakdown in team dynamics on a cross-functional team?

4. What are the advantages and disadvantages of including customers and suppliers on a cross-functional team? Are customers and suppliers included on cross-functional teams in your organization? To what extent and in what ways does it help or hinder team effectiveness?

5. What types of communications technology do cross-functional teams in your organization use? Which communications tools are the most and least effective?

Chapter Thirteen

Management's Role in Building a Team-Based Organization

There was a clear expectation of success from our sponsor.
She said, "Failure is not an option."
JOHN DEW, DIRECTOR, CONTINUOUS QUALITY
IMPROVEMENT, UNIVERSITY OF ALABAMA[1]

At a certain point in the natural history of an organization that is making extensive use of cross-functional teams, there is a realization that success is limited. You hit the wall. So you try more training. You renew your "vows." You say the right words again. But nothing seems to make a major difference. Things get better for a while but then tail off again. You realize that something more fundamental is at work here and, as a result, more substantive change is required to take the team process to the next level.

But first, let's take note of the distance we have come in the last ten years with the widespread use of cross-functional teams:

- Insurance companies are organizing their policyholder services employees into multiskilled teams able to provide better service to all customers in a region or line of business.

---

[1]Interview with the author, September 2001.

- In the pharmaceutical industry, drug development teams are managing multiyear projects that are shepherding new compounds from the laboratory through clinical testing and on to use by patients.
- In highly competitive service industries such as hotels and rental cars, teams of front-line service workers are being teamed with customers to come up with solutions to some of the customers' biggest problems.
- Consulting firms are reorganizing their staff experts into permanent multidisciplinary teams, aligned with their major customers or client groups.

THE CHALLENGE

At some point, there comes a realization that the organization talks a good team game but still practices command-and-control. The stated values that appear in corporate publications indicate support for team players, while the employee-appraisal process results in the top ratings going to technical experts who often have difficulty working with others. At the same time, the organizational structure is rigid and hierarchical, making cross-group collaboration a real struggle. Information flow is controlled at the top, and people regularly complain that they don't know what's going on. Recognition, if it exists at all, goes to "lone rangers" who work best on their own and rarely to people who share information and expertise in an effort to support their teammates. So, what happens?

Typically, the response is, "Let's give everyone some training in teamwork skills." Although I believe training is important and necessary, it is not sufficient to make the successful shift to a team-based organization. What is even more troubling is that the emphasis on training has detracted from a focus on the other critical aspects of organization change. I believe we already know how to train employees in team effectiveness, and yet we keep trying to perfect team-training techniques. In a major study of work teams in America, Wilson Learning Corporation found that almost 80 percent of the respondents named organizational barriers (including the entire infrastructure) as the major roadblock to effective teamwork (Leimbach, 1992).

Because we already know how to teach people to use the consensus method in team decision making, why do we keep developing more survival exercises? We have been lost on the moon, in the desert, at sea, and in at least a dozen other places. Do we need still more? We already have many five-, six-, and seven-step problem-solving models for teams. Why are we spending time developing variations on these same models? There are several very fine assessment tools for measuring team effectiveness. Do we really need another one? My point is obvious: we seem to be spending more time on doing what we already do well—training and developing teams—and thus adding little value to organizations struggling with the challenge of embedding teamwork in their organizational fiber.

Aligning the Organization to Support Cross-Functional Teamwork

Team building, coaching, facilitating, giving informal recognition, exhorting, and having good intentions can only take you so far. At a certain point, teams come up against a variety of environmental obstacles. The key to moving forward—to hitting the wall and fighting through it—is to ensure that the organizational systems are aligned in support of teams.

See Figure 13.1 for a description of the model that draws heavily on the work of Jamieson (1998). Absence of even one part of the whole can bring the team process crashing down. In the model, the teams operate in an environment that includes four elements: (1) strategy, (2) structure, (3) systems, and (4) culture.

**Figure 13.1. Aligning the Organization
to Support Cross-Functional Teams.**

Strategy

The key question here is, Does your organization's strategy include the use of cross-functional teams as a key success factor? Effective team-based organizations believe and so state in their strategic plan that judicious use of cross-functional teams provides them with a competitive advantage in bringing new products to the market faster, reducing costs, improving quality, and achieving high-level customer satisfaction.

More important, however, is that managers in the organization act as if the strategy document is more than just words on paper. They believe and behave in a way that demonstrates commitment to a team-based strategy. And, perhaps even more significant, managers are held accountable for their actions that encourage and support cross-organization collaboration. In practical terms, accountability translates into specific behaviors on the corporate performance appraisal form.

Some years ago at a telecommunications company known at the time as NYNEX, a cross-functional team was charged with the task of "making the vision a reality." The team devised specific actions that translated the wonderful words in the vision document into practical, everyday terms. The goal was to get to a place where involvement with teams is second nature and collaboration happens without a great deal of thought. In some organizations today, there are permanent cross-functional teams, ad hoc project teams, process improvement teams, and real management teams. In these organizations, involvement just happens. We have a problem? You get a few people together and come up with a solution. A new business opportunity comes your way? Form a cross-functional project team to explore the issue and prepare a recommendation. Everyone in the organization believes and acts as if cross-functional collaboration is the key to success. So, in the end, it is both having a team-based strategy ("talk the talk") and implementing the strategy on a daily basis ("walk the talk").

Talk the Talk

Organizations that want to succeed as a team-based organization must continually say the right words. The leadership team must send a clear and consistent message that cross-functional teamwork is our strategy for achieving world-class status. The message must first be contained in all written presentations. If you do not have a vision, values, or mission statement, then the first step is to create such a statement in concert with the leadership team. The vision should be a statement of your desired or preferred future, as opposed to your predicted future. A vision is more than an idea; it is a force—a picture that provides a future focus for the organization. Or as one of my clients put it simply: "It's where we want to be."

Here is how some organizations have stated the team aspects of their vision:

"Quality is our first priority and teamwork is our standard in all aspects of what we do."

"Our goal is to establish a climate of openness, mutual respect, and teamwork."

"We seek teamwork throughout the organization . . . participative goal-setting . . . and decision making at the lowest level."

With a clear message in hand, the leadership of the organization should use every opportunity to pound it home. At every company seminar, leadership meeting, awards dinner, or similar occasion, the cross-functional teamwork charge should be sounded. Company publications should also be used to promote the theme of teamwork. Stories in the annual report, status reports, in-house newspapers and newsletters, and corporate magazines should regularly carry stories of the benefits of teamwork and the valuable contributions of team players. Repetition is important because employees are used to quickly changing corporate themes, often referred to as the "topic *du jour*" or "flavor of the month." As a result, employees take the cynical view that if they do nothing and just wait, a new "priority" will emerge to replace the current fad. I work with managers who ask impatiently, "How many times do I have to make my teamwork speech?" And I always reply, "As often as possible and as many times as I ask you."

Walk the Talk

To those cynics who say, "Talk is cheap," I say, "You are correct but it is where we start." It is important to say the right words, but it is not enough. The leadership team of the organization must live by the words. They must act and work like a team. They must model cross-functional teamwork so the rest of the organization can look to them for guidance. It is by now an axiom that the most powerful motivator of employee behavior is the behavior of the boss. Most top-management teams and many middle-management teams are cross-functional. As a result, they are in a perfect position to demonstrate the value of cross-functional teamwork that sends a powerful message to others in the organization.

For example, on my first visit to the offices of a new client, I noticed a framed copy of the vision statement in every office and conference room. I remarked that this was an impressive display of the importance of the statement, to which the my client contact responded, "And the CEO measures every decision for its consistency with the vision." Later I wondered how he, as a mid-level manager, was so sure of this; he rarely interacted with the CEO. The point was that he probably did not know it for sure, but he believed it! And you can be sure he checked every one of his actions for their support of the company's vision.

One of my current clients is trying to install teamwork as strategy in their organization. They have decided that people do not know how to be team players and, therefore, we are conducting a course in teamwork for everyone in the division. However, the first group to be trained is the vice president and her direct reports. The message is going out to the rest of the organization that this is important and we need to learn these skills as well. Incidentally, a key unit of the course for the top team is a focus on what they can do personally and as a team to create a team-based culture.

By contrast, some years ago in another organization I was conducting a team-building course for a director-level group. When I urged them to work together across department lines, they responded, "You better tell our bosses first." They went on to tell horror stories of directions from their superiors not to work with this group, to hold up work needed by another, or to withhold information from someone else. The message was clear: we talk cross-functional teamwork, but we don't live it.

Structure

Structure is the way we organize ourselves to implement the strategy. It is the shape of the organization, including the relationship between work, people, and technology. In the true team-based organization, teams replace departments or functions. The organization no longer has, for example, a research function but rather is composed of teams responsible for a region, market, customer, or line of business. There are few team-based organizations. In most cases, cross-functional teams exist in a forest of functional departments that provide either easy access or significant barriers.

Systems

All systems in your organization must be aligned with and in support of teamwork. You cannot have a strategy that emphasizes teamwork and a structure that encourages cross-functional collaboration that is not supported by the organization's relevant systems. Relevant systems include information, performance management, training, and rewards.

Information

An information system that only flows up in an organization from individuals and teams must be rerouted. Teams cannot be held accountable if they do not get accurate and timely information that is relevant to their work. Information must flow up, down, and laterally to teams so they can complete their work and measure the results. People in the organization must be held accountable for information sharing; it must be incorporated in the performance appraisal process.

Performance Management

As I made clear in Chapter Eight, it is important to include specific team behaviors that support the strategy in the performance appraisal form. Second, performance on cross-functional teams must "count." The functional manager responsible for the appraisal must get feedback from team leaders on the performance of team members from that functional department. When the organization reaches a high level of maturity, some form of peer appraisal must be part of the overall performance evaluation process.

I believe we should begin with the appraisal process because it is a regularly scheduled activity that tells employees how their performance is measuring up. Therefore, it is extremely important that team player behaviors be included prominently among the factors that are rated. Many companies are already including team characteristics in their appraisal forms. Here are some examples from forms that I have collected:

- Understands and supports the goals of the team
- Consults with others and shares information
- Negotiates differences effectively
- Constructively challenges prevailing points of view
- Is open to unsolicited ideas and opinions
- Is friendly and approachable in working with others

Promotion is a specific and visible reward for performance. It is a way of both rewarding team players and sending a message to others in the organization that teamwork is our goal and team players are valued. As one manager said to me, "We promote team players, and we make it clear that profit-goal achievement alone will not lead to a promotion." However, to be really effective the promotion must be made public in a substantive manner. The reasons for the promotion must be made clear and specific. When a person is promoted because he or she is both technically competent and an effective team player, the accomplishments in both areas should be highlighted. A carefully worded promotional announcement makes it clear that getting ahead in the organization requires a combination of technical and teamwork skills. Here is an example of a short announcement (Parker, 1996, p. 139):

Promoted to Project Director

Donna Jamieson has been promoted to project director in recognition of her creativity as a systems developer on PBAT, YAMS and ORRIS. She continues to develop her technical skills via in-company workshops and external seminars and she recently completed course requirements for an M.S. degree in computer science from S.U. As co-chair of the user interface team and a member of the BIRKS Task Force, Donna has shown herself to be someone who can be depended upon to do her homework, to pitch in when other people need help, and make sure everyone gets a chance to participate in team decisions. She is honest, ethical, and willing to speak her mind on important organizational issues. Donna contributes technical excellence as well as positive team spirit to our organization.

Training and Development

Because Chapter Ten is devoted to team learning, I will simply mention that training sends a strong message of organizational commitment. Opportunities for team training for leaders and members, as well as team building for intact cross-functional teams, tell people that effective teamwork is so critical that we are prepared to invest in their development in this area. Learning opportunities must also include programs for senior management to learn how to support the work of cross-functional teams. For example, in one pharmaceutical company, we conducted three programs: (1) a team leader workshop, (2) a team member workshop, and (3) a workshop for the senior leadership team. In each of the three programs, the participants learned about effective teamwork from the perspective of their role. The concepts were the same but the focus differed.

Rewards

The rewards and recognition system must not focus on individuals (such as "employee of the month") but on teams so that recognition fosters collaboration. Individuals may continue to be recognized, but now they are recognized for being effective team players. Teams should be rewarded for accomplishments that support the overall organizational strategy. (See Chapter Nine for more on team recognition and rewards.)

However, the organization needs to start with the basic premise that people exhibit the behaviors that are rewarded and recognized. The formal awards program in the organization should allow teams to win awards. In addition, the criteria for individual awards should include team player behaviors. Many firms are moving to awards that go only to teams; that is, no one wins unless the team wins. This type of program encourages people to pitch in and help the team succeed.

One of the keys to a successful team awards program is allowing team members to select their own rewards as long as they stay within a budgetary limit, which explains the popularity of catalogue programs. Although everyone says they want money as a reward, studies continually show that employees want recognition for their contribution to the company. Noncash rewards provide recognition from management and peers. And perhaps more important, the recognition factor ("trophy value") lasts long after the money has been spent. In one company where the program provides cash awards, people also receive a plaque, which serves as a permanent reminder of their success.

One final but significant factor in team awards is the selection process. I strongly recommend a peer review process that is controlled by nonmanagement employees. Peer review means that employees develop the criteria, review the awards proposals, make the decisions, and present the awards. One company includes several management people on the committee to ensure organizational perspective. They also rotate committee membership so that all employees learn how the program works in practice.

Culture

Culture has been described as "the way we do things around here" (Deal and Kennedy, 1982). It includes and is influenced by a web of elements such the business environment, values, stories and myths, heroes and heroines, norms, and a network of "carriers." A strong culture tells people in an organization how to behave in most situations. For team members it tells you

- What the organization values
- Who the organization values
- How you are supposed to behave
- Who the "stars" of the organization are
- How success is defined
- Who will get rewarded
- What will get rewarded

If your organization has long valued individual technical excellence, thinly veiled competition, solo action, and private deals, then there is a need to emphasize sharing information, working collaboratively, making decisions in a participative way, and valuing empowerment. A body of teamwork stories will then evolve and circulate; the stories will create heroes and heroines of team players who have helped the crowd stand out rather than stood out from the crowd.

There is a crucial link between culture and strategy. An organization's culture must be aligned with the strategy if the strategy has any chance of succeeding. If you have a team-based strategy, the norms of the organization must emphasize collaboration, consensus, and communication. There is a crucial link between culture and structure. If the structure facilitates cross-organizational collaboration, then the culture must create heroes out of team leaders who succeed at managing a diverse group of people from a variety of functions. There is also a crucial link between culture and systems. For example,

- If the culture values information sharing, then teams will get the information they need to complete their task.
- If the culture values people who are team players, then the performance appraisal process will incorporate those behaviors into the system.
- If the culture values team collaboration, then the rewards program will include project team rewards that are based on a pre-announced formula.

Stories and Myths

Stories give people a flavor of the company; they tell people what type of behavior is valued. When these stories are told and retold and subsequently embellished, they become myths and the people in the stories become legends. Ultimately, they may translate into specific behavioral expectations called norms. Norms are simply the day-to-day informal guidelines that tell employees what is acceptable behavior.

For example, in the course of an organizational diagnosis, I was told, "You should have been there when Deborah told the vice president his marketing plan was all wet." This was an organizational story that was enhanced to the point of being a myth. In fact, Deborah did not say the plan was all wet. She just suggested some alternatives that were, in turn, accepted by the vice president. The point was that no one had ever had the courage to challenge the ideas of an upper-management person. However, the story served to establish a new team player norm that disagreement is acceptable.

What do you make of this myth, which is told about a legendary figure in the history of the company? "He once drove through a blinding snowstorm to make delivery to a customer." On the surface, this looks like a story about obsessive commitment to serve the customer. Although it is clearly a service story, it also promotes individual heroics rather than team success. It tells people that if you want to get ahead, look for opportunities to stand out from the crowd.

Another story in a similar vein seems to promote the value of team play over individual effort. In this example, a cross-functional new-product team composed of highly educated professionals worked all night loading trucks with product to meet a test-market deadline. People in the company enjoyed telling the story of these well-dressed MBAs who got their hands dirty doing what was necessary to meet their team objective.

Understanding the importance of positive cross-functional teamwork stories encourages leaders to use every opportunity to tell and re-tell these stories. The stories have the effect of making the vision and values come alive for people in the organization. They put life into the words and meaning into the actions of the company's heroes and heroines. Ultimately, the stories get folded into the daily life of the organization and eventually become the norms that shape and guide work-team behavior.

Resources

Teams cannot swim alone. They need resources to survive and thrive. Resources can mean many things.

Space

There is no substitute for good, well-equipped meeting rooms. Let's face it. As much as we hate meetings, teams do much of their work in meetings. The rooms should have good, basic meeting-room equipment such as flip charts or whiteboards, overhead and LCD projectors, and videotape players. And the allocation of the space should be well managed. In one organization, the administration of the meeting rooms is so ineffective that many teams have given up and simply use tables in the company cafeteria.

Technology

There are many new methods of electronic communication available today that can enhance the effectiveness of teams. And many of these methods can improve communication and often decrease a team's dependence on face-to-face meetings. Various groupware tools discussed in Chapter Twelve can increase the effectiveness of a team.

Training

We end where we began. Although training will not change an organizational culture, it can support and facilitate the change process. Training can do two important things to help create a team-based organization. First, training provides people with the skills and knowledge to help them be successful; second, it sends a message that teamwork is important, in fact, so important that we are investing in programs to upgrade the effectiveness of teams.

Several types of training are necessary. People need to learn how be team players; teams need to learn what constitutes an effective cross-functional team; team leaders need to learn basic leadership skills such as planning and facilitating meetings, making decisions, solving problems, resolving conflicts, and communicating; sponsors need to learn what they can do to support teamwork in the organization. (See Chapter Ten for a detailed description of team learning activities.)

Building a Team-Based Organization

We begin with the fundamental premise that teams are a critical factor in a successful business strategy. Although it is important to acknowledge the central role of cross-functional teams, it is not enough to simply set up teams, provide training, and hope for the best. Successful implementation of a team-based strategy requires a commitment to say the right words—that teamwork and team players are critical to our success—and to drive that message home as often as possible. In tandem with the words must come the actions that parallel the words and demonstrate that the leadership team of the organization is a living example of successful cross-functional teamwork.

Successful cross-functional teams and team players must be rewarded for their support of the organization's vision and values. And related to rewards is inclusion of team-player behaviors in the company's performance appraisal system. Both team-oriented awards and performance appraisals are tangible and visible support for team-work as the vehicle for implementation of the corporate strategy.

The leaders of the organization must work to create a team-based culture by telling organizational stories that perpetuate the heroes and heroines of teamwork. As these stories become embedded in the fabric of the organization, they translate into the daily norms that shape employee behavior in support of team play.

And finally, teams need resources of all types to increase their chances of success and to provide another bit of evidence that the organization is committed to teamwork as a serious business strategy. The Wilson Learning Corporation's study of teamwork concluded that the successful team-based organization "is one in which top management is strongly committed to breaking down barriers, eliminating, where possible, internal competition for resources, and avoiding the singling out of individuals for personal recognition and achievement. The . . . organization also provides a performance appraisal and compensation process that promotes interdependent achievement, but with individual accountability. The organization focuses not so much on individual achievement, but on individual contributions to group achievement" (Leimbach, 1992, p. 16).

Looking Back: Some Issues to Consider

1. In your experience, which of the four environmental factors (strategy, structure, systems, and culture) is the most important?

2. What are the advantages and disadvantages of a team-based organization in which the functional structure is replaced by permanent cross-functional teams organized around major customers, markets, or lines of business?

3. Is it possible to create a team-based culture where one does not now exist? Why or why not?

4. Should an organization wait until all the environmental factors are aligned before establishing cross-functional teams, or should they form the teams and then work to change the strategy, structure, systems, and culture? Why?

5. Assume that as you look at your organization, you conclude that all four factors need to change. Where would you start? Why?

Chapter Fourteen

Jump-Starting the Change to Cross-Functional Teams

You can't just superimpose a cross-functional team on a hierarchy and expect it to work.
SUZANNE BISHOP, SOFTWARE SUPPORT CONSULTANT FOR PHARMACEUTICAL RESEARCH TEAMS.[1]

OK, you're convinced. Cross-functional teams are a powerful vehicle for increasing the effectiveness of your organization. You want to start using these teams to streamline the product development process, improve the quality of your products and services, increase customer satisfaction, or reorganize the business. You want to know where to start. Or your organization may be littered with teams of all types and degrees of success. You are looking for ways to improve the functioning of your existing teams. But first, it is important to decide whether cross-functional teams are the way to go.

When to Use Cross-Functional Teams

Not every situation and not every organization is appropriate for cross-functional teams. Cross-functional teams are called for when

- Coordination of several different functions is critical for the success of the project or process.

---

[1]Bishop, 1999, p. 8.

- A wide variety of skills and knowledge is required for achieving the goals of the project.
- Commitment of a variety of organizations is needed for successful implementation of the project's outcomes.
- Speeding up the process is critical for success, and elimination of rework and duplication of effort are especially desirable.
- Alignment of the outcomes of the project with the overall strategic objectives of the organization is important.

When Cross-Functional Teams Should Be Avoided

Cross-functional teams are especially useful under the conditions described in the previous section. However, cross-functional teams are not a universal panacea. You should not use cross-functional teams when

- The functional silos in your organization are rigid and bureaucratic.
- Senior managers are unwilling to empower teams and individuals and consistently second-guess decisions.
- There are few people with the leadership skills necessary to manage a diverse team of people with a variety of skill sets, work styles, orientations, and team experience.
- Functional department heads are reluctant to give up their best people for projects outside their department.
- Rewards and recognition focus on individual performance and results.
- There is little history with participative tools such as quality processes and consensus building.

Guidelines for Key Players

If you decide to move forward with cross-functional teams, here are some things to consider.

If You Are a Senior Manager

First, understand that teamwork begins at home. Look around at your team. It is probably a cross-functional group and not really a team. Begin by making sure your team has a clear set of performance objectives (not just the company or division's objectives) and some joint output that requires the collaboration of team members. Ask for feedback on whether your team is perceived as an effective team. In other words, are you a model of cross-functional teamwork for all to see and emulate? If you engage in a team-building effort for cross-functional teams in your organization, start the process with your team. It sends a powerful message about the importance of the effort.

Second, think about the teamwork message you are sending to the organization.

- Are people clear that you value cross-functional teamwork?
- Do you send the same message out again and again? As Karen Soskin of Parke-Davis said, "Management has to be relentless and boring with commitment messages that are clear and repeated often. And keep it simple" (interview with the author, October 2001).
- Will team members be rewarded or at least acknowledged for collaboration with their colleagues in other departments?
- Do the functional department managers in your organization support the work of the cross-functional teams? Are these managers rewarded for their support?
- Have you made it clear that the cross-functional teams are empowered to carry out their project plan?
- Do you support risk taking, "good tries," and temporary setbacks? As Helena Gordon of Penn National Insurance points out, "Senior management supports the team, even when we suffer some bumps in the road" (interview with the author, October 2001).
- Do teams receive the resources they need to support their efforts?

You are still not deterred, but you are cautious. So you decide to begin with one cross-functional team. Here are a few tips for getting started from Sue Nador (2001):

- *Align the project with the organization's strategy.* You'll have a real chance for success if the members (and the stakeholders) know they are working on something that has an impact on the organization's success.

- *Pick the right people.* First and most important, pick a team leader with the right stuff, both technical and interpersonal. Then select members who have both the expertise and the skills required to work in a diverse environment.
- *Clarify your expectations.* Ensure that the team knows your expectations for the team in terms of outcomes and the members in terms of their roles and responsibilities.
- *Hold members accountable.* Insist on a project plan; empower the team to carry out the plan and hold members accountable for the outcomes.

If You Are a Team Leader

As a leader of a cross-functional team, you are probably aware of the potential of this diverse group of colleagues, strangers, and even enemies you are trying to lead. Where to begin? For a leader of a new cross-functional team, here are some tips:

- *First impressions are critical.* As pointed out earlier, the way a team starts out is a good predictor of how the team will end. The same axiom applies to the team leader. Begin the team-forming process even before the first meeting. To the extent possible, talk with every member of the team to explore their expectations, talents, and, perhaps most important, their concerns about the team and their role on the team. Team members will appreciate your interest and come to the first meeting with a more positive attitude.
- *At the first meeting, present what you know about the overarching goal and management's expectations for the team.* If possible, ask your management sponsor to attend the meeting to present the goals and expectations and to address questions and concerns.
- *At the first meeting, facilitate an icebreaker activity that focuses on members getting to know each other.* Make it a fun activity and, if necessary, ensure that remote members can participate in the exercise.
- *At the first meeting or shortly thereafter, engage the team in a goal-setting and planning process.* Develop the overarching goals or vision into specific objectives and a detailed project plan. (See Chapter Six for more on team goals.)

• *As soon as possible, use the project plan as the basis for a discussion with your sponsor about the level of empowerment delegated to the team.* Use these questions in your meeting with management (Rees, 1997):

• What decisions will be the sole responsibility of the team?
• What decisions will be made collaboratively between the team and management?
• What decisions will be reserved for management but with team input?
• What decisions will be reserved for management but without team input?

• *Once the team has goals and a plan, engage the members in an exercise designed to create a set of norms or operating guidelines.* Norms are the standards of behavior a team expects of its members. The key words are *standards* and *behavior.* Norms are what teammates come to expect from each other in terms of behavior.

• *If you have been handed a large team, develop a process for resizing the team in some fashion into a group capable of being effective.* See Chapter Eleven for ideas on dealing with large teams.

• *Early in the history of the team, reach out to the functional department managers who are providing resources to the team.* At these meetings, discuss the team's goals, its role, and the expectations you have for team members from the department; establish a process for regular communication with the manager.

• *As soon as possible, establish a process for regular communication with your management sponsor.* Determine the content, format, and frequency of communication that the sponsor needs and that you need.

If you are taking over an existing team, the place to start is by making a careful assessment of the team's strengths and weaknesses. Begin with the Survey of Cross-Functional Teamwork in the Resources section. How do you think the team stacks up? Ask other team members to do their own assessment. Get the whole team involved in evaluating the team and developing an improvement plan. When you have identified some areas for improvement, refer to the appropriate chapters in the book for ideas on what to do next.

Most important, recognize the importance of your role. According to Trent (1996), his research indicates that "of all the variables affecting a team, few exert as strong an influence on team performance as team leadership. This is true because the leader is in a position to influence some other variables that affect performance."

If You Are a Functional Department Manager

Let's assume a number of your people serve on cross-functional teams. The challenges are great for you because "rarely does the cross-functional team sabotage the efforts of the functional departments . . . rather it is the functional departments (that often control the resources and information vital to the success of the cross-functional team) that can and often do sabotage the efforts of the cross-functional team" (Bishop, 1999, p. 10). You must balance the need to achieve your department objectives with the need to provide support for the team's objectives. One way to do this is to talk with the leaders of cross-functional teams and your people who serve on these teams. In these meetings, get clarity on the best ways to meet both parties' needs and establish some norms for regular communication. This will also help facilitate the sharing of input from the leader for use in performance appraisal.

You should insist on two-way communication from the people in your area. Team members should report to you on the work of the team, and they should report to the team on the work in your area that is in support of the team. In addition, it is important to clarify the degree of empowerment you expect from the members representing your department. For example, what is their authority to commit resources and agree to take on work tasks that require other uses of department resources?

Finally, and perhaps most important, recognize that you will need to relinquish some control over the cross-functional team members from your department for project-related activities and understand that the team is shared by all departments (Bishop, 1999).

If You Are a Cross-Functional Team Member

Team members are often caught in the middle between the needs of the team and goals of their department. Conflicting priorities may be an ongoing challenge. Therefore, you must maintain a loyalty to both the cross-functional team and your functional department. Regardless of whether the lines are solid or broken, you will look to both the team leader and your manager for direction. Therefore, you must be continually communicating with both people if you have any hopes of maintaining your career and your sanity.

Here are some guidelines for team members:

- Clarify your role expectations with both your department manager and the team leader.
- Provide the team with updates on department-related activities.
- Report back to your department about team decisions, changes in milestones, and action items that have an impact on the department.
- Attend all team meetings. If unable to attend, provide the team leader with any outstanding action items, inform the leader of your absence, and send a fully informed and empowered substitute.
- Prepare for all team meetings by reading the relevant documents, gathering the necessary information, and formulating your opinions and concerns about the agenda items.
- During the meeting, stay focused on the issues and discussions.
- Volunteer for team roles such as scribe, timekeeper, parking lot attendant, and facilitator.
- Opt for team assignments such as participating in ad hoc task groups, making presentations, and visiting customers.
- Actively participate in team meetings by asking questions, seeking clarification, offering your opinion, sharing your expertise, actively listening, and facilitating a consensus.

If You Are a Human Resource Professional

You can look for ways to provide support for the leaders and members of cross-functional teams, as well as for the functional department managers. Training for leaders and members will be critical, and you can be the facilitator of the team learning process. Chapter Ten can help here. Coaching a team leader can be extremely helpful. You can help a leader by serving as a meeting planner, cofacilitator, or process observer. At some point, senior management will come to you for ideas on how to reward cross-functional teamwork. If management does not come to you, go to them with a proposal. Get a jump on reward strategies by reviewing Chapter Nine.

At the start-up of a new cross-functional team, you can help by

- Offering to design and facilitate a kickoff meeting
- Providing team-training and team-building sessions
- Coaching the team leader and sponsor on their respective roles
- Providing resource materials on key start-up issues such as goal setting, empowerment, and norms
- Serving as a process observer of team meetings and providing feedback to the leader

See Figure 14.1 for more start-up tips.

No matter who you are or where you are in the organization, never lose your sense of humor. The diversity of cross-functional teams will produce some conflicts, some strange and strained relationships, and some tense moments. But working with allies, enemies, and other strangers will also result in some wonderful and funny moments. Take the time to enjoy them.

Looking Back: Some Issues to Consider

1. What critical factor does an organization need to consider before making the transition to cross-functional teams? What factors in your organization tend to support the use of cross-functional teams, and what factors tend to hinder them?

2. What is the most important thing a senior manager can do to facilitate the creation and initial start-up of a cross-functional team? What role do senior managers play in your organization in regard to team formation?

3. You have just been assigned the role of leader of a new cross-functional team in an organization that has very little experience with these teams. What are the first three things you would do?

4. You are a manager of a functional department such as marketing. A new cross-functional product development team has

just been formed, and you have been asked by your boss to select a person from your department to serve on this team. What are your concerns? What questions do you have for your boss? How will you select the person from your department? What will you tell the person from your department?

5. You have just been asked to serve on a new cross-functional new-product team in your company. What concerns and questions do you have? To whom will you go for answers?

Figure 14.1. Ten Steps for New Team Start-Up.

1. *Set the direction.* Present management's expectations, overarching goal, specific objectives, key activities, and a project plan.

2. *Identify available resources.* What members, support groups, consultants, vendors, space, equipment, and budget will be available to the team?

3. *Define reporting requirements.* What type and frequency of reports and other communications are expected and to whom should reports be sent?

4. *Determine empowerment scope.* Get clarity on decisions the team may or may not make, including any spending limitations.

5. *Identify nonnegotiables.* Clearly understand the requirements or rules to which the team must adhere.

6. *Clarify roles.* Determine what is expected of each team member.

7. *Get acquainted.* Get to know your teammates, including who they are and what talents they bring to the team.

(Continued)

Figure 14.1. Continued.

8. *Establish team roles.* Identify what team roles will be necessary such as leader, facilitator, sponsor, scribe, and timekeeper.

9. *Agree on ground rules.* Draft a set of norms for key team behaviors such as decision making, resolving conflicts, communicating, and managing meetings.

10. *Provide orientation and training.* Hold a kickoff meeting and plan team-building or training sessions.

Resources for Cross-Functional Teamwork

This section includes tips specifically for team leaders, four case studies, and an assessment instrument.

Fighting the Forces of Evil

This is a message directed to leaders of cross-functional teams—first a description of some very bad things that can happen to a team, then a prescription for ways of treating those symptoms.

Case Studies

The four cases in this section resulted from interviews conducted during the data collection phase of this project. However, in each situation one or more of the team members, because of their intimate knowledge of the issues, created the case. The purpose of the cases is to help both practitioners and students learn more about how cross-functional teams develop, struggle with obstacles, and overcome internal and external barriers.

Survey

The Survey of Cross-Functional Teams is used as an assessment and team development tool. Typically, the process begins with each team member completing the survey, having it scored by an outside source, preparing a report, summarizing the results, and presenting the report at a team meeting. At the meeting, members identify strengths and areas where improvements are needed. At this point, subgroups are usually formed to address the improvement areas and return to the team at a specified time with recommendations for action. An abbreviated version of the survey is found in Parker (1997).

Fighting the Forces of Evil

In this section you will find a list of things that can give you a headache, an upset stomach, and insomnia. However, you will also find some tips for sleeping like a baby.

Ten Things That Will Keep You Up at Night

1. Key core team members consistently arrive late to team meetings; some leave early.
2. Your boss starts to attend your team meetings "because," in his words, "I just want to get an overview and keep on top of the project."
3. The most respected technical person on the team has angered most of her teammates by consistently criticizing their work as "incomplete" and "inadequate."
4. A functional department manager replaces an important representative from that discipline with a person with much less experience and expertise.
5. Senior management moves up by a month a key project deliverable without consulting you.
6. One day before the team is scheduled to implement a key project decision, your boss overrules the decision despite the fact that he knew the decision was being considered at team meetings for the past four weeks.
7. During team teleconferences you hear lots of clicking sounds indicating that team members are multitasking during meetings.
8. During the past two team meetings you are having great difficulty understanding a number of technical discussions.
9. An important member of the team complains to you that her manager "devalues and gives very little weight to" her participation on your team. Consequently, she did not receive

"appropriate credit" on her performance evaluation for her contribution to team goals.

10. You have a barbecue at your home to celebrate the achievement of an important team milestone but very few team members attend.

How to Get a Good Night's Sleep

1. When key members start to come late and leave early, move quickly to speak with each person privately. Try to determine if the problem lies with the team or within their functional department. Is the team meeting time no longer convenient for them? Have they taken on additional responsibilities that make participation on this team very difficult? Point out to them the negative impact of their behavior on team morale. Offer to alter the meeting time or day. Offer to speak with their functional manager about their responsibilities to the team. Be open to their feedback about the team since their disruptive behavior may be a sign of their frustration with your team.

2. When your boss attends your team meeting *and* you notice a significant change in team climate (for example, open communication and member participation dramatically decrease), you must speak with him or her. If your boss really just wants to get "an overview," offer to provide him or her with regular updates in whatever format is preferred. If, on the other hand, your boss has some concerns about the team and your leadership skills, you need to have a discussion about these concerns. Be open to the feedback and be ready to present other ways your boss can support your development as a team leader.

3. When a key technical person criticizes other team members in a destructive manner, you need to handle this issue quickly but carefully. You need the technical input that this person provides. However, you also need to point out that the nature of his or her comments are not having the desired effect. Strongly suggest that he or she present the comments in a positive manner. For example, rather than characterizing the work as "incomplete," suggest that the feedback focus on ways the work can be improved and either offer to help or recommend resources that will help the other team member.

4. When an important team member is replaced with a less experienced person, speak with the department manager. First, make sure he or she understands the importance of your project. Second, ask if there is another expert in the department who can be the replacement. Third, ask if the experienced person can be available to the team on an ad hoc basis or as an adjunct team member. Finally, offer to go with the functional manager to speak with senior management about what may be a resource issue. If the functional manager does not want to cooperate in any of the above actions, go to your senior management sponsor for help.

5. If senior management moves up the schedule for a key deliverable, go back to them with a tight presentation that points out the impact of this change and a proposal that outlines what you need to meet the new deadline. For example, one team that had this problem said "if you can live without this feature, we can meet your new schedule. However, if you must have all the original features, we will need an additional person for three months to get all the work done."

6. If your boss overrules a key team decision at the last minute, you need to respond to the issue in two ways: short-term and long-term. Most immediately, you must go back to the team with the news presented in the context of "I recognize that we all spent a lot of time on this issue, but this is the way it is and now we need to figure out a way to implement the new decision." You may need to let team members "unload" their feelings of frustration before you can move to an implementation plan. The long-term issue concerns the role of your boss and the relationship with the team. You need to have a serious discussion with him or her about such actions and the impact on team effectiveness. Together you need to come up with a way to avoid such situations in the future.

7. When you become aware that team members are multitasking during meetings, you need to quickly refer back to your team norms. However, if you do not have a norm about multitasking, engage the team in an exercise designed to develop guidelines for these and other disruptive behaviors that are especially relevant to multisite teams.

8. When you have difficulty understanding some technical presentations or discussions, other team members are probably having the same experience. As the team leader, you are not expected to understand everything completely. Therefore, you should "model" the desired behavior by asking questions when you do not understand something that appears to be critical and encourage other team members to do the same. By the way, it may be that some members of the team may be brilliant scientists or engineers but lack the ability to communicate information effectively. It may be helpful to establish a norm that encourages members to use jargon-free language, metaphors, and nontechnical terms whenever possible.

9. When a functional department manager does not "value" the contributions of team members on their performance evaluation, it is important for you to address this issue. Once again, approach the current issue directly but also think about a more strategic response. Speak with the department manager in question and offer to provide an assessment of the team member in any format desired up to and including completing the corporate performance management form. More broadly, you may want to make the same offer to all the functional managers who have employees on your team. Beyond that, propose a change in the organization's human resources process to require input from team leaders.

10. If only a few members attend your barbecue, get over it and do it differently next time. First, many team members may see such an event as just another workday rather than the fun activity that you had in mind. It is quite possible that they would rather spend any time off with their family and friends. Second, a celebration is still a good idea if properly planned. Next time, ask a small subgroup of the team to plan the event. That way, team members will get to do something they want, rather than something you want.

Case Study One

Creating the Climate for Cross-Functional Teams

Throughout the 1980s and 1990s, Parke-Davis was considered a mid-size pharmaceutical company. The company was heavily U.S.-based, with an ever-growing international presence. Parke-Davis had a history of over one hundred years of corporate existence. At one time, the company was the number one pharmaceutical company in the industry; world headquarters was in Detroit, Michigan.

In 1977, the very successful Warner Lambert Company purchased Parke-Davis. The decision was made to place the headquarters for Parke-Davis's worldwide research and development in Ann Arbor, Michigan, and the remainder of the business, such as sales and marketing, at the Warner Lambert headquarters in Morris Plains, New Jersey. As the sole pharmaceutical division within Warner Lambert, there was significant emphasis on growth, both in terms of the market share of existing treatments and in bringing new treatments to market. The vision was to restore Parke-Davis to the glory days when it led the industry.

Sue Whitt prepared this case. She was senior director and later vice president of Technical Operations (Tech Ops) during the period described. She has over twenty years of progressive corporate experience in leadership and operations management, including her last position as senior vice president of development operations for Pfizer R&D. Whitt is currently a team and leadership consultant in Ann Arbor, Michigan, and owner of Leadership Works Consulting. She can be reached at www.leadershipworksconsulting.com.

The Drug Development Process

Pharmaceutical companies tend to work in highly matrixed and cross-functional environments. The drug development process is an extremely complex one that requires expertise from a great many disciplines over a long period of time. Traditionally, a research group of scientists works to discover new compounds, a development group conducts clinical trials in humans, a regulatory group works with the regulatory agencies throughout the world, and a sales and marketing group launches a new drug and then is involved in promoting the commercial success of the product.

Parke-Davis was not very different from its competitors in terms of the high-level structure for the drug development process. Product development time in the pharmaceutical industry has traditionally been quite long—often a decade or more to develop a compound into a safe and effective product. A lot of change can take place during a decade. For example, company leadership may change, and there may be corporate restructuring, staff turnover, modifications to existing regulations, new regulations, and technology changes. All can affect how the science is conducted and the operations are run. Business conditions external to the company can also pose concerns. For example, during the 1990s the pharmaceutical industry had a great many mergers and acquisitions that resurfaced the commercial playing field for the industry.

The Role of Technical Operations

All mid- to large-size pharmaceutical companies have an operations component within the clinical development organization. At Parke-Davis, Technical Operations (Tech Ops) was the operational arm of the Worldwide Clinical Development organization. Tech Ops provided a wide variety of services to the organization. Data management, statistics, and research report writing services were provided, along with records management and clinical systems services. Tech Ops, like most operational arms of a development group, represented approximately half the staff of Worldwide Clinical Development. In 1995, there were over two hundred Tech Ops staff, which grew to over four hundred by

1999; staff were located in Ann Arbor, Michigan, Fresnes, France, and Freiburg, Germany.

One factor to note is that even though Tech Ops had long been a stand-alone component of Worldwide Clinical Development, it had never been well respected by the therapeutic areas that made up the balance of the organization and that held the organizational power. Clinicians within these therapeutic areas had for years created a culture in which Tech Ops was seen as a second-class organization whose role was to follow and not lead. The Tech Ops organization was mocked as ineffective and inefficient. It was consistently used as the whipping boy when deadlines were missed, and there was a lack of trust among the departmental silos throughout the clinical organization. Fear and inappropriate competitiveness also existed. In summary, a highly dysfunctional culture was embedded in the organization. But even though Tech Ops had operational issues to address (some serious ones at that), the group was more competent than this saga suggests. Their unfortunate history did, however, place an additional burden on change efforts.

Conditions That Created the Need for Cross-Functional Teams

In 1994, it became increasingly obvious to the senior leaders of Tech Ops that changes must occur if the group was going to have a viable future. Change was a business imperative. Tech Ops needed to improve the speed of its deliverables or ultimately go out of business.

Need for Speed

The external environment was full of contract research organizations (CROs) proclaiming they could perform the same work Tech Ops performed but in a fraction of the time. For example, it may have taken Tech Ops six months to release a database for analysis after a final patient visit, but CROs were claiming they could do it in six days.

As might be expected, customers (physicians and clinicians) were drawn to the claims of the CROs. The high cost of pharmaceutical drug development was a key driver in the need for faster development time. Industry consultants estimated that a pharmaceutical company would lose approximately $1 million a day for each day the drug was not on the market and being sold. Given the potential lost revenue, the substantial cost of using a CRO during clinical development paled by comparison. Thus clinicians were very willing to use a third party to conduct the clinical operations associated with drug development. Several senior-level clinicians were quoted as saying, "If we don't figure out a better way, we'll be out of business."

Need for Single Point of Contact

Creating a single point of contact for customers via a Tech Ops team leader was another necessary step for organizational survival. This contact would provide an easy entry point for customers, allow Tech Ops to manage their own activities through the team leader, and help even out the power base in the organization. Until this time, the clinicians, who held the organizational power, would go from group to group within Tech Ops to determine the status of a project. Typically, staff within a single Tech Ops department would tell the clinicians all the perceived problems with another Tech Ops department. This information, which was often inaccurate, was used inappropriately within the larger organization. Needless to say, these types of dialogues undermined the credibility of the Tech Ops organization and continued to fuel the dysfunctional culture. Using a central Tech Ops point of contact helped facilitate communications such as status reporting, problem definition, and escalation.

Staff Burnout

Another internal reason for going to cross-functional teams was an attempt to eliminate the staff burnout that led to turnover. One of the results of an inefficient operation, regardless of the cause, is staff overwork. Tech Ops staff typically had to work long hours prior to the final release of deliverables. Working these long hours for months at a time was also necessary during the interim release of deliverables. On completion of these extremely challenging efforts, staff were burned out and dissatisfied; they lacked energy for the next challenge. Moving to cross-functional teams seemed a way to minimize handoffs and streamline operations, thus eliminating some of these burdens on the staff and reducing turnover.

Organizational Change

Tech Ops senior leaders, along with our customer's senior leaders, conducted an analysis of our operations. Working over several months, we developed different strategies. Several senior-level participants said, "It was a highly successful and engaging process." Ultimately, it was determined that if Tech Ops was going to achieve the increased speed required, then it had to make changes in three interrelated areas: (1) organizational structure, (2) technology, and (3) process (see Figure C1.1).

It was critical that all three changes be initiated concurrently. The process changes had short- and long-term components, but all were aimed at streamlining our efforts and being more efficient. We started with the "low-hanging fruit" processes and then moved to the more complex processes, which were often embedded in our technologies. The technology changes were mostly long term (took longer than a year). Primarily, we had to focus on replacing our entire clinical trial database system with a new and improved system. In addition, we needed to adopt new technologies that could maximize the use of electronic data capture for clinical trials. The technology changes were necessary to stay technologically current and to address some of the upcoming Y2K computer issues. The last and the most important area focused on organizational structure. This was the foundation component of our change initiative.

Figure C1.1. Change Management in Technical Operations.

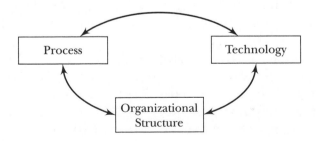

The organizational structure changes consisted of formal changes in organizational reporting lines and in a campaign that emphasized team behaviors as a critical success factor. The formal changes reorganized Technical Operations into the following (see Figure C1.2):

Primary groups—Data Acquisition and Management Team (DAMT), Data Output Integration Team (DOIT), Cross-Functional Tech Ops Teams

Support role—Cross-Functional Tech Ops Teams

The vision was that most employees would have a technical home in either the DAMT or the DOIT groups and a team home on one of the cross-functional Tech Ops teams that focused on a specific drug program. The role of Organization and Team Development was to provide guidance in the establishment of the new structure and ongoing support to the team leaders and teams.

Establishing the Cross-Functional Teams

Time and attention were paid to the process of establishing the Tech Ops teams. For several months, we designed approaches to the establishment of team leaders and teams, as well as the impact on the technical departments in Tech Ops and our customers. In May 1995, we implemented the new Tech Ops structure.

Four New Cross-Functional Teams

We started with four cross-functional teams targeted at specific drug programs. Each team had a goal statement with an event signifying completion. In these cases, it was the submission of the new

Figure C1.2. Technical Operations Organizational Structure.

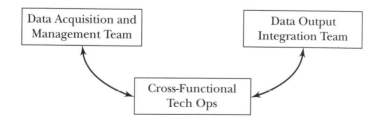

drug application (NDA) to the Food and Drug Administration. We felt it was extremely important that the newly established teams realize that they were involved in an effort with a beginning and an end; they were not an ongoing team. We believed the establishment of a clear goal with an end point would be motivating to colleagues and would help fuel their commitment. It is important to understand that three of the four drug teams had NDA submissions within a year or so and that this is the most stressful time for staff on these projects. Team leader Debra Gmerek commented, "These teams are critical to the success of our drug submissions and the future of Parke-Davis. We had to figure out how to reduce the inefficiencies in our processes and deliver a good product effectively."

Team Leader Selection

The teams were carefully crafted, starting with the team leaders. We selected highly qualified individuals to become team leaders. A list of competencies for the role was developed, and candidates were screened against these requirements. The individuals selected had years of experience in the industry, and each was well respected by our customers and our staff for their competencies. The team leaders reported directly to the vice president of Tech Ops.

The team members were selected next. This was a more straightforward process and was driven primarily by existing staff assignments. As part of the preparation work, roles and responsibilities were generated for the team leaders, the heads of the technical

**Figure C1.3. Cross-Functional Team
Member Reporting Relationships.**

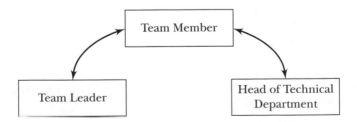

departments, and the team members (see Figure C1.3). Many hours were spent discussing the team members' reporting structure. More specifically, the questions were (1) where was the solid-line reporting? and (2) where was the dotted-line reporting? In the end, we explained it as the team members having two equally important reporting lines. Furthermore, there would be a high degree of collaboration and a shared accountability between the team leader and the head of the technical department.

Team Behaviors

Another critical component of the process of establishing the new organizational environment was team behaviors. Work had begun in this area, and now was the time to increase the emphasis. Two major components were areas of focus: values and compensation.

Values

We had developed Tech Ops to be a values-based organization, that is, based on the hypothesis that in order to increase organizational effectiveness (clearly required if we were to become viable), we must increase opportunities for participation, shared power, and truth telling.

Participation was defined this way: Look for and create opportunities to be involved in the operation and planning of the organization, especially in regard to changes that will directly affect your effectiveness in the organization. Show commitment toward creating compatible and productive work groups. If difficulties should arise, work together with those involved to resolve issues.

Shared power was defined this way: Look for and create opportunities to share power in this organization. Encourage and support other colleagues to make decisions on appropriate issues. Assume joint responsibility for project success, be willing to negotiate a common ground, and seek resolution for any problems that may arise. Refrain from talking negatively about other colleagues, departments, or teams (for example, do not "bad mouth").

Truth telling was defined this way: Strive to tell the truth in a constructive manner to others in this organization. Truth telling includes giving objective information, such as technical specifications, as well as subjective information such as reactions, feelings, and thoughts. Even when it is difficult, strive to disclose relevant truth and seek the same from others.

These values were initially embraced at varying degrees throughout the organization. The senior leadership of Tech Ops immediately recognized the importance of the values. Mary Black, then senior director of DOIT, said, "These values form a solid foundation that we can utilize to drive our organization to world-class performance."

Compensation

Second, we felt strongly that if we wanted true team behaviors, we would need to change the compensation system to reward individuals who were demonstrating appropriate behaviors. The senior leadership of Tech Ops was ready to "put their money where their mouth was" and pay people for performance in both technical contributions and team behaviors. Colleagues' pay would be based one-half on their technical contributions and one-half on their team behaviors. Those in formal leadership roles would have their pay based on one-third leadership, one-third team behaviors, and one-third technical contributions. As in many large companies, technical contributions had been rewarded in the past. But the complexity of the drug development process and the highly cross-functional nature of the drug development effort meant that effective teamwork was a critical success factor. This change was seen as critical to the success of instilling team behaviors. Carol Brodbeck, then head of clinical systems, said, "Making this change shows colleagues at all levels that we are very serious. Our customers will also know that we intend to put our money where our mouth is and demand team performance."

Training

Work began with the Tech Ops Management Team. Various workshops were held to address intrapersonal, interpersonal, and large-team-based behaviors. Members of the initial teams attended special sessions to discuss roles and responsibilities, behaviors, and goals. Further discussions took place regarding our values and the need to increase our organizational effectiveness. It is important to note that all existing and new Tech Ops colleagues attended a three-day course on team skills that addressed these topics. Mary

Sylvain, then team leader on one of the NDA submission teams, said, "The quality and focus of this training is fantastic. Staff are immersed in important subjects targeted at the individual and group dynamics, all set in the context of project work." The feedback received on this training was consistently very positive.

Communication

Communicating this new structure was an extremely important part of the process. We sent out communications to our customers explaining the new structure and conducted presentations whenever possible to explain the changes. For our own staff, we had presentations and written materials to explain the changes. These communications covered the reasons we were making the changes, what the new structure looked like, what the impact of the changes would be, and how we would define success. Upper- and mid-level management, including the team leaders, were expected to follow up these initial presentations with staff discussions and question-and-answer sessions. The communications resulted in much good feedback and many questions. On a weekly basis, the Tech Ops Management Team met and were able to discuss issues and concerns that were being raised throughout the organization.

The Role of Team Leader

The role of team leader was mission critical. No other position in Tech Ops held greater responsibility for the practical implementation of our new vision. The team leader was a crucial change agent.

Central Point of Contact

The new structure provided a central point of contact for our customers. This greatly facilitated relations with the clinicians, and they appreciated having one person to deal with. Many comments were received from senior clinical leaders who said, "I am so thankful to have this streamlined approach for working with Tech Ops." One of the key responsibilities of the team leader was to be the project manager and, as such, know the status of activities and the open issues. This greatly facilitated conversations with our clinical customers, and the team leader was typically able to address customer issues before they bubbled up to senior management.

Trainer and Coach

The team leader had the greatest responsibility for the on-the-job education associated with our team behaviors. The team leader was clearly in the best position to observe the team behaviors and could best illustrate both the direct benefits and the lost opportunities. Team leaders were involved in the ongoing coaching of staff and their formal performance evaluations. Maira Rieger, then Clinical Communications Department director, spoke passionately about the importance of this role: "Developing our colleagues is a primary focus of leadership. Ensuring that they understand our goals and have the resources necessary to achieve is mission critical."

Communicator and Implementer

As Tech Ops implemented changes in process and technology, the team leader played a major role in ensuring successful completion. Although the team leader created a single point of contact for our customers, many Tech Ops staff felt it actually complicated the lines of accountability within Tech Ops. Traditionally, employees went to their technical boss for assistance. Now they were sometimes confused about where they were supposed to go for help. This was especially confusing when new technologies or processes were being implemented. Team leaders were able to make connections within the Tech Ops organizations and bring resources to their teams as necessary to assist with implementing changes.

The Role of Senior Management

Senior management support was important. The clinical executive committee (CEC) was made up of all the vice presidents in clinical development; the vice president of Tech Ops was a member. This group initially supported the reorganization into cross-functional teams. A very skeptical group, they needed to see sustained benefits from the structure. They heard of these benefits from their senior clinical staff and maintained a generally supportive position. They were not called on to provide active and visible support on a regular basis; rather, they were called on when there was a problem.

This approach worked, as most CEC members were perceived as long-time nonsupporters of Tech Ops and, as such, had little credibility with Tech Ops staff. The head of the CEC—the senior vice president of clinical development—was a strong supporter of the team structure and publicly praised the approach and the successful results. His comments were extremely uplifting to the Tech Ops organization, which made up approximately half of all the clinical staff. His support of the effort was fundamental to sustaining and refining our organizational structure.

Other Supports

Organizational development experts provided other support. We worked with our internal human resources director during the design phase. As we moved toward implementation, he supported our use of external consultants to assist with the efforts. Two consultants with whom we had previous experience were selected. During initial implementation and then beyond, a substantial number of consulting hours were used.

The consultants provided a wide range of services: executive coaching to individual Tech Ops leaders, consulting with the entire Tech Ops Management Team, working with individual teams to address team behavioral matters, teaching the three-day course on teamwork, and coaching individuals in Tech Ops at all levels who wanted to work on personal behaviors. Funding for these efforts came directly from the Tech Ops budget. Many members of the Tech Ops Leadership Team said, "I appreciate not only the competence of our consultants but the fact that they bring an external and broad perspective to our efforts." In my personal experience, I always believed that the "commitment to the consistent application of organization development principles could propel an organization to achieve the unbelievable."

How Obstacles Were Overcome

Obstacles to organizational change can come from both inside and outside a group. Internal obstacles probably created more challenges for Tech Ops than obstacles from outside did. The nature of our change to cross-functional teams was fully in the realm of responsibilities of the vice president of Tech Ops. Once it was broadly agreed with all clinical leadership to move Tech Ops to this type of organization, the Tech Ops senior leadership was able to do the bulk of the design and implementation work.

Internal Obstacles

Internally, resistance came from some of the first-line managers and staff. Typically, this resistance was fueled by fear. These fears were usually calmed through communication and education. The movement to cross-functional teams required team behaviors, and this was a stretch for some colleagues; most members quickly learned what was expected. Of course, some disliked the requirement that half their pay would be based on team behaviors, and they left the organization within the first twelve to eighteen months.

External Obstacles

Outside Tech Ops, the senior leaders in the CEC created some obstacles. Although supportive at first, these vice presidents started to resist Tech Ops when they realized that Tech Ops was becoming a strong, well-functioning organization. With a single team leader at the helm, Tech Ops staff had a point person who could escalate operational concerns. If, for example, a clinical senior staff person wanted a nonstandardized approach used when it wasn't necessary, the staff person could use the team leader to challenge this organizationally powerful customer. In the past, the individual Tech Ops staff person would typically feel powerless and give in to personality-driven customer requests. This caused many problems and was often the reason operations took so long. When it became recognized that Tech Ops could not be fractured so easily, concern grew at the senior level regarding this change in the power base. Statements such as "Tech Ops Takes Over" were used to express frustration at their loss of control. We did overcome these situations by having the vice presidents express their specific concerns and providing explanations of why certain operational approaches were used. Eventually, they got used to the new model and the changing power base.

Drug Development Teams

Another small but important obstacle was the acceptance by larger drug development teams in the division that the Tech Ops team leader was the single point of contact for operational matters. These larger drug development teams, whose scope went from early research through sales and marketing, were used to having a senior clinician represent all the activities occurring within the clinical organization. This approach did not work well. Drug development executives were often quoted as saying, "We need concise, factual information regarding the operations in clinical." Typically, the leaders who attended the drug development meetings were not up to speed on the operational issues, as their expertise was in drug efficacy and safety. As a result, operational matters were often not represented; sometimes they were misrepresented, or Tech Ops was used as the scapegoat for project delays. With the birth of the new team leader role, we had to work with the leaders of these large drug development teams to get them to sit at the table with the Tech Ops representative. Over a year or so, we were able to get the Tech Ops team leaders onto these teams. The leaders played an important role and were ultimately recognized as the operational experts who were sought out for their knowledge and input.

How the Structure and Process Changed over Time

As we experienced success with the four initial teams, the Tech Ops Management Team decided to expand the cross-functional team model to include other drug programs and our colleagues in Europe.

In the early part of 1997, we migrated all of the staff to cross-functional Tech Op teams. Because of the large number of staff, the majority of the teams were focused on a therapy area (for example, anti-infective or cardiovascular); a few teams remained with a focus on an immediate submission. In going to therapy-based teams, we did lose that initial goal orientation and a clear end point. However, there was a gain in that team leaders had increased staffing flexibility. For example, there may have been five different drug programs in a therapy area. The single team leader could move staff from drug program to drug program as changes occurred. Many staff members commented, "I am pleased that I have the ability to work within a fairly constant group of team members." Staff liked having more flexibility, and many also liked being able to stay focused in a therapy area.

Tech Ops hired many new staff members, particularly in 1997 and 1998. This, coupled with the movement to predominantly therapy-based teams, required some team structure changes. As a result, the initial pyramid structure whereby each team member reported to a team leader and a technical department manager was no longer viable. A movement was made to have the first-line manager from the technical department assigned to the team, along with the technical staff. Thus the team members had direct accountability to the first-line technical manager (now on the team full-time) and of course the team leader. This first-line technical manager was called a primary contact (PC). The PC had a dual reporting relationship to the team leader and the head of the functional department. Role definitions were created for the PC, and a new round of education had to occur to ensure that everyone understood the new roles.

Our European colleagues were brought more directly into the Tech Ops structure during 1997. These individuals received the same training and consultant usage as their U.S. counterparts. In addition, cultural training was conducted for colleagues who resided in the United States, France, and Germany.

It is interesting to note that we did experiment with a Team Coordinator Model but unanimously agreed not to implement the approach. The coordinator role was different from a team leader in that the coordinator was just a project manager. The members had no kind of formal reporting to the team coordinator. We concluded that it was the lack of formal reporting of the staff to the leader that made this model unsuccessful. It was harder to make changes occur, particularly in process and technology, in this model.

Results

In summary, the movement to cross-functional Tech Ops teams was extremely successful. The initial teams demonstrated the benefits associated with this model primarily through speed, increased employee satisfaction, and increased customer satisfaction.

Speed

We achieved our "fast-and-good" vision through an overall acceleration of the NDA preparation process. This increase occurred from our baseline in 1994 through 1999. We saw an increase in speed for several major milestones. For example, we reduced the time to develop a clinical database by approximately 75 percent. The time from the end of a clinical study to the release of the database was reduced by more than 50 percent. The time to release planned statistical analyses after a database is released for large Phase II and III projects was cut back to an amazing three days; unplanned analyses were typically available in a few weeks; for Phase I studies, we were able to release data within hours of the database release. In addition, we recognized significant improvements in the time to prepare interim data summaries from several weeks to days.

Increased Employee Satisfaction

Colleagues were surveyed in different ways and times during the period 1996 to 2000. In general, colleagues of all levels indicated that they found the team experience to be more satisfying than previous models. Some of that increased satisfaction was due to the realization of our values, which provided for greater participation and for a sharing of power and of truth telling. The increased satisfaction was also due to the realization of a more efficient team process that resulted in less stress and burnout, particularly in the weeks prior to the delivery of the NDA. Employees liked the increased flexibility that came with being assigned to therapeutic-based teams. On several occasions, just the Tech Ops leadership team was surveyed on their satisfaction of working together and leading the organization. The results of these surveys were also positive. Many leaders were quoted as saying, "This is the best leadership culture I have ever worked in. We have operationalized the fact that we are jointly responsible for the success of all the drug programs and the development of our colleagues. I feel very supported in this team." Usha Rafferty, one of the team leaders, said, "Our approach to teams and values has built a sense of community and connection to one another."

Increased Customer Satisfaction

Our clinical customers were extremely pleased with the increased speed and their new ability to work directly with a single point of contact—the team leader. Although formal surveys were not used, customer interviews did occur. Furthermore, these customers were very vocal about the positive results. Many customers commented, "Tech Ops can really deliver, and the projects are all getting the attention they need." One of the clinical drug directors on a major multi-year project commented, "No one in Tech Ops would even have agreed to such timelines in the past; they would have probably outsourced the work. Now they are consistently getting the job done." As the negative Tech Ops comments subsided, employees in the larger organization, such as the research division, took note. Many inquired about the change and how we had become so successful.

These results were seen time after time throughout the late 1990s. A large number of metrics continued to be gathered on numerous components of the cross-functional process. Our fast-and-good philosophy had been achieved through the tremendous efforts of the many Tech Ops colleagues worldwide.

There was another benefit to the organization, although it was not measurable. The significant amount of training and consultant time focused on team skills, leadership, change management techniques, intrapersonal examination, decision making, meeting facilitation, and project management resulted in Tech Ops colleagues being very well prepared to lead and participate in initiatives throughout the division. Many were able to use these skills to help bring effective operations to teams they were involved in, and others were able to use these skills in new jobs throughout the division. In summary, our efforts were successful at building leadership at all levels throughout the organization.

Lessons Learned

Significant learnings occurred during and after the transition to cross-functional teams. We learned that it was important to

- Spend time up front to define roles and responsibilities
- Conduct debriefings on teams and projects to learn from our experiences

- Communicate the rationale for the changes to all staff and customers
- Select highly qualified team leaders and provide them with a significant level of coaching and support
- Create a values-based organization in which the values remained in place throughout the process of creating organizational change
- Have external organizational consultants to assist the leadership team, keeping the number of consultants to a minimum, and using the same individuals over the multiyear process
- Create metrics and publicly display and share the data
- Reward teams for their successes, using a variety of monetary and nonmonetary approaches
- Keep the vision alive, thus helping all colleagues connect their work to business goals and to achieving the ultimate vision
- Recognize that it takes all the components working together to achieve success (functional experts, team members, management personnel, employees who provide administrative support, and the external consultants)
- Create a climate in which people know that it is OK to make mistakes, thus helping many deal with change and move more quickly to the new, desired state
- Use a shared vocabulary to discuss the changes taking place in the organization, including using similar organizational models for addressing issues such as change management, leadership, and behavior
- Involve the international colleagues as soon as possible, thus increasing the success of the global teams
- Change the compensation system so that pay is based on both technical contribution (50 percent) and team behaviors (50 percent)
- Colocate the work areas of staff from multiple technical disciplines—a highly effective way to increase communication and thereby improve decision making
- Have ongoing training

All colleagues attending the three-day team course shortly after being hired laid a great foundation for their initial orientation. Having concentrated leadership training and forums helped to build skills for these individuals. And finally, having short (for example, sixty- to ninety-minute) sessions focused on key organization development topics and made available to all colleagues was a big hit with the staff.

Here are some things we didn't handle well and might have done differently:

• *Early on, we didn't have a process in place for adding new members to the team.* Because of limited staffing, members would have to be moved from one team to another. Effectiveness suffered until a good "on-boarding" process was in place that defined the role of the technical department and the role of the team leader.

• *We thought we could convert all colleagues to the new world order.* Accept that this is not possible. Some individuals will not be willing or able to make the change and will need to move on to another place of employment. Don't spend too much time trying to convert these individuals; the people who are willing to make the change need your time and attention. Make the performance expectations known to all, and then manage accordingly; move people out of the organization when necessary.

• *We should have implemented a 360-degree feedback mechanism.* If we'd had a way for team members to provide feedback directly to one another, it would have been most beneficial. Over time, it was commonplace for management personnel to get input from the peers and customers of an individual; however, this information would be given to the supervisor for later discussion with the staff person. Ideally, we should have created a mechanism for individuals to regularly obtain direct feedback, which would have fit with our truth-telling value. Creating a culture in which this type of feedback could occur may have increased our effectiveness.

• *More emphasis should have been placed on regular communications to all colleagues in Tech Ops regarding the status of the change efforts.* That would have been particularly valuable when changes were going well. The use of the Web is the perfect mechanism to supplement the many presentations and group meetings that did occur.

• *Additional emphasis should have been placed on the management in the technical departments.* Within a very short time after the movement to cross-functional teams, the technical department management voiced concerns that they were no longer a critical part of the operations organization. Obviously, the positive results generated from the early role-definition work were not sufficient to sustain these leaders. Additional work had to be done to ensure that everyone understood the importance of both the team leaders and the technical department management.

• *Metrics were not put in place fast enough and not communicated widely enough.* It was a great struggle to obtain the metrics data and then to generate the reports needed to review the information. Time was lost in understanding what was happening on the teams and in being able to market the great progress that had actually occurred.

• *More involvement of first-line management should have occurred on a group basis.* The single head of the respective technical department brought his or her first-line department managers together. However, bringing all the first-line leaders together cross-functionally was not done early in the change process. As a result, opportunities were lost for sharing perspectives and experiences.

Critical Success Factors

I was a senior director in Tech Ops and an internal team development consultant from the beginning of this change initiative in May 1995 and subsequently became the vice president in the latter part of 1996. As our work developed and matured throughout the late 1990s, I was struck by the critical importance of several factors in developing successful teams. Summarized next are seven critical success factors that have been proven to bring about results.

Vision: Say It Over and Over and Over Again

First you must have a vision. Second, make the message simple and clear. People want to know where they are going. Third, communicate it over and over and over. Don't miss an opportunity to discuss the vision, including its importance to the business, along with the role of the individual in achieving the vision. All members of the management should espouse these messages. In my experience, you can't overcommunicate these important elements!

Have a Never-Ending Drive to Succeed But Don't Forget the Compassion

Achieving large organizational change in an effective manner is not for the timid. It requires an enormous commitment. Being a risk-taker is a requirement for the individual leading the function. The senior leader of the group and those surrounding this individual must embody an insatiable desire to achieve the goal. This level of energy will be needed to weather the storms along the way. Direction setting and decision making are two primary activities for the organization's leaders. However, because everyone reacts to change differently, the leaders of the group must also demonstrate genuine compassion for the thoughts and feelings of the staff, all the while giving them the confidence and resources needed to move quickly and effectively into the new model.

Listen a Lot and Learn Even More

To successfully implement a major change such as moving to cross-functional teams, it is imperative that the leaders of the organization actively seek out the relevant opinions of the staff. Establish regular forums where staff can come to express their ideas and create other opportunities for ad hoc discussions. Even more important, leaders must learn from these discussions and incorporate the necessary elements into the workplace. People feel valued when they are listened to, and creating a culture where people are valued is mission critical to sustaining long-term positive change. During these discussions, ask questions and challenge people to propose solutions to problems and to express potential new ways of working.

Create a Values-Based Organization

In today's economic climate, one of the few things that we can count on is that change will continue to occur at an ever-increasing pace. Leaders have the responsibility to implement changes in their organization. Change requires a consolidated effort in today's changing world. As a result, it is important that organizations create a set of values that do not change. These values should represent the kind of cultural environment that is the foundation for the organization. Of course, having values is not enough; behaviors must coincide with these values. Tremendous benefits can be reaped from the stability associated with leaders behaving in accordance with values that remain constant. In doing so, employees will have something to hold on to during turbulent times. Do not underestimate the importance of walking the talk; people are always watching.

Select the Right Leaders and Keep On Training New Ones

Establishing cross-functional teams requires that outstanding leaders be placed in the role of team leader. Select the very best candidates when you initiate this type of organizational structure. From the very beginning, work with these leaders to be sure they understand the vision and values; supplement any deficiencies they may have with targeted training; create a forum for the team leaders to come together and discuss what is working well and what is not; and, finally, have a coach for the team leaders whom they can use to receive organizational development feedback. In addition, identify employees with high leadership potential and develop them to take on future roles in the organization.

Measure Key Operations and Communicate the Results Against Plan

Developing metrics to measure key operations is mandatory. Furthermore, communicating the results of the metrics is also mandatory. The metrics are a wonderful business tool that should be used to help all employees learn how well the actual activities are charting against plan. Significant information can be generated by discussions around the meaning of the metrics data. Ideally, metrics are regularly used at both team meetings and senior leadership meetings. Implementing metrics is typically a controversial matter, particularly in an R&D environment. People are fearful that the metrics will not be used or that they are taking time to generate data that no one will look at. Reviewing metrics at the level of team meetings has the benefit of demonstrating that these data are important to the business and are not a vehicle for retribution. Reviewing metrics also demonstrates that the data are actually used to run the business. Finally, be sure to share relevant metrics data with your customers. Let them know how your team is progressing. Share the good news, and let the customers share in the positive results. Share the bad news as well; typically, the metrics data present a better story than the creative imagination of a disgruntled customer.

Have a Sense of Humor and Encourage Fun

Implementing significant organizational change is difficult work that can take years to fully realize. A great deal of personal effort goes into making these efforts successful. The pressures associated with implementing change can create a tense environment. Leaders are wise to create a culture in which time is taken to allow folks to have some fun. Humor is a great way to reduce stress. Create situations in which people can come together to have fun. Use different vehicles, as people's tastes vary widely. Have team members in charge of creating these activities. These types of nonmonetary rewards go a long way toward improving the health of a team.

Looking Back: Some Issues to Consider

1. Parke-Davis created cross-functional teams in response to a business crisis. What are the advantages and disadvantages of an organizational change at this time?

2. The new structure initially caused some confusion among team members about their reporting relationships. How could this confusion have been minimized or eliminated?

3. How do you feel about the decision to change the performance appraisal process to one where 50 percent of your evaluation was based on your team performance and 50 percent on your individual technical performance? How did this help the cross-functional teams succeed? How would it work in your organization?

4. What metrics are necessary for defining success when dealing with cultural change?

5. What role did the commitment of the leaders in Tech Ops play in the success of this organizational change?

6. How do you feel about the use of the three values as a foundation for effecting cultural change in this organization? How much impact do you think these values had in the short term and in the long term?

7. In selecting individuals to become cross-functional team leaders, what experience and personal attributes do you think are most important?

Case Study Two

A Virtual Cross-Functional Team Story [1,2]

*Coming together is a beginning, staying together is
progress, and working together is success.*
HENRY FORD

The following describes a significant IBM cross-functional team
effort to design, develop, and deliver an education offering within
IBM Global Services. This endeavor involved multiple individuals
from various organizations worldwide.

Background on IBM

In January 2002, the International Business Machines (IBM) Corporation was recognized as the world's largest information technology company, the world's largest hardware company ($33B),
and the largest IT services ($35B) and IT rental and financing
($3.4B) company. IBM is also the world's largest business and tech-
nology consultancy—growing that business in just eleven years
from $4B to $35B in annual revenue.

IBM strives to lead in the creation, development, and manufacture of the industry's most advanced information technologies,
including computer systems, software, networking systems, storage

---

[1]Reprinted by permission from International Business Machines. Copyright ©
2001, 2002.

[2]This case is a collective work product of the Global Services Team. For further
information on the case, contact Fred Stevens at fstevens@us.ibm.com or Jane
Ellingwood at jelling@us.ibm.com.

devices, and microelectronics. IBM's worldwide network of solutions and services professionals translates these advanced technologies into business value for their customers.

IBM Global Services

IBM Global Services (IGS) is the world's largest business and technology services provider, with year 2000 revenue of more than $33.2 billion. The organization is the fastest-growing part of IBM, with more than 169,000 professionals serving customers in 160 countries. Since 1991, IGS has helped companies of all sizes manage their IT operations and resources—ensuring their technology investments contribute to profitable growth.

The IGS portfolio offers deep technical and strategic expertise to address customers' demand for the following:

Business Innovation Services: BIS is the consulting arm of IBM Global Services. BIS delivers industry-based e-business strategy, process, design consulting, and end-to-end solution integration across five sectors: Communications, Distribution, Financial Services, Industrial, and Public.

Integrated Technology Services: IBM's ITS ensures the reliability and security of systems and networks, provides support and training to IT departments and end users, and maintains hardware, software, and networks. Like BIS, ITS seeks alignment of its infrastructure solutions around industry-based value propositions to meet the real business needs of IBM customers.

Strategic Outsourcing Services: IBM's Strategic Outsourcing works with customers to evaluate their business objectives and identify which IT operations can be outsourced for competitive advantage. This releases customers from the cost of keeping up with rapidly changing technology and constant retraining and recruitment in a marketplace where IT skills are in short supply. IBM is increasingly combining traditional Strategic Outsourcing deals with major BIS consulting engagements—a winning combination that delivers high value to customers and good business to IBM.

IBM Learning Services: IBM Learning Services is the world's largest IT training provider, offering training in over fifty countries and more than twenty technical areas. This unit delivers e-learning solutions that enable customers to broaden the scope of education and training, maintain the right skill level in their workforces, and reduce the travel and productivity costs associated with traditional classroom training.

E-business Hosting: This unit combines offerings in Web hosting, wireless hosting, and storage utility services, as well as hosting solutions for e-markets and application services providers.

Application Management Services: AMS outsourcing, which was formally managed as part of the Strategic Outsourcing line of business, develops and manages enterprise applications for IBM internal business organizations as well as for IBM's commercial customers.

Cross-Functional Participation Transforms Business Needs into Education

Virtual teaming, collaboration, cross-geography, cross lines of business—do these ever seem like the buzzwords du jour? Sometimes they are. At other times, they are realities that can lead to innovative and exciting results. The new Managing Technical Careers (MTC) e-learning course, released on October 15, 2001, was the end product of a dynamic team and a partnership among several IBM Global Services organizations.

The team was created to respond to an education need identified by the IBM Global Services Americas Professional Development Team (PDxT). The PDxT needed to develop a course to provide IBM Global Services' managers with information and education experiences to help them become more effective as coaches and career counselors for their technical employees. The course was completed in just four months at a savings of several thousand dollars for the sponsoring organization.

Exceptional Results from a Cross-Functional Team

By combining the thoughts, experiences, and desires of an extensive group of subject-matter experts, the PDxT and technical resources program managers (TRPMs) provided managers with a simple, easy-to-learn guide on coaching their employees in pursuing technical careers in IBM. The result was a modular, e-learning Lotus NotesBook course called Managing Technical Careers. The course was delivered ahead of schedule and within budget as a result of cross-teaming with individuals highly motivated to achieve the important goals of the business.

Collaboration of Brain Power and "Teaming" Translates into a Very Successful Project

Jane Ellingwood, chairperson of the PDxT and program manager for professional development programs in IBM Global Services Americas, had the following to say about the course and the teamwork involved:

> The design and development of the Managing Technical Careers course represent a collaborative effort of the IBM Global Services Americas Professional Development Council, the IBM Global Services Americas Technical Resources Program Managers, the IBM Global Services Institute, IBM Learning Services, IBM Management Development, and IBM Global Services Americas Human Resources.

IBM Global Services Americas Professional Development Council was the course sponsor. Members of the PDxT worked in partnership with the IBM Global Services TRPMs, with involvement from the Human Resources Team. The IBM Global Services Institute (IGSI), the learning agent for IBM Global Services, managed the development and delivery of the Managing Technical Careers course. IBM Learning Services designed, developed, and is delivering this e-learning course. IBM Management Development worked in concert with IBM Learning Services to create a set of interactive scenarios especially designed for the course. This was a unique partnership opportunity for a number of players who had not previously collaborated with each other.

The PDxT sponsors a number of key professional development initiatives in support of professionals and managers within IBM Global Services Canada, the United States, and Latin America. The PDxT also partners closely with its corresponding organizations in Asia Pacific and in Europe, the Middle East, and

Africa, working in conjunction with partner organizations at the global level.

The TRPMs are leaders responsible for the identification, development, retention, and promotion of current and future top technical talent and leaders. The TRPMs for IBM Global Services work closely with their TRPM counterparts from other IBM business units. They also partner closely with the Professional Development Team within IBM Global Services Americas.

IGSI manages the IBM Global Services investment in education to ensure IGS has the right skills at the right time and at the right place. IGS must have the skills in place to compete effectively in the IT services business to grow our business and revenue. Having the right education to augment other forms of learning is one of the key ingredients in meeting these demands for skills that translate into revenue and profit.

Establishing the Team

After the PDxT worked with IGSI to submit an initial request for new education, IGSI's education solutions manager, Fred Stevens, identified and selected the members of the core development project team. He selected team members based on the initial scope of the project and the expertise required. The customer sponsor selected Ray Paskauskas as the overall customer project manager. Ray is the IBM Global Services Canada technical resources program manager and leader of the technical subteam of the PDxT. An initial conference call was scheduled within twenty-four hours, which is a rapid turnaround time within IBM's highly matrixed organizational environment.

The Cross-Functional Core Team Members

Jane Ellingwood, program manager, PDxT and Professional Development Programs, IBM Global Services Americas, Somers, NY

Ray Paskauskas, IGS Canada technical resources program manager, Markham, Ontario

Jerome Murphy, education program manager, IBM Learning Services, Greensboro, NC

Fred Stevens, education solution manager, IBM Global Services Institute, Armonk, NY

Joanne Allen, development project manager, IBM Learning Services, Atlanta, GA

Kristine Saracelli, Americas technical resources program manager, IBM Global Services, Research Triangle Park, NC

Pam Sullivan, delivery solutions manager, IBM Global Services Institute, Atlanta, GA

Jennifer Pressley, communications leader, IBM Global Services Institute, Atlanta, GA

Hector Bird, executive project manager, IBM Global Services Institute, Boca Raton, FL

Mary Owen, development solutions manager, IBM Global Services Institute, Tampa, FL

Dick Richardson, curriculum development manager, IBM Management Development, Charlotte, NC

Numerous SMEs from multiple geographies, including Europe, Asia Pacific, Latin America, and Africa

The Role of the Team Leader

The nature and scope of this project required multiple leadership functions. The customer sponsor, Ray Paskauskas, was the team leader responsible for coordinating subject matter resources, pilot participants, and reviewers, and for providing source material. The overall project manager, Hector Bird, coordinated the other project participants and was responsible for scope, schedule, and cost. The development project manager, Joanne Allen, owned and coordinated development activities and resources. This project management process ensured clarity of roles and responsibilities throughout the project and contributed to the project's success.

The Role of Senior Management

IBM senior management played a small but critical role in this project. Their support enabled a team of professionals and leaders who are responsible for overseeing professional development and the development of technical resources within IBM Global

Services to make this project a success. After this team developed the requirements for a new course, senior management reviewed the requirements and gave the green light to proceed.

Senior management trusted the team to deliver the customer's expectations in a timely and effective manner. This is exactly what happened. Once the goals and objectives were communicated, the respective team leaders and team participants proceeded to accomplish the required tasks. There were several "check points" presentations to senior management during the development and delivery planning stages of the project. However, the team was empowered to do what they felt was needed to accomplish the objectives. Their initiatives helped to eliminate unnecessary reviews with senior management.

The Team Faced Its Share of Challenges

The course was originally scheduled for release at the end of 2001, with a project duration of six months. Because of the customer sponsor expectations, the schedule was reduced by two months, with completion scheduled for October. How were they going to complete the project under this rigid timetable? The due date was now moved up!

Another requirement was the need to coordinate a significant amount of input from a number of subject matter experts (SMEs) assigned to the project. They were now faced with consolidating the feedback, communicating changes, keeping the project on track, and delivering it two months earlier than expected.

An additional challenge was the organization and geographic dispersion of team members. The team had members from various organizations across multiple regions (Canada, the United States, and Latin America). How were they going to pull this project together when team members were in different locations? There was no travel budget for the project, and some of the members of the project team did not know each other or had met only over the telephone.

Another obstacle was the customer's desire to make the e-learning group experience more than just independent learning. This was the first time the team was faced with a request of this nature.

How the Team Overcame the Challenges

The rapid deployment method and the sponsors' high level of commitment provided the answer to Problem 1.

The project team agreed to release the course ahead of schedule but, in return, asked the sponsor to meet certain conditions:

- The sponsor agreed to turn in subject matter experts' requests within twenty-four hours.
- The sponsor also agreed to hold daily project status calls in the pilot phase of the project. In addition, IGSI and Learning Services instituted an "accelerated development schedule" to shorten the time it takes to develop a course, including
    Performing development and delivery activities in parallel
    Assuming "risk of acceptance" by conducting a modular pilot versus a complete course pilot
    Continuously validating content requirements with the sponsor deploying the course on the appropriate server using the rapid deployment method (RDM)
    Accelerating the course pilot with close to one hundred SME participants from eight countries

The RDM substantially decreased the number of architectural reviews and costs normally associated with server deployments. This method allowed the team to save the customer money and deliver the course at the right time. In addition, the sponsor team's high level of commitment and the responsiveness of the subject matter experts in course development and reviews dramatically impacted the acceleration of the project schedule.

Weekly status calls and consistent follow-up were the solution to Problem 2.

Another requirement was the need to consolidate significant amount of input from a number of subject matter experts assigned to the project. The skilled leadership of the project manager was a key factor in keeping the project on schedule through communications of changes as well as responsibilities. The project manager collected and consolidated the SME's feedback and conducted concise, weekly project status calls with the team. Items covered in each meeting were current actions, closed actions, open items, and new actions that needed closure. Follow-up through detailed e-mails was a great contributor to the success of the project. This project management enabled the team to meet the aggressive timetable and budget costs for the project. All constituencies were represented and participated with accountability. Partway through the project, Kris Saracelli provided backup in the team leader's absence for several weeks and stated, "Hector's project management style, both with me individually and with the project team overall, made the transition from Ray to me during a critical time in an already accelerated project schedule possible. The whole team helped me move quickly from a SME role to that of a leader. I don't think the transition impacted the project at all."

Virtual teaming was a big help in eliminating Problem 3.

The team members were not located in the same geographic area but conducted business through e-mails, regular conference calls, and Lotus Notes. The team did not hold one face-to-face meeting for the purpose of this course. However, this did not hamper the end results and successful solution of the project. Furthermore, this may have enabled the team to design and deliver a solution that was intended to serve an audience—IBM Global Services managers—who work in this same kind of environment.

To address Problem 4, managers and executives took the course together and actively participated in conference calls.

The customer suggested an approach that would enable a group of managers to go through the Managing Technical Careers course together, with a formal opening and closing experience to serve as "bookends" around the taking of the course. This was a unique request in the ever-evolving field of e-learning, but IGSI and Learning Services responded quickly. Conference calls with appropriate executive speakers were designed. Each business unit or organization within IBM Global Services was encouraged to have groups of managers and their executives take the course together and participate actively in the opening and closing conference calls. This provided more "control" around what was otherwise an independent learning experience, and gave the managers more incentive to actually complete the course. This motivated them to be prepared for the closing conference call.

THE CROSS-FUNCTIONAL TEAM
BRINGS THE PROJECT TOGETHER

The PDxT and TRPMs collaborated with many organizations to understand what was needed for the Managing Technical Careers course. The group evaluated recent survey results and employee feedback, as well as input from the management and executive teams and others. Ray Paskauskas knew that the team needed to provide education to increase managers' awareness of the careers available for technical professionals, the respective roles of the employee and management in career development planning, and the factors involved in implementing a development plan. The top priority was to create a course for managers that would provide guidance and coaching that would, in turn, enable the management team to more effectively guide and coach their technical professionals. This led to the proposal to create the (MTC) e-learning course.

Determining the exact content required selecting subject matter experts from IGS managers, technical leaders, the IBM Management Development Center, new hires, and seasoned professionals. These SMEs represented a cross-section of all IGS business units and technical development programs.

Hence, the project team used e-mail and conference calls to conduct business and telephone calls to conduct interviews. When it came time to conduct the pilot of the course, nearly one hundred managers and professionals from seven countries in the Americas plus Japan participated in the course pilot. The pilot was conducted through conference calls and Lotus Notes, and the pilot results were positive.

Feedback on the Course

Although intended for managers of all types of technical professionals in IBM Global Services Americas, this course has already received broad exposure and positive feedback, as shown in these samples:

"It's got to be one of the best written that I've seen from IBM."

"Regardless of how long you have been in IBM, or in management, this course is great. I especially like all of the informational links it provides."

"Thank you for inviting me for the pilot. The content is excellent."

"The course is comprehensive. It's a great learning vehicle for a new manager and a great refresher for an experienced manager."

The Managing Technical Careers Course Serves as a Model for Future Courses

A global version of Managing Technical Careers was designed after the Americas version was released. The global version will cover not only the Americas but also IBM Global Services' business units in Asia Pacific and in Europe, the Middle East, and Africa.

Even more exciting was the release of a companion course, Managing Your Technical Career (MYTC), designed for technical professionals. This course grew out of the success of the Managing Technical Careers (MTC) course. The new MYTC e-learning course was designed for a global audience from the start, as a result of great interest from all of IBM Global Services' geographic organizations around the world.

The global versions of both Managing Technical Careers and Managing Your Technical Career are excellent examples of reuse of intellectual capital and building upon successful programs. They represent additional positive outcomes from the release of the first version of Managing Technical Careers.

Adhering to the IBM Global Services principle of sharing and reusing intellectual capital, the team is moving forward to explore all the various ways that Managing Technical Careers can impact the key business imperatives of attracting, developing, and retaining employees within IBM today.

Feedback from the Sponsor

Jane Ellingwood, program manager, PD Programs and PDxT for IGS Americas, said at the conclusion of the project, "Some of the exciting results of this effort have cascaded throughout our organization as well as outside IBM. Really great things happen when lots of people work together across boundaries and with great attitudes to create and deliver something new and exciting."

Comments from Team Members

Speaking in his role as project manager, Hector Bird remarked, "The team members understood their individual roles and trusted each other. Each person made it a point to communicate well with others on the team. Everyone embraced the challenges we faced, and everyone was willing to assist to get the job done."

Speaking in her role as IGS Americas technical resources program manager Kris Saracelli noted that "the Managing Technical Careers course has been so well received that we have created a similar course for the technical professionals—Managing Your Technical Career. The combination of the two will greatly improve the partnership between manager and employee in the development of our technical professionals worldwide."

Fred Stevens, IGSI's education solutions manager, stated, "Teamwork was extraordinary. All members were dedicated to meeting a challenging schedule, on time, and within budget. Whenever problems presented themselves, the team members were quick to work toward a solution. The customer was responsive. The development team and the development project manager were aggressive, flexible, highly motivated, and committed to the project's success. A sense of urgency resonated from the very beginning." Fred also stated that he believes the reason for the project's success started with an unwavering desire on the part of everyone on the team to achieve the customer sponsor's objectives.

Lessons Learned

What worked? Each of the following was a critical success factor:

- *Clear goals:* At the outset, the team developed a clear set of deliverables, a timeline, and an implementation plan. The plan served as a guide throughout the project.
- *Empowerment:* The team was empowered to do whatever was necessary to achieve the goals without checking every decision with management. There was a high level of trust in the team.

Empowerment allowed the team to meet the challenging deadlines on schedule.

- *Virtual teaming:* The team was able to meet objectives while operating as a true virtual team without the benefit of any face-to-face meetings. The people selected for the team were experienced and comfortable working in a virtual environment.

- *Communications technology:* The project demonstrated the fact that a virtual team can succeed without the use of sophisticated technology systems. The two primary tools used by the team were e-mail and audio teleconferencing.

- *Customer involvement:* The customer was an active member of the team throughout the life of the project, providing valuable input that ensured the product met their needs.

- *Management support:* Senior management supported the team by quickly approving the plan, trusting and empowering the team to make key decisions, and not interfering in the work of the team.

- *External relations:* The team succeeded, in part, because of effective relationships with many IBM organizations that provided input and resources as well as quick turnaround on the team's requests.

- *Team members:* The team had the right people from the standpoint of both team skills and their technical experience, especially their experience in working in a virtual environment. There was excellent collaboration between all organizations. The team did a great job of tracking outstanding issues and following up on action items on a weekly basis. The team would have benefited by doing a more thorough job of sharing information about their respective professional backgrounds at project launch. This would help with understanding the perspective each team member brings to the project.

Critical Success Factors

The following are critical to a team's success:

- Understand and be aware of how to handle potential inhibitors to schedule.

- Disregard organizational boundaries in an effort to arrive at the best solution.
- Continually focus on the business imperatives throughout the project.
- Be sensitive and responsive to the concerns and considerations of other team members in the design of projects.
- Have empathy with geographical, cultural considerations.
- Understand that common goals and targets are mandatory of all team members.
- Provide open and frequent (risk-free) communications.
- All team members pull their own weight and share a common objective.
- Capitalize on team members' strengths.
- Capitalize on new technologies, such as Lotus Notes delivery vehicles for education.
- Maintain constant focus on meeting and exceeding customer expectations.
- Keep all commitments to the team and to the project.
- Use common tools.
- Realize that strong project management skills are a must.
- Develop a sense of trust among all team members.
- Be willing to accept and try ideas that are different from the norm, even if it means modifying the established process.
- Use a bit of humor when discussions get tense and the pressure to complete tasks is high.

Looking Back: Some Issues to Consider

1. The customer sponsor (the PDxT) had several people playing leadership roles. How do you think this helps a team succeed? What are the potential downsides? Would it work in your organization?

2. As you read the story on this team, what do you think was the most important factor in their success?

3. How would you prioritize the Lessons Learned and Critical Success Factors in the successful execution of your own projects?

4. How do you think your organization might make better use of conference calls, e-mails, and other technologies to enable cross-functional teams to work together without having to come together in person? What are the trade-offs of having face-to-face meetings during a project or working solely in a virtual project environment?

5. This case seems to suggest that selecting the right people as team members was extremely important. In your organization, to what extent does the sponsor or team leader have the freedom to select the members of a cross-functional team?

6. In this situation, the team was energized by a very challenging due date for completing the project. How important are stretch goals for a team?

7. What does this case tell us about what it takes to have a successful virtual team?

8. Senior management empowered the PDxT Team to accomplish the objectives. How does empowerment work in your organization?

9. How do you deal with geographic and cultural differences within your own organization and team projects?

Case Study Three

A Network of Cross-Functional Teams Responds to the 9/11 Crisis [1,2]

International Business Machines (IBM) is a fully integrated company focused on customer satisfaction as its number-one priority.

The IBM Software Group

IBM's Software Group is the world's second-largest software business and the world's largest middleware business. It has the industry's leading portfolio of middleware products, for example, software between an application program and the lower-level platform functions. A specific example of middleware is WebSphere Application Server product. The organization has about 35,000 employees working in some thirty locations around the world. The IBM Software Group is a traditional hierarchy. Yet hidden within this structure is an imposed matrix management organization requiring the functional organization structure to bend to the business needs of other business processes. The Customer Satisfaction Team is one of the matrix organizations stretching across those pillars.

---

[1]Reprinted by permission from International Business Machines Corporation, copyright © 2002.

[2]This case study was prepared by Frank Brinkman, senior software engineer, IBM Software Group, Data Management Division, Silicon Valley Laboratory, Customer Satisfaction Project Office, San Jose, California.

Role of the Customer Satisfaction Team of the Software Group

IBM established a customer satisfaction process to be the advocate of the customer within the company. This specific team is the customer satisfaction team in the Software Group, which develops and sells middleware software. The objective of the Customer Satisfaction Process is to represent customers when the IBM Company does not meet their expectations during their use of normal business processes. This is a fast-response team designed to assess, gather a rapid response team to address the needs of customers, and deliver a solution to the customer with the goal of restoring company loyalty.

The Conditions That Created the Need for the Team

The terrorists' attacks on the World Trade Center and the Pentagon on September 11, 2001, created major emergencies for the businesses located in those centers because their IT infrastructure was severely disrupted. Their personnel were traumatized and incapable of working immediately following the disaster. Yet IBM needed to be ready for an immediate, urgent, and possibly overwhelming volume of requests for assistance. IBM estimated that it had about 150 customers in the Twin Towers alone. The anticipated requests would be for new hardware, replacement software, and services. The most urgent need was to be able to enable the New York Stock Exchange and the banking industry to return to operation as soon as humanly possible.

Establishing the Network of Teams

The scope of the disaster precluded one simple team from being able to respond. The requests for assistance would be beyond the ability of any one services- or product-focused team to respond effectively. The IBM team is really a group of teams working in close concert. Each team works independently but in a coordinated fashion to maximize the effort and minimize the overlap in responsibilities.

In the minutes before the buildings collapsed, I spoke with my counterpart in IBM Americas. IBM Americas is the sales and distribution organization focusing on Americas customers from the tip of Argentina to northern-most parts of Canada. She has management contacts in Americas Sales and Services. I had the contacts for IBM software development. Each of us called a meeting of our respective teams to gather the response team to discuss what actions needed to be put in place. By 4 P.M. in the afternoon, we had 24/7 teams assembled and ready to respond to urgent requests from the customers. It was organized in layers to relieve the Customer Account Executive Team working directly with the customer on-site as much as possible. The layers were as follows:

- *Customer Account Executive Teams.* Responsible to coordinate all assistance required by the customer to restore normal business processes. All communication with the customer was focused through these teams. The intent was to minimize the disruption of the customer to a set number of people and not overwhelm them with requests from all parts of IBM.
- *Hardware Team.* Responsible to obtain and facilitate rapid installation of replacement hardware.
- *Advanced Technical Sales Support Team.* Responsible for receiving and prioritizing all software and services requests.
- *Americas Software Sales Team.* Responsible for on-site assistance to obtain and install software. We integrated our software recovery processes with the IBM-wide processes. Americas software sales representatives were in contact with the customer obtaining the software necessary to reestablish the customer's infrastructure.
- *Software Group Team.* Responsible to provide replacement software, technical problem resolution, installation advice, and counsel.

Each team met daily, both early in the morning and late afternoon for briefing and coordination of action plans.

All paperwork or authorization requirements that hindered responsiveness were waived. Records were to be kept of what was supplied by account teams for later reconciliation with the customer.

The Teams and the Team Members

The Software Group Team is composed of seven subteams focused on specific middleware software, Application and Integration Middleware, Data Management, Lotus, and Tivoli being the four largest teams. I am responsible for both the Software Group Team and the Data Management Team.

The Role of the Team Leader

The team leader had to be

- *A good listener*—correlating many facts and rumors into a set of needed action plans with a vision.
- *Compassionate*—understanding the emotional capabilities of the team members and customers to ensure the success of the team.
- *Decisive*—making decisions with incomplete information amid the chaos of urgency and heightened emotions.
- *Excellent communicator*—constantly clarifying and communicating concise and clear information.
- *"Egoless"*—have the ability to be wrong, apologize, be flexible to change, and continue to act with a passion to reach the goal.
- *Empowering*—there is too much for a single person to manage or accomplish alone. The leader must empower others to act on his or her behalf and then guide them when they are wrong, strengthening them, not criticizing them.

The Role of Senior Management

Senior management's role was supportive. They had to communicate with their peers in the companies (customers) affected by the crisis. Yet they needed to enable the teams when a business need came up. For example,

> All tunnels into Manhattan were closed. All airports were closed. The only way into the business district was via trains. The only way to get software to the New York area was via the Internet. The Sales Reps purchased CD/RW drives, accessed the IBM Passport Advantage

Web site, and downloaded software. They then hand-carried the CDs to the customers for installation.

Software Fulfillment recognized a need to get software that is only stored on computer tapes to the New York area. Permission to use IBM executive aircraft to fly the tapes was approved in a two-minute telephone conversation.

Other Supports

In this crisis, many people wanted or needed to do something to help. IBMers worldwide focused their energies to respond to the business need. In some cases, they felt left out if they were not called on to provide immediate assistance. Many had difficulty waiting.

How Obstacles Were Overcome

In addition to the obstacle mentioned earlier of the ability to get software delivered to the New York area and into the hands of the customer, there was the waiting.

Waiting was one of the most difficult parts of this project. Our team was in place and ready almost immediately. Then came the long wait. The wait was interminable. It was the anticipation and yet anxiety to be doing something to help.

Due to the loss and emotional trauma suffered by the employees and management directly affected by this disaster, several days went by before that first call came in. It was received with a sigh and relief. This feeling of helplessness was overcome with a concentration on the little tasks that could improve the ability to respond when a call came.

In the early hours of the crisis, there was a lack of information on what customers were affected and what software was installed at their site. Proactively, we had the technical support community review all the "trouble" reports received from the customers in certain zip codes and compiled a list of software companies and software that possibly needed to be replaced.

Internet communication to and from Manhattan was disrupted and was not reliable. Communication with the Americas sales team was impacted by the destruction of the telecommunication equipment that was in and on the World Trade Center Towers. There was a restriction on calls being placed to Manhattan. Cell and satellite phones were used to communicate in urgent situations. In some cases a "personal relay" of information was set up.

How the Team Did Its Work

Each team operated independently. They came together to exchange actions taken and outstanding issues each morning and afternoon during shift change, enabling continuous effective operations. When cross-team assistance was needed, that communication occurred immediately between team leaders and requestors. Action plans were agreed upon and implemented.

A "Playbook" was created. This document described the team organization and actions necessary to respond to a disaster of this magnitude.

Results

All customers were restored for the opening of the New York Stock Exchange on Monday, September 16, 2001.

Lotus Team was recognized for lending their expertise and resources to the critical relief agencies. They volunteered their services to the Department of Information Technology and Telecommunications. Within twenty-four hours the team created and installed key applications for several disaster recovery organizations. For the Office of Emergency Management, the team created an application that stored data regarding the structural integrity of the three hundred buildings directly affected by the attacks. For the New York Human Resources Administration, it built a system for maintaining and tracking the case information of the 20,000 victims who lost loved ones, jobs, or homes on September 11, 2001. For those tracking the vast amounts of donations submitted in the weeks following the tragedy, the team built a materials inflow-outflow process and workflow application. All of these applications were completed in record time, so that agency personnel could quickly provide help for those who needed it most.

The Playbook methodology was adopted by the other geographic teams responsible for Europe, the Middle East, Africa

(EMEA), and Asia Pacific (AP) as the basis for their disaster recovery plans.

Software Fulfillment was recognized for their personal sacrifice of time and talent to facilitate immediate delivery of replacement software, in spite of the disruption of the normal distribution processes.

Lessons Learned

What worked? Each of the following was a critical success factor.

- *Creation of a layered approach to handling requests.* It might be called a triage approach where a request is handled by a small team and then directed to the right team to manage.
- *Delegating work efforts and expecting it to be handled without constant status checking or interference.* A combination of trust and empowerment, coupled with commitment.
- *Publishing all current status on the intranet Web site.* All executives, managers, and other IBMers were directed to a common Web site for the latest information on the IBM recovery teams. No meetings were to be held with executives or management to provide status reports. This was a real timesaver. It also provided a single, consistent message to all.
- *Coordination with teams on the ground.* Lotus worked closely with New York City disaster recovery teams providing critical resources and applications to assist in the communication and collaboration to assess damage to quickly identify the needs of emergency personal at Ground Zero and organize the requisite resources.
- *Software Fulfillment created a 24/7 CD-burning process for software.* Under normal circumstances, each CD software order is custom built to specific software maintenance levels. In this disaster, we needed to be prepared to deliver volumes of CDs that the custom build process would have difficulty producing.
- *Instant communication. Lotus Sametime Connect Instant Messenger* service was invaluable as a quick means of communication with all parties. This tool enabled multitasking. I knew who was available at any moment. When people were busy, I was able to leave messages on their terminal. When needed to, I could create a chat room to gather the key team leaders to

understand the issues and make decisions. I could be on a teleconference and still be participating in ongoing *Sametime Connect Chat* sessions. I was able to instantly disseminate the new information to other team members, be involved in multiple *Sametime* session discussions, or respond to information requests. I had ten different *Sametime* sessions up at the same time.

What didn't work:

- *Communication.* Communication was critical to all teams, and sometimes they did not get the needed information in a timely manner. Constant attention had to be paid to ensure there was clear, concise communication and that all necessary parties got the message. Correcting the communication problems took the most time.
- *Altering the normal software delivery processes.* Customers needed immediate access to replacement software without the normal time-consuming purchasing processes. The America Sales Reps were given access via a special user ID and password. They were given carte blanche authority to download software for customers. They kept track of the software given to the customer for later reconciliation.
- *Normal delivery processes failed due to lack of transportation capabilities.* Airports, airlines, cargo carriers, and personal aircraft could not fly. Permission to use IBM corporate executive jets was obtained to facilitate delivery of software. This option was available but not used during the crisis. Cargo carriers returned to service to provide the overnight service needed from Boulder, Colorado, to New York and Washington, D.C.

CRITICAL SUCCESS FACTORS

Teams need the following in order to succeed:

- *Clear purpose.* A clear and concise overarching goal with an urgency that was obvious.
- *Clear team roles.* Each team understood their roles and responsibilities. Ambiguities were quickly discussed and resolved. They were not left unspoken.

- *Clear plan.* Triage approach to focus request to the right team. The Advanced Technical Support Team had the responsibility to understand the request and route the request to the proper teams on a 24/7 basis.
- *Communication mechanism.* Status communication to management and executives via a common Web site structured to provide all necessary communication. No special meetings were held to communicate status.
- *Commitment.* The Americas Software sales reps downloaded the requested software from their homes or locations where they could get a reliable Internet connection. They hand-carried the software to the customer.

Looking Back: Some Issues to Consider

1. Although this team operated in a most unusual environment and under unique conditions, what are the lessons from this case that can be applied to your cross-functional team?

2. This leader minimized outside interference in the operation of the team so the team could focus on the task at hand. In what ways is this approach applicable to your cross-functional team?

3. Cross-team communication was a problem for this team, as it is for all cross-functional teams that need to coordinate with other teams. What are some ways to overcome this barrier?

4. What do you think of the so-called triage concept? What are some other applications of this concept? How would it work in your organization?

5. The customer satisfaction team got high-level member commitment because of the enormity of the crisis and the desire to "do something to help." What lessons about commitment can we draw from this case that can also be applied to "normal" cross-functional teams?

Case Study Four
A Permanent Cross-Functional Team in the Public Sector

Clark County, Nevada, encompasses nearly eight thousand square miles of land within the southern tip of the State of Nevada. Clark County is roughly the same size as the state of New Jersey or twice the size of Los Angeles County, California.

One of seventeen counties located in Nevada, Clark County contains five incorporated cities, fourteen unincorporated town advisory boards, and six citizen advisory councils, along with numerous other communities. The county government is responsible for providing regional and municipal services to residents in the unincorporated portion of the county, much as a city or town does.

The U.S. Census 2000 population estimate for Clark County was 1,375,765—an 86 percent increase over the 741,749 people who were estimated to live there in 1990. Approximately five thousand people have moved to Clark County every month during the past ten years. All of the municipal governments in the urban valley are pro-growth and have encouraged this development; the number of housing units has increased by 76 percent within this same time period. In order to help developers with large parcels of land slated for master-planned communities, the county created the Major Projects Review Team.

This case was prepared by Marta Golding Brown, team leader of the Major Project Review Team, Clark County, Nevada. She may now be reached at P.O. Box 6048, Lancaster, California 93539, 702-592-2396, or ccar5525@aol.com.

Background and Structure of Clark County Development Review

Clark County, Nevada, is responsible for reviewing and approving projects submitted for development in the unincorporated areas of the county. The standard review of these projects requires each project to address land use and entitlement issues with the Comprehensive Planning Department, project improvements such as transportation and drainage issues with the Public Works Department, and zoning and building code compliance with the Building Department. This review, although much abbreviated here, is comprehensive and carries a development project from the start (with planning approvals) to the finish (with building permit issuance) and eventually a constructed development.

Role of the Major Projects Review Team

The purpose of the Major Projects Review process is to provide standards and procedures for accepting, processing, hearing, and taking final action on applications for lands designated for future development or lying beyond the area projected to meet the near-term urban growth. The Major Projects Review Team completes much of the review described; the team is colocated in the county's Planning Department. The team's review provides a comprehensive consideration of proposals for large projects and for projects outside the infrastructure required to support them, such as sewer and water lines, parks, and schools.

By centralizing the comprehensive consideration of large projects, the Major Projects Review Team can assess the effects the projects will have on the neighborhood and community overall. This helps the Board of County Commissioners and the Planning Commission determine proper land use and zoning for the projects. Once land use has been approved, improvement plans are submitted for each project, and the team setting encourages the cross-verification of information received with the current approvals. The team also meets weekly with project developers who want to brainstorm new ideas; that way, they can work through any perceived obstacles early in the project rather than force costly delays on developers when construction is eminent.

Business Conditions That Created the Need for the Team

The development process is very competitive in the Las Vegas Valley. Developers continually seek to have the competitive edge of faster reviews on their projects. Faster reviews mean less interest to carry on undeveloped land, thus increasing the profit margin of projects. The Major Projects Team can provide this service because they have only a certain number of projects to deal with and can remain familiar with the issues surrounding master developments as well as smaller projects within those developments. Also a development code is locked in with the project development agreement. These codes are revised in a fairly frequent process, and planners working with smaller projects are continually working with the updated code requirements rather than code from several years ago.

Having the same individuals working on the projects requires less research time because either team members are dealing with an issue in another arena and have the information readily available, or a teammate can step in to provide the information. This reduces the time required to resolve issues and consequently reduces review times. One developer said, "The Major Projects Team is required to process and approve applications based upon formerly applicable county development standards. The team's familiarity with the development agreements, the locked-in codes, as well as the master studies and overall development plans for the properties, is a great advantage."[1]

Steps in the Process of Establishing the Team

Staff saw the benefits early to creating a cross-functional team to assist these large master-planned communities. It would definitely be a benefit to staff, and we felt it would assist the developers as well. But the financial people at the county, as well as the developers, needed to be convinced. It was determined that the team could not be financed from the county's general fund, and an "enterprise account" would be created to handle team finances. In addition, to provide the customized team support envisioned, high-level staff would be hired to handle these specialized projects.

---

[1]Mark Dunford, vice president, America West Homes.

Compensation for the higher salaries would be provided through the higher fees paid by the developers.

The development community was reluctant to accept the change at first; they were concerned about paying higher fees with no guaranteed return on investment. Much of putting the original team together had to do with choosing the right individuals for the positions created. Once the benefits were shown to all, about two years later the county approved additional positions for the team; developers now ask to have their projects handled by the team.

Team Members

The Major Projects Review Team is a cross-functional team in the Comprehensive Planning Department. The team is composed of a senior drainage engineer, a senior traffic engineer, two associate engineers, two principal planners, two senior planners, and a building plans examiner. The team leader is an assistant planning manager. The team completes work that is typically handled in three county departments: Planning, Public Works, and Building.

The Major Projects Review Team completes the following tasks for large major projects:

- Development agreements
- Land use applications
- Right-of-way acquisition
- Final review and approvals on vacations, subdivisions, and right-of-way
- Zoning plan check
- Review of traffic and drainage studies and improvement plans
- Major and minor subdivision reviews and approvals

Role of the Team Leader

The team leader is a working member of the team. The leader is responsible for the negotiation of all development agreements and oversight of the agreements until all points are fulfilled. The leader is responsible for team administration and management and is a liaison between team members and other departments, management, and the development community on issues that cannot be resolved by the individual team members. If roadblocks need to be removed to assist the team with completing their work, it is the leader's role to remove the obstacles as quickly as possible.

Role of Senior Management

The role of senior management was initially to overcome the obstacles of establishing a cross-functional team. The team had to break down departmental barriers that exist not only in Clark County, Nevada, but across the nation in local governments. Traditionally, engineering and planning practitioners don't work in the same department or group. County management and some department management accepted a vision from a staff study showing a cross-functional team approach to large comprehensive project approvals within the county. This study was based in part on county management's desire to create a *Seamless Government*.[2]

The first team leader was challenged with establishing a team with respected senior staff members from the various departments. These staff members needed to be trusted by the sponsoring departments and respected by the development community. They had a clear understanding of their goals and the importance of keeping a strong working relationship with the other departments. Once the initial team was established, the original team leader was promoted to another position, and a second team leader was hired. The second team leader has focused on rounding out the team and removing administrative obstacles whenever possible.

The team is still focused on the initial mission, but as a result of their successes, county management is attempting to create a second team with a somewhat different mission and is forming a new cross-functional department to review all county development applications.

Other Supports

After the original study was completed showing how a cross-functional team could aid the current process for large developments, two staff members were hired within the Planning Department

---

[2]*Seamless Government: A Practical Guide to Re-engineering in the Public Sector,* Russell M. Linden (San Francisco: Jossey-Bass, 1994).

who had experience working on successful cross-functional task forces in other jurisdictions. These task forces were convened when appropriate to provide feedback to developers on projects but remained employees of the traditional departments. They became internal advocates for the newly proposed process. They clearly aided the Planning Department in taking the lead on the creation of the Major Projects Team.

In addition, one of these study team members was hired by the Planning Department to oversee the development agreements the developers of large projects had with the county. All of these things, combined with the financial viability for developers, allowed the team to move forward.

How Obstacles Were Overcome

It took several years for the vision to be approved and a funding source to be identified and adopted by the Board of County Commissioners. Once all of the approvals from the county's leadership were received, the next set of hurdles was working with the individual departments to allow staff appointed to the new team to complete reviews not traditionally handled by the Planning Department. The departments agreed to allow the individuals to report to a team leader administratively but remain technically under the sponsoring departments. For some team members, it meant the requirement of issuing letters under another department's letterhead, and some were only allowed to use the Planning Department's letterhead. Not all members were treated alike by the other departments or even within the same sponsoring department. However, the team learned to look beyond these differences and to the end goal, which was the efficient and effective review of large comprehensive development projects. Admittedly, it has been difficult.

Results

The Major Projects Team has successfully broken down the barriers in development review, "where most public agencies tend to compartmentalize the work flow. By breaking down the compartmental barriers, the work flow is handled more efficiently because all the team members understand the complexity, history, assumptions, and constraints associated with each approval in a more global sense and time spent re-educating is minimized with each work item. All in all, the team has been a tremendous asset to the success we have had at Southern Highlands."[3] This also creates ownership of the project by team members. They are able to see a project from beginning to end rather than just a small portion as the paperwork passes their desk.

The result of having the Major Projects Team complete development review has been the acceptance by the development community of how well a cross-functional team can work. In fact, a large national developer approached county management to either expand the team or create additional teams. A modified second team was created, with support from the Major Projects Team.

In addition, the county manager believes the process has worked so well that he has combined the operative portions of the three departments normally involved in development review into one department. They will officially combine in July and are working together now to create their ultimate organizational chart. The Major Projects Team will be part of this new department. The new director believes "the Major Projects Team is being viewed as a model for the future organization of this new department. The challenge we are looking forward to is elevating customer service to the level that the Major Projects Team now provides."[4]

Lessons Learned

The lessons learned by this team include seeing that true autonomy in decision making is preferable, as the relationships created with the sponsoring departments are tentative at best. Any bump in the road seemed to be an excuse to erode a piece of the approvals given to the team. We continually strive to provide the best service possible to our developers. When other departments control some steps in the process, it can mean a delay in the total service provided, thus reducing the effectiveness of the team and the savings in time they provide.

---

[3]Mark Teepan, development manager, Southern Highlands Development Corporation.
[4]Phil Rosenquist, director, Clark County Development Services Department.

Critical Success Factors

The following factors are critical to the success of cross-functional teams.

Have a Clear Purpose

It is critical to establish a clear mission for the team. The team must understand why they were created and what they are expected to accomplish. The second step is to clearly define goals to complete the established mission.

Empower the Team

Provide the team with as much autonomous control of the process as possible. Allow decisions to be made by team members, and place the responsibility for those decisions squarely on the team. Everyone tends to keep each other in check, and it also provides the opportunity for people to brainstorm the process and provide positive improvements. We have also found that it allowed the county's development process to be reviewed in its entirety, not as the fragments that staff typically works with.

Provide Resources

Provide team members with the tools needed to complete the job and resources to remove obstacles. The Major Projects Team received a seed loan from the county's general fund. The funds helped establish the team by providing the necessary equipment and overhead. It was made clear to the original team members that this was a loan and they were responsible for their new enterprise fund—a novel concept to most public employees. It was like running a business. You needed to identify the right projects (customers) and convince them it was to their benefit to pay up to five times the normal amount of fees to have their projects reviewed by this "experimental" team. They also reviewed the budget each quarter and questioned the expenditures shown on the reports. It was with pride that the original seed money was repaid to the general fund two years later.

Carefully Select Team Members

The Major Projects Team was created with individuals well acquainted with the county's development review process; they volunteered to participate in something new and innovative. Most team members had worked in at least one other county department, in another agency, or for a private development firm. This wide breadth of experience resulted in more informed decisions and comprehensive input during brainstorming sessions with developers. It also provided people who weren't afraid to try new things and didn't have the mind-set that "we've always done it this way." Since the team wasn't a sure thing in the beginning, people who were willing to take a chance were the only ones willing to apply for the positions. This has aided the team when difficult situations have arisen with other departments and the development community. They stand up for what they think is right and are willing to fight for a common cause if it makes good, logical sense. They are truly team players in every sense of the phrase.

Involve Customers

The team has fostered openness by the participating developers, which has encouraged them to think and act in a different way. Development is proprietary, and no information is submitted to a public body until the developer is willing and able to release the information. Developers and team members have developed a level of trust with releasing information verbally to discuss appropriate solutions to design issues. In many instances, staff members and consultants of developers have actually become extended members of the Major Projects Team. If developers choose to participate on the team, they also reap the benefits of being an extension of the team. We kick around ideas together and brainstorm the best solutions for problems as they arise. By working collaboratively, solutions can be derived when a variety of options can still be financially accommodated.

Have Open Communication

Honest and candid communication has been the key to communication on the Major Projects Team. Sometimes it is brutally honest, but everyone knows where things stand at all times.

Share Leadership

When questions or discussions arise around a topic, the responsible team member or the one having the most experience is the one who takes the lead. Leadership roles clearly rotate on the team to the member with the most experience. Other team members may offer an opinion or ultimately provide the solution during discussion, but the responsible team member makes the final call. If the decision is out of the person's realm of authority, he or she will take the information to a person with technical expertise in the traditional department to assist with the decision. A meeting with the developer and that individual may be needed, but the team member is a heavy contributor to the decision.

Looking Back: Some Issues to Consider

1. What are the advantages of the Major Projects Review Team being a *permanent* cross-functional team in the county government? How do you think it might have worked if an ad hoc project team had been created to review each new development application?

2. What are the advantages of a cross-functional team composed of *full-time* team members?

3. How does a cross-functional team that takes over responsibilities formerly held by functional departments maintain effective relationships with those stakeholders?

4. The Major Projects Review Team involves customers (developers) on a regular basis in their work. To what extent is that approach applicable to your team?

5. Selecting the right people was a critical success factor in this case. To what extent do you have the freedom and opportunity to select the members of your cross-functional team? If you don't have that freedom, how do you address the issue of getting the talent needed to do the job effectively?

Survey of Cross-Functional Teamwork

This survey includes a list of factors that contribute to the success of cross-functional teams. Please review the list and do two things: (1) indicate the extent to which you believe each factor is *important* to the success of your cross-functional team, and (2) *assess* your team in regard to each factor.

Success Factors	Importance					Assessment					Comments
	Unimportant	Somewhat important	Important	Very important	Critical	Strongly disagree	Disagree	Neutral	Agree	Strongly agree	
	1	2	3	4	5	1	2	3	4	5	
1. *Leadership Effectiveness* The leader has high-level technical and team-management skills.	1	2	3	4	5	1	2	3	4	5	
2. *Empowerment* The team's authority to act is clear and consistent with the team's responsibility.	1	2	3	4	5	1	2	3	4	5	

3. *Shared Goals*
   The team has developed a vision, mission, and clear set of goals, and these are shared by all team members.

   1 2 3 4 5   1 2 3 4 5

4. *Recognition*
   Individual members receive appropriate recognition for their contributions to team efforts.

   1 2 3 4 5   4 2 3 4 5

5. *Role Clarity*
   Members are clear about what is expected of them and of their team members.

   1 2 3 4 5   1 2 3 4 5

(continued)

Success Factors	Importance					Assessment					Comments
	Unimportant	Somewhat important	Important	Very important	Critical	Strongly disagree	Disagree	Neutral	Agree	Strongly agree	
6. *Boundary Management* The team does a good job of developing relationships with other teams, clients, and key stakeholders	1	2	3	4	5	1	2	3	4	5	
7. *Performance Appraisal* Each team member's performance appraisal includes his or her performance on the cross-functional team.	1	2	3	4	5	1	2	3	4	5	

8. *Team Training* Team leaders and members have been trained in team-effectiveness skills.	1	2	3	4	5		1	2	3	4	5
9. *Team Size* The team is small enough to ensure effective communication, and decision making or subgroups or core teams are used to facilitate effective teamwork.	1	2	3	4	5		1	2	3	4	5
10. *Management Support* Management actively supports the work of the team by modeling team behavior, rewarding teams and team players, and providing necessary resources.	1	2	3	4	5		1	2	3	4	5

(continued)

Success Factors	Importance						Assessment						Comments
	Unimportant	Somewhat important	Important	Very important	Critical		Strongly disagree	Disagree	Neutral	Agree	Strongly agree	
	1	2	3	4	5		1	2	3	4	5	
11. *Interpersonal Excellence* There is a high level of trust, resulting in open communication, successful conflict resolution, active listening, consensus decisions, good meeting management, and an appreciation of cultural and style differences.												

12. *Customer-Client Focus*   1   2   3   4   5
The team's primary
emphasis is on
satisfying the
customer's and
client's needs.

In general, our cross-functional team is successful. (Please circle one.)

1. Strongly disagree   2. Disagree   3. Neutral   4. Agree   5. Strongly agree

References

Alexander, S. "Virtual Teams: Going Global." *Info World,* Nov. 13, 2000, *22,* 55–56.

Allaire, P. A. *Xerox 2000: Putting It Together.* Stamford, Conn.: Xerox Corporate Communications, Feb. 1992.

Ancona, D. G., and Caldwell, D. "Beyond Boundary Spanning: Managing External Dependence in Product Development Teams." *Journal of High Technology Management Research,* 1990a, *1*(2), 119–135.

Ancona, D. G., and Caldwell, D. "Improving the Performance of New Product Teams." *Research-Technology Management,* Mar.-Apr. 1990b, 25–29.

Ancona, D. G., and Caldwell, D. "Cross-Functional Teams: Blessing or Curse for New Product Development." *MIT Management,* Spring 1991, 11–16.

Ancona, D. G., and Caldwell, D. *Speeding Product Development: Making Teamwork Work.* Cambridge, Mass.: Sloan School of Management, 1992.

Anderson, C. "Curing What Ails U.S. Health Care." *Quality Progress,* Apr. 1992, 35–38.

Austin, N. K. "Updating the Performance Review." *Working Woman,* Nov. 1992, 32–35.

Be Prepared for Meetings. Mill Valley, Calif.: Kantola Productions, 1991. Videotape.

Beckert, B. A. "Changing the Culture." *Computer-Aided Engineering,* Oct. 1991, 51–56.

Belasco, J. A. "Empowerment as a Business Strategy." *Executive Excellence,* June 1991, 15–17.

Bennis, W. G., and Slater, P. *The Temporary Society.* New York: Harper-Collins, 1968.

Bishop, S. K. "Cross-Functional Project Teams in Functionally Aligned Organizations." *Project Management Journal,* Sept. 1999, 6–12.

Block, P. *The Empowered Manager: Positive Political Skills at Work.* San Francisco: Jossey-Bass, 1987.

Bouchard, T. J., and Hare, M. "Size, Performance and Potential in Brainstorming Groups." *Journal of Applied Psychology*, 1970, *54*(2), 51–55.

Bouchard, T. J., Draden, G., and Barasaloux, J. "Brainstorming Procedure, Group Size and Sex as Determinants of the Problem Solving Effectiveness of Groups and Individuals." *Journal of Applied Psychology*, 1974, *59*(2), 135–138.

Brown, S. L., and Eisenhardt, K. M. "Product Development: Past Research, Present Findings and Future Directions." *Academy of Management Review*, 1995, *20*(2), 343–378.

Brunelli, M. A. "How Harley-Davidson Uses Cross-Functional Teams." *Purchasing*, Nov. 4, 1999.

Carmel, E. *Global Software Teams*. Upper Saddle River, N.J.: Prentice Hall PTR, 1999.

Champion, M. A., Medsker, G. J., and Higgs, C. "Relationship Between Work Group Characteristics and Effectiveness: Implications for Designing Effective Work Groups." *Personnel Psychology*, 1993, *46*, 823–850.

Ciborra, C. U. (ed.). *Groupware and Teamwork*. New York: Wiley, 1996.

Clark, K. B., and Wheelwright, S. C. "Organizing and Leading `Heavyweight' Development Teams." *California Management Review*, Spring 1992, 9–28.

Cleland-Hamnett, W., and Retzer, J. "Crossing Agency Boundaries." *Environmental Forum*, Mar.-Apr. 1993, 17–21.

Cohen, S. G., and Bailey, D. E. "What Makes Teams Work: Group Effectiveness Research from the Shop Floor to the Executive Suite." *Journal of Management*, May-June 1997, *23*, 239–252.

Cohen, S. G., Ledford, G. E., and Spreitzer, G. M. "A Predictive Model of Self-Managing Work Team Effectiveness." *Human Relations*, 1996, *49*(5), 643–676.

Combs, G., and Gomez-Meija, L. R. "Cross-Functional Pay Strategies in High Technology Firms." *Compensation and Benefits Review*, Sept.-Oct. 1991, 40–48.

Culotta, E. "Teamwork Is Key to Solving Complex Research Problems." *Scientist*, Mar. 8, 1993, 20–22.

Davis, S. M., and Lawrence, P. *Matrix*. Reading, Mass.: Addison-Wesley, 1977.

Deal, T. E., and Kennedy, A. A. *Corporate Culture*. Reading, Mass.: Addison-Wesley, 1982.

Dealing with Conflict. Carlsbad, Calif.: CRM Learning, 1992. Videotape.

Deming, W. E. "The Merit System: The Annual Appraisal: Destroyer of People." Paper presented at "A Day with Dr. W. Edward Deming," University of Michigan, 1987.

Dowler, T. *SBDM: Another Look at School-Based Decision-Making*. Frankfort, Ky.: Kentucky Education Association, 1991.

Dowst, S., and Raia, E. "Design '88: Teaming Up." *Purchasing*, Mar. 10, 1988, 80–91.

Doyle, M. F. "Cross-Functional Implementation Teams." *Purchasing World*, Feb. 1991, 20–21.

Duarte, D., and Snyder, N. *Mastering Virtual Teams*. San Francisco: Jossey-Bass, 1999.

Dumaine, B. "How Managers Can Succeed Through Speed." *Fortune*, Feb. 13, 1989, 54–59.

Dumaine, B. "The Bureaucracy Busters." *Fortune*, June 17, 1991, 35–50.

Edwards, M. R. "Making Performance Appraisal Meaningful and Fair." *Business*, July Sept. 1989, 17–25.

Edwards, M. R. "Accurate Performance Measurement Tools." *HR Magazine*, June 1991, 95–98.

Eisenhardt, K. M., and Tabrizi, B. N. "Accelerating Adaptive Processes: Product Innovation in the Global Computer Industry." *Administrative Science Quarterly*, 1995, *4*, 84–110.

Eisman, R. "The Rewards of Teamwork." *Incentive*, Feb. 1990, 52–55.

Elliott, V. "Motivating Bank Employees to Think Like Business Owners." *Bankers Magazine*, May-June 1991, 70–74.

Fern, E. F. "The Use of Focus Groups for Idea Generation." *Journal of Marketing Research*, 1982, *19*, 1–13.

Fried, L. "Team Size and Productivity in Systems Development." *Journal of Information Systems Management*, Summer 1991, 27–35.

Gerwin, D. "Team Empowerment in New Product Development." *Business Horizons*, July 1999, 8–25.

Gordon, J. "Work Teams: How Far Have They Come?" *Training*, Oct. 1992, 59–64.

Govindarajan, V., and Gupta, A. "Building an Effective Global Business Team." *MIT Sloan Management Review*, 1996, *4*, 63–71.

Hackman, J. R., and Vidmar, N. "Effects of Size and Task Type on Group Performance and Member Reactions." *Sociomet*, 1970, *33*, 37–54.

Hall, E. T. *The Silent Language*. New York: Doubleday, 1959.

Hall, E. T. *Beyond Culture*. New York: Doubleday, 1976.

Halverson, C. B. "Managing Differences on Multicultural Teams." *Cultural Diversity at Work*, May 1992, 10–11.

Hansen, C. J. "Writing the Project Team: Authority and Intertextuality in a Corporate Setting." *The Journal of Business Communication*, 1995, *32*(2), 103–122.

Hastings, C., Bixby, P., and Chaudhry-Lawton, R. *The Superteam Solution*. San Diego, Calif.: University Associates, 1987.

Henkoff, R. "Making Your Office More Productive." *Fortune,* Feb. 25, 1991a, 72–84.

Henkoff, R. "For States: Reform Turns Radical." *Fortune,* Oct. 21, 1991b, 137–139.

Hill, C. H., and Yamada, K. "Motorola Illustrates How an Aged Giant Can Remain Vibrant." *Wall Street Journal,* Dec. 9, 1992, pp. A1, A18.

Hills, C. H. "Making the Team." *Sales and Marketing Management,* Feb. 1992, 54–57.

Hoerr, J. "Benefits for the Back Office, Too." *BusinessWeek,* July 10, 1989, p. 59.

Hofstede, G. "Cultural Constraints in Management Theories." *Academy of Management Executive,* 1993, *7*(1), 81–93.

Huret, J. "Paying for Team Results." *HR Magazine,* May 1991, 39–41.

Hutt, M. D., Walker, B. A., and Frankwick, G. L. "Hurdle the Cross-Functional Barriers to Strategic Change." *Sloan Management Review,* Spring 1995, *36,* 22–30.

Jamieson, D. "Aligning the Organization for Team-Based Operation." In G. Parker (ed.), *Handbook of Best Practices for Teams.* Amherst, Mass.: HRD Press, 1998.

Jassawalla, A. R., and Sashittal, H. C. "Building Collaborative Cross-Functional New Product Teams." *The Academy of Management Executive,* Aug. 1999, 50–63.

Jehn, K. "A Multi Method Examination of the Benefits and Detriments of Intragroup Conflict." *Administrative Science Quarterly,* 1995, *40*(2), 245–282.

Johnson, R. "Milacron Survives in Dog-Eat-Dog Industry by Forming Wolfpack." *Total Quality,* Sept. 1992, 6.

Kaeter, M. "Cross-Training: The Tactical View." *Training,* Mar. 1993, 40–46.

Kanin-Lovers, J. "Motivating the New Work Force." *Journal of Compensation and Benefits,* Sept.-Oct. 1990, 50–52.

Karvelas, K. *Winning with Teamwork.* Franklin Lakes, N. J.: Career Press, 1998.

Katzenbach, J. R., and Smith, D. K. "The Discipline of Teams." *Harvard Business Review,* Mar.-Apr. 1993a, 111–120.

Katzenbach, J. R., and Smith, D. K. *The Wisdom of Teams.* Boston: Harvard Business School Press, 1993b.

Katzenback, J. R., and Smith, D. K. "The Discipline of Virtual Teams." *Leader to Leader,* Fall 2000, *22,* 16–25.

Kessler, E., and Chakrabarti, A. K. "Innovation Speed: A Contextual Model of Context, Antecedents and Outcomes." *Academy of Management Review,* Oct. 1996, 1143–1191.

Kettley, P., and Hirsh, W. "Learning from Cross-Functional Teamwork." *IES Report,* Oct. 2000, *356.*

Kohn, A. *No Contest*. Boston: Houghton Mifflin, 1986.

Kull, D. "Software Development: The Consensus Approach." *Computer and Communications Decisions*, Aug. 1987, 63–69.

Kumar, S., and Gupta, Y. P. "Cross-Functional Teams Improve Manufacturing at Motorola's Austin Plant." *Industrial Engineering*, May 1991, 32–36.

Larson, C. "Team Tactics Can Cut Product Development Costs." *Journal of Business Strategy*, Sept.-Oct. 1988, 22–25.

Larson, C. E., and LaFasto, F.M.J. *Teamwork: What Must Go Right/What Can Go Wrong*. Newbury Park, Calif.: Sage, 1989.

Lawler, E. E., III. *High-Involvement Management: Participative Strategies for Improving Organizational Performance*. San Francisco: Jossey-Bass, 1986.

Lawler, E. E., III. "Gainsharing Theory and Research: Findings and Future Directions." In W. A. Pasmore and R. W. Woodman (eds.), *Research in Organizational Change and Development*. Greenwich, Conn.: JAI Press, 1988.

Lawrence, P. R., and Lorsch, J. W. *Organization and Environment: Managing Differentiation and Integration*. Boston: Harvard Business School, 1967.

Lawrence-Lightfoot, S. *Respect: An Exploration*. Reading, Mass.: Addison-Wesley, 1999.

Leavitt, D. "Team Techniques in System Development." *Datamation*, Nov. 15, 1987, 78–86.

Leimbach, M. P. *Meeting the Competitive Challenge*. Eden Prairie, Minn.: Wilson Learning Corporation, 1992.

Lewis, A. C., Sadosky, T. L., and Connolly, T. C. "The Effectiveness of Group Brainstorming in Engineering Problem Solving." *IEEE Transactions in Engineering Management*, 1975, *22*, 119–124.

Linden, R. M. *Seamless Government: A Practical Guide to Re-engineering in the Public Sector*. San Francisco: Jossey-Bass, 1994.

Lipnack, J., and Stamps, J. *Virtual Teams*. New York: Wiley, 1997.

Lockwood, T. "Designing Automobiles for Global Value: Ten Market Trends." *Design Management Journal*, Fall 2001, 46–52.

Loehr, L. "Between Silence and Voice: Communicating in Cross-Functional Project Teams." *IEEE Transactions on Professional Communication*, Mar. 1991, *34*(1), 51–56.

Lovelace, K., Shapiro, D. L., and Weingart, L. R. "Maximizing Cross-Functional New Product Teams' Innovativeness and Constraint Adherence: A Conflict Communication Perspective." *Academy of Management Journal*, 2001, *44*(4), 779–793.

Lyons, T. F., Krachenberg, A. R., and Henke, J. W. "Mixed-Motive Marriages: What's Next for Buyer-Seller Relations?" *Sloan Management Review*, Spring 1990, 29–35.

Magjuka, R. J., and Baldwin, T. T. "Team-Based Employee Involvement Programs: Effects of Design and Administration." *Personnel Psychology,* 1991, *44,* 793–812.

McCall, M. *High Flyers: Developing the Next Generation of Leaders.* Boston: Harvard Business School Press, 1998.

McClenahen, J. C. "Not Fun in the Sun." *Industry Week,* Oct. 15, 1990, 22–24.

McCorcle, M. D. "Critical Issues in the Functioning of Interdisciplinary Groups." *Small Group Behavior,* Aug. 1982, *13*(3), 291–310.

McGee, E. C. "Peer Evaluation: Coaching for Coaching." In G. Parker (ed.), *The Handbook of Best Practices for Teams.* Amherst, Mass.: HRD Press, 1998.

McKeown, J. J. "New Products from New Technologies." *Journal of Business and Industrial Marketing,* Winter-Spring 1990, 67–72.

Meeting Robbers. Carlsbad, Calif.: CRM Learning, 1995. Videotape.

Melymuka, K. "Born to Lead Projects." *Computer World,* Mar. 27, 2000, *34,* 62–64.

Merrick, N. "Remote Control." *People Management,* Sept. 26, 1996, *40*(19), 40–41.

Miller, C. "How to Construct Programs for Teams." *Reward and Recognition* (Supplement to *Training*), Sept. 1991, 4–6.

Mower, J., and Wilemon, D. "Rewarding Technical Teamwork." *Research-Technology Management,* Sept.-Oct. 1989, 24–29.

Murray, T. "Team Selling: What's the Incentive?" *Sales and Marketing Management,* June 1991, 89–92.

Myerson, D., Weick, K. E., and Kramer, R. M. "Swift Trust and Temporary Groups." In R. M. Kramer and T. R. Tyler (eds.), *Trust in Organizations: Frontiers of Theory and Research.* Thousand Oaks, Calif.: Sage, 1996.

Nador, S. "The Fine Art of Team Selection." *Canadian HR Reporter,* Oct. 22, 2001, 15, 19.

Norman, C. A., and Zawacki, R. A. "Team Appraisal-Team Approach." *Personnel Journal,* Sept. 1991, 101–104.

"Non-Financial Rewards Motivate and Drive Performance." *IIE Solutions,* Mar. 1996, 1–2.

Nulty, P. "The Soul of an Old Machine." *Fortune,* May 21, 1990, 67–72.

O'Dell, C. "Team Play, Team Pay—New Ways of Keeping Score." *Across the Board,* Nov. 1989, 38–45.

O'Dell, C., and McAdams, J. *People, Performance and Pay.* Phoenix: American Compensation Association; Houston: American Quality and Productivity Center, 1987.

O'Hara-Devereaux, M., and Johansen, R. *Globalwork: Bridging Distance, Culture, and Time.* San Francisco: Jossey-Bass, 1994.

"Organizational, Individual Factors Pose Biggest Barriers for Teams." *Total Quality,* Dec. 1992, 5.

Orsburn, J. D., Moran, L., Musselwhite, E., and Zenger, J. *Self-Directed Work Teams: The Next American Challenge.* Homewood, Ill.: Business One Irwin, 1990.

Parker, G. M. *Parker Team Player Survey.* Tuxedo, N.Y.: Xicom/Consulting Psychologists Press, 1991.

Parker, G. M. *Team Players and Teamwork: The New Competitive Business Strategy.* San Francisco: Jossey-Bass, 1996.

Parker, G. M. *Cross-Functional Teams Toolkit.* San Francisco: Jossey-Bass/Pfeiffer, 1997.

Parker, G. M. *25 Instruments for Team Building.* Amherst, Mass.: HRD Press, 1998.

Parker, G. M. "New Teams in the Workplace." *US1: The Newspaper,* Jan. 8, 2000a, p. 25.

Parker, G. M. *Being a Team Player.* Beverly, Mass.: Interactive Training, 2000b.

Parker, G. M. *Team Depot: A Warehouse of 585 Tools to Reassess, Rejuvenate, and Rehabilitate Your Team.* San Francisco: Jossey-Bass/Pfeiffer, 2002.

Parker, G. M., and Kropp, R. P., Jr. *50 Activities for Self-Directed Teams.* Amherst, Mass.: HRD Press, 1994.

Parker, G. M., McAdams, J., and Zeilinski., D. *Rewarding Teams: Lessons from the Trenches.* San Francisco: Jossey-Bass, 2000.

Patti, A. L., Gilbert, J. P., and Hartman, S. "Physical Co-Location and the Success of New Product Development Projects." *Engineering Management Journal,* Sept. 1997, 31–37.

Pearson, P. H. "The Interdisciplinary Team Process, or the Professionals of Babel." *Developmental Medicine and Child Neurology,* June 1983, 390–395.

Penzer, E. "A Philadelphia Story." *Incentive,* July 1991, 33–36.

Perry, M., Pearce, C., and Sims, H. "Empowered Selling Teams: How Shared Leadership Can Contribute to Selling Team Outcomes." *The Journal of Personal Selling and Sales Management,* 2000, *19*(3), 35–51.

"Pulling Together Can Pay Off: Reveals New IPD Research on Team Pay." *Management Services,* Mar. 1996, 1–2.

Rees, F. *Teamwork from Start to Finish.* San Francisco: Jossey-Bass/Pfeiffer, 1997.

Renzulli, J. S., Owen, S. V., and Callahan, C. M. "Fluency, Flexibility and Originality as a Function of Group Size." *Journal of Creative Behavior,* 1974, *8*, 107–112.

Robinson, R., Oswald, S. L., Swinehart, K. S., and Thomas, J. "Southwest Industries: Creating High-Performance Teams for High-Technology Production." *Planning Review,* Nov.-Dec. 1991, 10–14, 47.

Sato, K. "Trust and Group Size in a Social Dilemma." *Japanese Psychological Research,* 1988, *30,* 88–93.

Schmidt, J. B, Montoya-Weiss, M. M., and Massey, A. P. "New Product Development Decision-Making Effectiveness: Comparing Individuals, Face-to Face Teams and Virtual Teams." *Decision Sciences,* Fall 2001, 575–600.

Sellers, P. "How to Remake Your Sales Force." *Fortune,* May 4, 1992, 96–103.

Senge, P. M. "The Leader's New Work: Building Learning Organizations." *Harvard Business Review,* Fall 1990, 7–23.

Sethi, R. "New Product Quality and Product Development Teams." *Journal of Marketing,* Apr. 2000, 1–14.

Sherman, S. "A Brave New Darwinian Workplace." *Fortune,* Jan. 25, 1993, 50–56.

"Shifting the Corporate Culture." *Working Woman,* Nov. 1992, 25, 28.

Smart, K. L., and Barnum, C. "Communications in Cross-Functional Teams." *Technical Communication,* Feb.-Mar 2000, *47,* 19–21.

Stratton, A. D. "StorageTek and Excellence Through Quality." *Journal for Quality and Productivity,* Dec. 1991, 6–9.

Team Building II: What Makes a Good Team Player? Carlsbad, Calif.: CRM Learning, 1995. Videotape.

Thomas, K., and Kilmann, R. *Thomas Kilmann Conflict Mode.* Tuxedo, N.Y.: Xicom/Consulting Psychologists Press, 1971.

Townsend, A. M., DeMarie, S. M., and Hendrickson, A. R. "Virtual Teams: Technology and the Workplace of the Future." *Academy of Management Executive,* Aug. 1998, *12*(3), 17–29.

Torres, C., and Spiegel, J. *Self-Directed Work Teams: A Primer.* San Diego, Calif.: Pfeiffer, 1990.

Trent, R. J. "Understanding and Evaluating Sourcing Team Leadership." *International Journal of Purchasing and Materials Management,* Fall 1996, 8–25.

Tuckman, B. W. "Developmental Sequence in Small Groups." *Psychological Bulletin,* 1965, *63*(6), 384–399.

Vasilash, G. S. "Chrysler Gets Serious About Success." *Production,* Jan. 1992, 58–60.

"Vendor Certification Improves Buyer/Seller Relationships." *Total Quality,* May 1990, 1–3.

Vogt, J. F., and Murrell, K. L. *Empowerment in Organizations.* San Diego, Calif.: University Associates, 1990.

Wallace, R., and Halverson, W. "Project Management: A Critical Success Factor or a Management Fad?" *Industrial Engineering*, Apr. 1992, 48–50.

Wellins, R. S., Byham, W. C., and Wilson, J. M. *Empowered Teams: Creating Self-Directed Work Groups That Improve Quality, Productivity, and Participation.* San Francisco: Jossey-Bass, 1991.

White, M. "Linking Compensation to Knowledge Will Pay Off in the 1990s." *Planning Review*, Nov.-Dec. 1991, 15–17.

Whiting, R. "Core Teams Take the Front Lines." *Electronic Business*, June 17, 1991, 50–54.

Wolff, M. F. "Teams Speed Commercialization of R&D Projects." *Research-Technology Management*, Sept.-Oct. 1988, 8–10.

Yu, L. "Marketers and Engineers: Why Can't We Just Get Along?" *MIT Sloan Management Review*, Fall 2001, 13.

Zaccaro, S. J. "Social Loafing: The Role of Task Attractiveness." *Journal of Personality and Social Psychology*, 1984, *43*, 1214–1222.

Index